Exploring the World of Data Processing

Exploring the World of Data Processing

CLAUDE J. DE ROSSI
Systems Analyst
General Electric Company

Reston Publishing Company, Inc.
Reston, Virginia 22090
A Prentice-Hall Company

LIBRARY OF CONGRESS CATALOGING IN PUBLICATION DATA

DeRossi, Claude J
    Exploring the world of data processing.

    1. Electronic data processing. 2. Electronic digital computers—Programming. 3. Programming languages (Electronic computers) I. Title.
QA76.D37   001.6'4   74-28054
ISBN 0-87909-259-9

© 1975 by
Reston Publishing Company, Inc.
A Prentice-Hall Company
Box 547
Reston, Virginia 22090

All rights reserved. No part of this book may be reproduced in any way, or by any means, without permission in writing from the publisher.

10 9 8 7 6 5 4 3 2 1

Printed in the United States of America

To Dave, Ang, and Del

Contents

	PREFACE	xv
1.	**A BRIEF HISTORY OF DATA PROCESSING**	1

Early Devices, 1
Charles Babbage, 3
Dr. Herman Hollerith, 4
ENIAC, 5
Dr. John von Neumann, 6
Summary, 7
Questions, 8

2. **WHAT IS A COMPUTER?**   9

A Visit to a Computer Center, 9
Computer Systems, 10
Computer Applications, 11
Summary, 15
Questions, 15

3. **THE BUSINESS WORLD—A WORLD OF PAPER**   17

Profits, 17
Data and Information, 18
Paper Work, 18
Electric Accounting Machine Equipment, 18
Three Levels of Data Processing, 19
Summary, 19
Questions, 21

viii   Contents

4. **EAM EQUIPMENT**   22
   The Punched Card, 22
   Keypunch, 24
   Sorter, 25
   Collator, 25
   Interpreter, 26
   Accounting Machine, 26
   Reproducer, 27
   Control Panel, 28
   Summary, 28
   Questions, 29

5. **FILE PROCESSING**   30
   Files, 30
   Records, Fields, and Characters, 31
   Unit Record Principle, 31
   Magnetic Tape, 32
   Blocks, 33
   Tape Handlers, 34
   Buffers, 34
   Central Processing Unit, 36
   Basic Data Processing Cycle, 36
   Summary, 37
   Questions, 37

6. **CONVERTING FROM EAM EQUIPMENT TO A COMPUTER**   39
   Conversion, 39
   The Computer Becomes Entrenched, 40
   Increasing Capacity, 41
   Summary, 42
   Questions, 42

7. **COMPUTER INPUT/OUTPUT DEVICES**   43
   Card Reader, 43
   Magnetic Tape, 45
   Disk, 46
   Drum, 47
   Data Cell, 47
   High-speed Printer, 49
   Optical Scanner, 50

Contents   ix

      MICR, 50
      Typewriter, 51
      Printers, 51
      Photography, 52
      Computer Output Microfilm (COM), 52
      Voice, 52
      Card Punch, 53
      Summary, 53
      Questions, 53

8. **COMPUTER OUTPUT MICROFILM**　　　　55
      Advantages of COM, 56
      Applications of COM, 57
      Summary, 58
      Questions, 58

9. **BINARY BITS**　　　　59
      Decimal Numbers, 59
      Binary Numbers, 60
      Words, 62
      Cores, 62
      Summary, 64
      Questions, 65

10. **INTEGERS**　　　　66
      Positive Integers, 66
      Two's Complement, 67
      Negative Integers, 67
      Adding in Binary, 68
      Summary, 70
      Questions, 71

11. **FLOATING POINT**　　　　73
      Mixed Numbers, 73
      Floating Point, 73
      Combining the Characteristic and Mantissa, 75
      Representing Whole and Mixed Numbers, 75
      Excess-64 Method, 76
      Summary, 80
      Questions, 81

12. HEXADECIMAL AND OCTAL CODES — 82
Using Integers and Floating-point Numbers, 82
Hexadecimal Code, 84
Octal Code, 88
Interrelationships of Number Systems, 89
Summary, 90
Questions, 90

13. COMPUTER MEMORIES — 92
Computer Components, 92
Memory Configurations, 92
Bytes, 96
EBCDIC, 96
Summary, 97
Questions, 98

14. INSTRUCTIONAL FORMATS — 99
Machine-Language Programming, 99
Hypothetical Learning Computer (HLC), 99
Programs, 101
Accumulator, 103
Index Registers, 104
Summary, 105
Questions, 106

15. MACHINE-LANGUAGE PROGRAMMING — 107
One-address Computers, 107
Tag, 108
Two-address Computers, 108
Three-address Computers, 108
Index Registers, 109
Summary, 112
Questions, 112

16. ASSEMBLY-LANGUAGE PROGRAMMING — 113
Machine-language Programming, 113
Assembly Language Programming, 114
Coding Forms, 114
Source Deck, 116
Assembly, 116

Contents   xi

       Execution, 117
       HLC Ops, 118
       Counting Using Index Registers, 121
       Address Modification, 122
       Summary, 124
       Questions, 124

17. A SURVEY OF FORTRAN—PART I   **126**

       Universal Languages, 126
       FORTRAN, 127
       Calculations, 128
       Coding Form, 128
       Statements, 129
       Source Deck, 131
       Input Data, 131
       Job Control Language (JCL) Cards, 131
       Compilation, 132
       Execution, 133
       Debugging, 133
       Object Deck, 133
       Summary, 133
       Questions, 134

18. A SURVEY OF FORTRAN—PART II   **136**

       Integer Numbers, 136
       Real Numbers, 136
       Variable Names, 137
       Assignment Statement, 138
       PRINT And FORMAT Statements, 139
       IF Statement, 140
       STOP and END Statements, 140
       READ Statement, 141
       FORTRAN V, 142
       Summary, 142
       Questions, 143

19. COBOL CONCEPTS   **144**

       COBOL Objectives, 144
       Business Files, 145
       COBOL Coding Form, 145

xii   Contents

    Source and Object Decks, 146
    Divisions, 147
    COBOL Vocabulary, 151
    Summary, 151
    Questions, 153

20. THE BASIC LANGUAGE   154
    BASIC's Development, 154
    Timesharing Mode, 155
    BASIC's Vocabulary, 155
    Seven BASIC Statement Types, 156
    Summary, 163
    Questions, 164

21. FLOWCHARTING   165
    Flowchart Concepts, 166
    Flowchart And Program Examples, 166
    Flowchart Symbols, 167
    Summary, 172
    Questions, 174

22. BATCH MODE   175
    Computer Usage Modes, 175
    Batch Mode Programming Steps, 175
    Computer Center Procedures, 177
    Summary, 179
    Questions, 179

23. REMOTE BATCH   181
    Remote Batch Mode, 181
    Terminals, 183
    Obtaining Output, 183
    Costs, 186
    Summary, 186
    Questions, 187

Contents   xiii

24. CONVERSATIONAL TIMESHARING   188
Conversational Timesharing Mode, 188
Timesharing Languages, 189
System Commands, 196
Summary, 202
Questions, 203

25. SOFTWARE   205
Software, 205
Assembler, 205
Compiler, 206
Operating System, 209
Multiprogramming, 209
Summary, 210
Questions, 211

26. APPLICATIONS   212
Scientific Applications, 213
On-line Applications, 214
Business Applications, 215
File Miantenance, 215
Sequential and Random File Maintenance, 220
Summary, 225
Questions, 226

27. SYSTEM DESIGN   228
Procedures, 228
System Study, 229
Costs, 230
Designing the System, 230
The Feasibility Study, 230
Conclusions and Recommendations, 233
Summary, 233
Questions, 234

28.	**THE FUTURE**	**235**

      Finance, 236
      Education, 236
      Transportation, 237
      Entertainment, 238
      Medicine, 239
      Government, 239
      Summary, 239
      Questions, 239

GLOSSARY   **240**

INDEX   **252**

Preface

This text provides an overview of the world of data processing. It is intended for persons who need to have a general understanding of the field but who do not need the in-depth knowledge that would enable them to program computers or design business information systems.

The book may also be used as the first text by those who intend to pursue a data processing career, since it places the entire field in perspective and prepares the way for further study.

This book may be used either as a text for self-study, or it may be used as the main text in a one-semester course for business students in junior college or at a four-year school. In high schools, this book may be used in data processing courses for mature students.

I would like to express my appreciation to those who have helped me prepare this book. To L. W. Rank and Reston Publishing Company go my thanks for their very helpful advice in the preparation of this manuscript. To my wife, Cynthia, my gratitude for the expert typing she did.

CLAUDE J. DEROSSI

1 | A Brief History of Data Processing

In the beginning, say a couple of million years ago, there was no great need for data processing. Anything a person possessed could probably be counted on the fingers of one or two hands. Or, if the hands were not enough, there were the toes of both feet in reserve.

It appears that the fingers were adequate since the base of the business, scientific, and social numbering system that we use today is 10. There are ten symbols or digits in that system, zero through nine.

EARLY DEVICES

Eventually, the need for computing devices began to arise; one of the earliest devices that we see in use to this very day is the abacus (see Fig. 1-1).

FIGURE 1-1. Abacus

Using the abacus, persons may add, subtract, multiply, and divide. Skilled operators are able to implement these operations so expertly that they can outperform persons using electric desk calculators.

The abacus was invented around 3000 B.C. The next computing device worthy of mention was Napier's "bones." In the early 1600s, John Napier, a Scottish mathematician, invented a sort of multiplication table inscribed upon a set of rods. Though strictly not a machine, the invention could be used to assist in the performing of multiplication and division problems. Napier is remembered not only for these "bones," but also for the invention of logarithms.

In 1632, William Oughtred invented the slide rule, a mechanical device that is still used today. This was the first mechanical calculating device.

A few years later (1642), Blaise Pascal, a French mathematician, invented a mechanical calculator that could add and subtract (see Fig. 1-2). It could also divide by repeated subtractions or multiply by repeated additions. For example, to multiply 3,497 by 534, the following additions would be performed:

```
3497  ⎫
3497  ⎬  4 times
3497  ⎪
3497  ⎭
34970 ⎫
34970 ⎬  3 times
34970 ⎭
349700 ⎫
349700 ⎪
349700 ⎬  5 times
349700 ⎪
349700 ⎭
```

Toward the end of the 1600s, a German mathematician, Gottfried von Leibnitz, invented a machine that really represented an improved Pascal device. This machine could multiply and divide directly.

FIGURE 1-2. Pascal's Calculator

Leibnitz, too, is remembered for an achievement other than a calculating device. He is credited by many as being the inventor of the calculus. (Others feel that calculus was invented by the British mathematician, Sir Isaac Newton.)

In the early 1800s, a Frenchman, Joseph Marie Jacquard, developed a loom that used punched cards as the control for the weaving of intricate patterns in cloth. Though there does not seem to be much connection between looms and computing devices, the punched card idea was later picked up by the Britisher Charles Babbage in the middle 1800s.

CHARLES BABBAGE

There are many who will claim that Charles Babbage was the real inventor of today's electronic marvel, the automatic digital computer. Despite the fact that the two machines that Babbage worked on were never completed, they were so computerlike that there is much merit in the statement that he was the inventor of computers.

Babbage was an inventor and a mathematician. He used desk calculators and he foresaw their possibilities. Therefore, in 1812 he began building a device called a "difference machine." Later (1822),

FIGURE 1-3. Babbage's "Difference Machine"

he got a better idea and began developing an "analytical engine." At first, Babbage had the support of the British government in his work, but then the project became expensive and the support was withdrawn. Babbage had another problem. He needed intricate parts to use in his machine, but the technology of the 1850s was not equal to the task; he could not get the parts made.

Babbage's analytical engine was not built, but later his designs were transformed into real machinery and the device functioned as expected.

DR. HERMAN HOLLERITH

In 1890, the name Dr. Herman Hollerith entered the data processing world. He was a statistician working in the United States Census Bureau who was assigned the challenge of speeding up the compilation of census statistics. This compilation was taking so long between census years that there appeared to be real danger that it would take over ten years to evaluate the results of a census.

Dr. Hollerith utilized the punched card principle as Babbage had done. He first used small punched cards upon which to store the information that had been obtained. Later, the size was increased to 7-3/8 × 3-1/4 in., the exact size of the dollar bill used in those days.

To process these cards, Hollerith invented a card punch machine, a sorter, and a tabulator. These machines so effectively reduced the time required to process the census that it was clear that a new era had dawned, the era of automatic data processing.

FIGURE 1-4. Dr. Herman Hollerith's Machine

ENIAC

Over the next years, there were improvements in data processing machines. Eventually, the machines began to take on characteristics which caused them to behave more and more like the computing devices of today. A significant machine built in the early 1940s was Mark I. Under the direction of Dr. Howard Aiken of Harvard University, the machine was built and tested. It was slow by today's standards but was nevertheless an impressive machine for the automatic processing of data. Later in the 1940s, ENIAC (Electronic Numerical Integrator and Calculator) was built. This is considered to be the first electronic machine. (Mark I was electromechanical.) The men primarily responsible for ENIAC's appearance were J. P. Eckert and

Dr. J. W. Mauchley of the Moore School of Engineering at the University of Pennsylvania. ENIAC was much faster than Mark I (over one thousand times as fast), since it used vacuum tubes instead of relays. It was such a successful machine that it was used for computations until well in the 1950s.

DR. JOHN VON NEUMANN

An important name associated with the development of computer design is that of Dr. John von Neumann. In 1946, Dr. von Neumann joined Messrs. Burke and Goldstine in authoring a report to the U.S. Army Ordinance Department in which it was suggested that instructions to be performed by a computer (its program) be stored in the computer's memory. The major problem with ENIAC was that it depended upon wired plugboards for control. These plugboards contained the computer's program. Since they were external devices requiring hand wiring, they were inflexible and awkward to use.

The suggestion was universally adopted, and virtually all computers built from the 1950s to the present have been of the kind that stores programs in memory.

Many manufacturers entered the field of computer manufacture. Some of them were UNIVAC, Remington Rand, Control Data Corporation, National Cash Register, General Electric, Radio Corporation of America (RCA), International Business Machines (IBM), and others. Some of these corporations are no longer building computers. Almost from the beginning, IBM has dominated the field of computer manufacture and sales. Its latest series of computers, System 370, has had a profound influence on the design of competing machines.

Since their inception, there have been four generations of computers. The first generation was characterized by the vacuum tube. Computers used many thousands of them to act as switches. The problem with tubes is that they are bulky and expensive, they generate a great deal of heat, they break down frequently, and they function relatively slowly. While many important machines were built in the first generation era, it was apparent that improvements in hardware were necessary.

In the early 1960s, vacuum tubes were replaced by transistors. This improvement enabled machines to become faster and more reliable. Memory sizes were greatly enlarged. The programming languages that computers could be conditioned to understand were increased. The second-generation computer had arrived.

Third-generation computers were developed in the mid-1960s. The major improvements in this generation involved the miniaturization of components, the closer blending of hardware and software features, the introduction of remote access and timesharing, and the expansion of secondary storage capabilities.

Since the beginning of the 1970s, a fourth generation of computer systems has begun to emerge. It is a little early to determine exactly what constitutes a fourth-generation machine. Memories are becoming much larger, and calculating speeds are increasing. There is even greater miniaturization of components and the blending of hardware and software components. Multiprogramming is now available. New types of main memory storage devices are being developed; programming languages are becoming more sophisticated; operating systems are becoming more powerful. If there is to be a single word which is to characterize fourth-generation computers, it may be "intelligent." More and more computers are taking on attributes that once were thought to be the sole possessions of humans.

It can be safely said that the past is mere prologue. Over the coming years, there will surely be startling breakthroughs in the development of data processing systems. Compared with the machines of the future, today's sophisticated devices will almost certainly appear as toys.

SUMMARY

While it is difficult to determine when computing actually began, it seems clear that, except for the abacus, there was no urgent need for computing devices until the seventeenth century. In the 1600s, the names Napier, Oughtred, Pascal, and Leibnitz became associated with computing and computing devices. Later, Jacquard and Babbage began work for which they are remembered today. Babbage may, in a sense, be credited with inventing the automatic computer.

In the closing years of the 1800s, Hollerith made significant progress in the development of data processing techniques and equipment.

Then, in the 1940s, Messrs. Aiken, Eckert, Mauchley, and von

Neumann participated in the development of mechanical and electronic computers. The early computers MARK I and ENIAC led to the introduction of the models which are so well-known today.

The major developments in computer technology have fallen into roughly four generations. The first generation was characterized by the use of vacuum tubes, the second by the use of transistors, the third by the integration of hardware and software features, and the fourth by the extraordinary capabilities of modern machines. The fourth generation of computers may become known as the intelligent generation.

QUESTIONS

1. What is the name of the oldest computing device known? Approximately when was it invented?
2. What was the contribution of Pascal to data processing? In what way was Leibnitz's contribution similar?
3. How are the works of Jacquard and Babbage related?
4. What were the *two* devices that Babbage worked on? Why weren't they completed?
5. What was the contribution that Dr. Herman Hollerith made to data processing?
6. What was the important idea that von Neumann offered to the field?
7. How were the MARK I and ENIAC devices similar? How did they differ?
8. Which computer manufacturer has the dominant position in the data processing field today?
9. Give the general characteristics of the first three computer generations.
10. Give some conjectures as to what attributes fourth generation computers may have.

2 | What Is a Computer?

Since we shall be discussing computers in this book, let us first ask: "What is a computer?"

There are many answers to that question, some giving only half the truth. For example, a computer has been compared to a robot, a machine that follows instructions. Yet, if you look at a computer you will not see arms and legs, eyes and ears. Clearly, a computer does not have the appearance of what you and I would call a robot.

A computer has been called a giant adding machine. But where are the keys to push and the crank to turn? There are not any, so a computer is not really a mere adding machine. It has been called a machine that processes data. Well, this description may be true enough, but what does the expression "process data" mean? That description does not seem to help very much as we try to learn what a computer is.

A VISIT TO A COMPUTER CENTER

Suppose we take a more direct approach and visit a computer center. Here, at least, we can actually walk up to a computer, see what it actually looks like, and listen to it operate. We can even talk to the persons who make it run.

Walking into the computer room (see Fig. 2-1), we are first struck by the fact that the room is cool, almost cold, in fact. Most rooms housing large computer systems are kept air conditioned, we are told. Because they are transistorized, computers use relatively little power, but they still give off a considerable amount of heat. Heat is injurious to computer components, hence the air conditioning. Some computers require coolness to the degree that if the temperature in the computer room rises, they will shut themselves down. One computer that we are familiar with types out a message before doing so. It tells the computer operators that it is experiencing a potentially dangerous temperature and that it will shut down until the climate can be made acceptable.

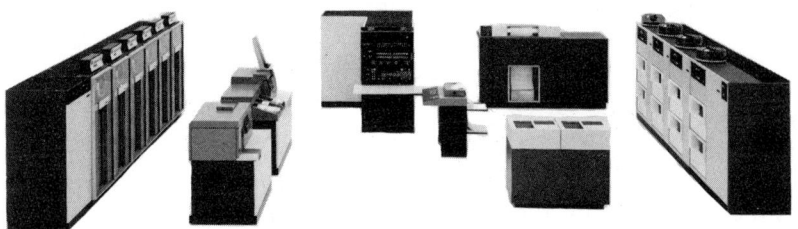

FIGURE 2-1. Computer System

As we look around the room we see that it is filled with several free-standing cabinets—some twenty or thirty of them. These cabinets contain the components of the computer. In other words, a computer is not just a large box filled with electronic gear; it is composed of many smaller units. In the cabinets we find tape drives, disk units, memory modules, input/output units, and several other devices of various types. At this time you probably do not know what a tape drive is, or a disk unit, or any of the other devices that have been mentioned. Those items will be described and explained in this book.

The room that you are in may have the floor space that one would ordinarily expect to find in twenty or more fair-sized living rooms. Each square foot of the area seems to have been carefully planned to hold some type of electronic component—all part of the one computer system.

COMPUTER SYSTEMS

You might have expected to be overwhelmed by the sounds of activity around the computer components. True, there is some noise.

The card reader, reading punched cards, sounds like a muffled machine gun; the printer, printing lines on computer paper, sounds like dozens of typewriters in action, but the noise is not nearly what you might have expected. One can easily converse with the computer operators while observing their actions around the computer console.

The computer console consists of a desk at which one or more computer operators may stand or sit. There may be a panel on the console with lights that appear to be rapidly flickering on and off. There may also be a typewriter that the operator uses when he wants to type a message to the computer. The typewriter also goes into action when it wants the operator to know something or to do something. For example, the computer may type a message directing the computer operator to mount a reel of tape on a certain tape handler. The operator is given a certain length of time to do so. If he does not accomplish the task within that length of time, the computer reminds him.

In the last paragraph we again mentioned some devices with which you may not be familiar: card reader, printer, and tape handler (see Fig. 2-2). These devices will be fully discussed later.

COMPUTER APPLICATIONS

The operators show us the jobs that are ready to be submitted to the computer, and communications between operators and computer, and the jobs which have been completed. A "speedometer" upon the console tells us that the computer is currently executing about one million instructions per second. In more understandable terms, the computer is doing in one second the work that would require one full year for a human to accomplish if he worked twenty-four hours a day. And, of course, we are not even mentioning accuracy. The computer's work would almost certainly be error-free, while that of the human would probably contain thousands of mistakes, if not hundreds of thousands.

Upon leaving the computer center, we may be impressed with what we have seen, but have we come closer to an understanding of what a computer really is? We have seen decks of punched cards being "read" by a card reader, reels of magnetic tape being mounted on tape handlers and dismounted from them, thousands of pages of reports being printed by high-speed printers, but as yet we do not really know what was happening behind the activity.

12   What Is a Computer?

FIGURE 2-2. A Tape Handler

Despite the fact that you do not yet really have an understanding of what computers are or what they can do, you do know that in our world computers cannot be ignored. They influence our lives in the fields of business, science, medicine, weather forecasting, power generation, and many other fields. Computers are used by corporations, government bodies, law enforcement agencies, schools, and other establishments. Let us explore some of the ways that computers affect your life.

Business

The business world affects us all, whether or not we wish it to do so, and the business world functions as smoothly as it does largely because of the assistance of data processing systems. Business concerns need to establish and maintain voluminous records in master files; they need to pay employees periodically; they need to control the manufacture and storage of parts and devices; they must communicate with their stockholders, their bondholders, and their pensioners. There are thousands of other functions that business concerns must perform. Many of these functions affect you whether you are a student, farmer, housewife, factory worker, salesman, teacher, proprietor, inventor, manager, or government official, or whether you follow any of a thousand other pursuits. All of these persons receive computer-prepared checks, bills, announcements, advertisements, and other documents. Even the unemployed hobo hitching rides on freight trains is dependent upon the computer-prepared schedules under which the railroads operate.

Science

In the beginning, computers were used almost exclusively in the areas of science. They were used to develop astronomical schedules, to calculate ballistic projectiles, to compile mathematical tables. Though most computer processing is now performed in the field of business, the scientific area still occupies an important segment of the data processing spectrum. Computers are used to help design components for machines and electronic devices. They are being used in areas of pure research to find ways of using atomic energy, to find new power sources, to clean up the environment, and to purify the air and the waters.

Computers are, of course, indispensable in exploring the universe around us, to find out where man came from, where he is now, and where he is going. The spacecraft on its way at this very moment to the remote recesses of space maintains a life line to one or more computers on Earth. As answers come to Earth from outer space, computers help man analyze these messages and thus help him understand himself.

Education

In the field of education, computers enable students and teachers to perform more effectively. With their assistance, persons may delve more deeply into areas that were once thought too time-consuming for ordinary efforts. When students are relieved of tedious and error-prone repetitive tasks, they can investigate more thoroughly the whys of their subjects rather than just the whats.

Imaginative new devices and techniques have been developed to help students learn. As an example, students may sit at teletype-like terminals and communicate directly with a computer. In a question-and-answer conversational mode, the computer can instruct students in areas of mathematics, history, physics, chemistry, and others.

Medicine

In the field of medicine, computers are being used to help improve the health of people. Libraries of symptoms can be stored in memory banks and interrogated when needed. In those libraries, there can also be stored references to articles and papers concerning various diseases and their treatment. By use of terminals connected to diagnostic devices, doctors are able accurately to monitor the bodily functions of patients, even when the doctor and his patients are located at distances hundreds, if not thousands, of miles from each other. Any of us may someday owe our lives and well-being to the fact that a doctor can analyze our problem over ordinary phone lines.

Other Areas

The areas of human endeavors involving the computer are almost literally too numerous to mention. The federal and state governments use computers to prepare, monitor, and analyze budgets. They use computers to check the returns of taxpayers, to send millions of monthly paychecks to retirees on Social Security, to document the results of the most recent census, and for many other purposes.

In law enforcement, computers are used to study the methods of operation of lawbreakers and to store these MO's in data banks for later reference. Computers are used to help trace stolen goods, to study the causes of crime, and to research methods of preventing crime. These are only a few of the ways that computers are used in enforcing the law.

In the area of transportation, power generation, communication, weather forecasting, and others, computers are used in ways which affect your daily life. They help determine the time that your bus will appear at the corner bus stop, the amount of electricity that will be available for use at your home, the kinds of programs that you will be able to see on television, and the type of clothing that you will wear tomorrow as you make your way to school or to work.

It is indeed important that we study computers, since they have such profound effects upon the way we live. What are computers? Why do some people refer to them as robots, while others say that they are nothing more than overgrown adding machines? To find the answers to these and other questions, let us first take a look at the world of business (Chapter 3).

SUMMARY

In this chapter, we took you on an imaginary tour through a computer center. We observed that a computer is not just one electronic device housed in an elaborate cabinet; it is, instead, a system of devices each in its own cabinet. We saw a console, the nerve center of the system, where operators and machine communicate. We saw a card reader transmitting information to the computer; a printer printing hundreds of lines of output per minute. We saw reels of tape spinning.

It all seemed wonderful and mysterious, but we gained this impression only because everything was so new to us. After having learned more about computers and data processing, much of the mystery will be dispelled, but the fascination will still remain.

Computers profoundly affect the lives of us all. In the fields of science, business, transportation, education, law enforcement, and others, computers are doing the tedious work that humans are not very good at; they are controlling processes at speeds that the reactions of humans cannot hope to match; they are opening new horizons of discovery and adventure in our world.

QUESTIONS

1. A computer has been compared to a robot. Give some reasons why this description is appropriate. Give reasons why it is not.
2. Why is a computer room cool?
3. How many free-standing cabinets would you expect to find in a computer room? Is this number subject to some variation? Why?

4. What is the name of the device from which a computer system is controlled?
5. What device permits operators and the computer system to communicate with each other?
6. How many instructions may a computer execute per second under ideal conditions? (While there may be some variation to the answer to this question, depending upon the machine used, give a response that you believe is typical.)
7. What are computers doing in the field of business?
8. How is science advanced with the aid of computers?
9. What are some ways that computers assist in the field of law enforcement?
10. How can computers help people learn?

3 | The Business World — A World of Paper

PROFITS

The business world is concerned with operating at a profit. An individual company may manufacture a product or provide a service. With rare exceptions, its every activity is concerned with obtaining more funds than it expends. If at the end of the year the company's income exceeds its outgo, the company is said to have "made a profit"; if the reverse is true, the company is said to have "suffered a loss."

In its profit-oriented activities the company may require that data be processed. The data may be test results obtained in the laboratory, or they may be inventory figures. The scientists employed in the company may want to use the test results to develop a better product; the managers of the company may want to use the inventory figures to help reduce manufacturing costs.

Both groups of people are concerned with the effect that their actions ultimately have upon profits. The scientific persons know that by offering a better product, the company will gain an edge on its competitors. The managers know that by reducing manufacturing costs, they will be able to price their product more attractively, thus tending to increase sales.

DATA AND INFORMATION

Both scientists and management need to convert the data they have obtained to a form that is more meaningful. That form is called "information." From information company officials are able to make wise decisions regarding the future actions that the company is to take.

Data alone may be too unorganized to enable a company official to make a wise business decision. The data must be converted to information. In this process, some data may be discarded, some may be combined. The results of the processing are in a form which a person may easily understand; for example, a report. Using the report, a manager can more readily make the kinds of decisions that tend to create profits for the company.

As you have probably seen, data processing may be done for either scientific or business purposes. In this text, we shall concentrate more upon business applications, since three-fourths of all data processing being done today is on business applications.

PAPER WORK

Regardless of a company's primary function, it probably has to process a great deal of paper work. This paper may take the form of customer orders, inventory listings, pay vouchers, material requisitions, and many others. Much of the paper may be processed manually; that is, no machines are needed to handle the documents. Some of it is shuffled from desk to desk, then is finally filed. Additional documents follow material as it is being formed into products to be sold. When the documents are no longer needed, they are thrown away.

ELECTRIC ACCOUNTING MACHINE EQUIPMENT

Other documents require processing in electric machines which, though similar in structure and appearance to computers, are not really computers. There are, for example, machines that punch data processing cards (keypunches), machines that sequence them (sorters), machines that perform calculations and produce printed reports (accounting machines), and others. The machines that we have just mentioned come under the general heading of EAM (Electric Accounting Machines) or unit record equipment. Often EAM equipment is all a small company needs to do its data processing. In the next chapter we shall discuss more thoroughly EAM data processing.

THREE LEVELS OF DATA PROCESSING

Many companies must use electronic computers when processing the vast amounts of paper with which they deal. Only by utilizing the great speed and flexibility of electronic computers are they able to keep track of where the business has been and in what direction it should be going.

There are, therefore, three levels of data processing (see Fig. 3-1). They are

1. Manual
2. Semi-automatic using EAM equipment
3. Automatic using electronic computers.

Small companies do all of their data processing employing only manual methods; larger companies use a combination of manual and semi-automatic methods; the largest companies employ all three levels.

SUMMARY

In this chapter, we observed that the primary reasons that businesses exist is to make profits. Managements of business concerns need to process data so that their products may be more profitably marketed.

In the operation of a business, much paper is generated. The paper work associated with processing the paper may be done manually, by using EAM equipment, and/or by using electronic computers. Small companies may require only manual means or EAM equipment; large companies may require all three methods.

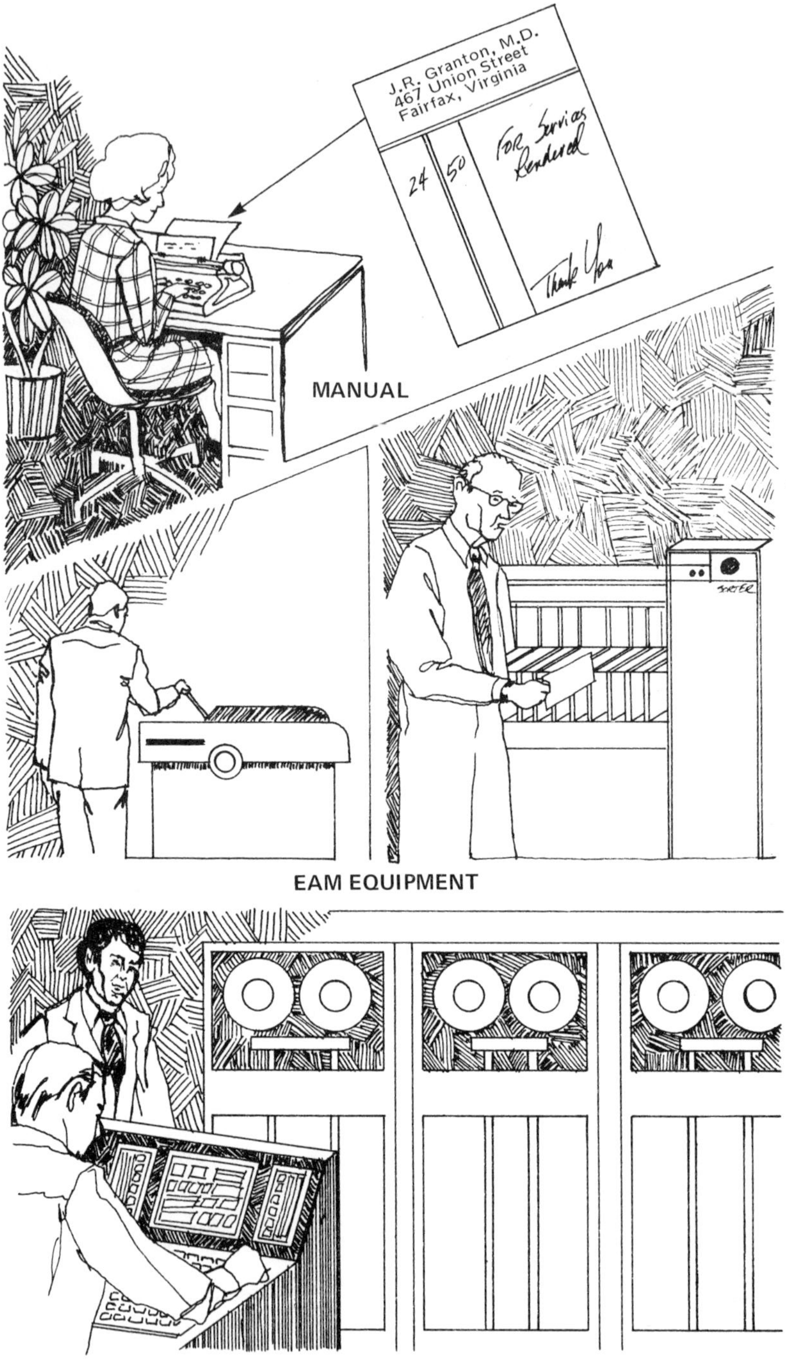

FIGURE 3-1. The Three Methods of Data Processing

QUESTIONS

1. What is the primary objective of most business concerns?
2. Is it to a company's benefit to offer a better product at a lower cost? Why?
3. What is the difference between data and information?
4. Of the two forms of data processing (scientific and business), which is more prevalent in industry today?
5. What are some forms of paper work that are required in today's business world?
6. What does the term "EAM" mean? Give some examples of EAM devices.
7. What are the three levels of data processing? Which two methods might a small company employ?
8. Which of the three levels of data processing would a large company employ?

4 | EAM Equipment

The age of EAM equipment began with the U.S. Census of 1890. The government realized that processing census data was requiring more and more time. Unless something was done, it would take more than ten years to process the data which was taken only once every ten years.

The government asked a well-known statistician, Dr. Herman Hollerith,* to devise an automatic means whereby census data could be processed more efficiently. Doctor Hollerith borrowed from the ideas of Joseph Marie Jacquard of France, who in 1801 developed a loom that used punched cards to control its operation. Hollerith invented and built several devices that could punch holes in 3 × 5 in. cards and process them. The equipment worked very well, and the census of 1890 was processed in less than half the time it would have otherwise required.

THE PUNCHED CARD

Three-by-five cards later gave way to the size that we see today, 7-3/8 × 3-1/4 in. Figure 4-1 shows an example of a punched card that is used in today's business world. Study the card carefully and observe these points:

1. There are eighty columns on the card, each of which is capable of holding a single character of data. That character may be a letter of the alphabet, a digit, or a special sign.

EAM Equipment

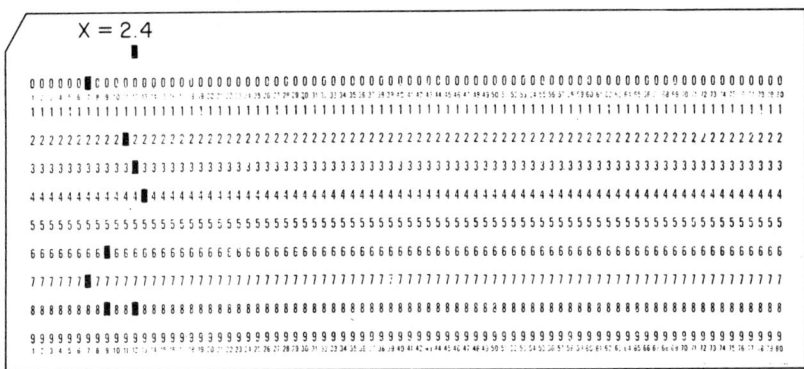

FIGURE 4-1. Punched Card

2. There are twelve rows. Starting at the very top, those rows are named "12 row," "11 row," and "zero" through "nine" rows. When characters are to be recorded upon a card, one or more holes are punched at the intersection of rows and columns. For example, if the letter Q is to be punched in column 17 of a card, holes are punched at the intersections of rows eleven and eight in column 17.

3. Each character has its own combination of punches to represent it. Letters use two punches in a column; digits use one punch; special symbols use one, two, or three punches. These punches are made in accordance with a code known as the Hollerith code.

These cards are often called IBM cards, because they were originated and popularized by the IBM Company. Strictly speaking, they should be called data processing cards, since many other computer manufacturers use them.

Other types of punched cards do exist. There are, for example, the Remington Rand card, which enables 90 characters of data to be recorded upon it, and the IBM System/3 card, which enables 96 characters to be recorded upon it. The most distinguishing feature of the Remington Rand card is the fact that round holes are punched into it. The most distinguishing feature of the IBM System/3 card is the fact that it is only about one-third the size of the standard 80-column card. Over 98 percent of all data processing being done today uses the 80-column card.

KEYPUNCH

Holes are punched in cards by keypunch machines. Figure 4-2 shows an IBM 129 Card Data Recorder. This machine and those similar to it look and perform very much like typewriters. An operator depresses keys upon its keyboard. Holes are punched on cards in the Hollerith code or in whatever other code is desired.

FIGURE 4-2. IBM 129 Card Data Recorder

The best-known keypunch machines in extensive use today are the IBM 026, 029, and 129 and the Univac Series 1700 machines. The IBM 5496 punches holes for use with the smaller System/3 cards.

Much of the data that are to be processed is originally punched upon data processing cards. Then the cards are fed to EAM devices or to electronic computers. Both classes of machines employ card readers. A card reader is a device that detects the locations of holes upon cards and provides electrical circuits that enable the punched data to be transferred from one place to another. In some card readers, metal brushes actually feel the cards, locating the holes; on other card readers, beams of light are directed at the cards. Where light passes through holes, electric circuits are created. Optical card readers, those using lights, tend to be faster than the ones that use brushes. The trend is toward optical card readers.

In addition to keypunch machines, several other types of devices come under the heading of EAM equipment. These are sorters, collators, interpreters, accounting machines, and reproducers.

SORTER

The IBM 083 Sorter is used to arrange punched cards in a numeric sequence either ascending or descending. Sorters are capable of processing cards at a rate of up to 2,000 cards a minute.

A typical application for a sorter would be to place in sequence several thousand cards containing a customer account number punched within columns 16 through 25. This area on the card (field) contains 10 digits. To sort the cards, ten passes are made through the machine. The machine is first set to position 25 for the first pass; then 24 for the second pass, etc.

In addition to sequencing, a sorter can be used for sorting in alphabetic sequence. Two passes are required through the machine for any one character position. Thus, if customer names located within columns 66 through 80 are to be alphabetized, 30 passes through the sorter are required.

COLLATOR

Figure 4-3 shows an IBM 088 Collator.

FIGURE 4-3. An IBM 088 Collator

The collator can perform four different kinds of operations:

1. Sequence checking
2. Merging
3. Matching
4. Selecting

Sequence checking means that the machine examines decks of cards to make sure that they are in the proper sequence to permit their processing.

Merging means that two decks of punched cards are combined to form a single deck. The decks are combined upon the basis of some key field found on both decks—for example, social security numbers found within columns 1 through 9 of both decks.

Matching means that two decks of cards are examined to determine whether certain contents on certain fields are identical in both the first (primary) and second decks (secondary). Cards fall into one of four pockets: matched primary, unmatched primary, matched secondary, and unmatched secondary.

Selecting means that certain required cards are extracted from a deck of punched cards for special processing.

Collators operate at rates of speed of up to 1,300 cards per minute.

INTERPRETER

The IBM 557 interpreter is able to print upon the face of a punched card the information that has been punched on the card. As you already know, a keypunch machine may optionally print along the top of the card what has been punched on it. Sometimes, though, cards are punched by machines other than keypunches. It is often desirable to pass those cards through an interpreter so that the contents of the cards may be more easily understood.

Interpreters operate at about the rate of 100 cards per minute.

ACCOUNTING MACHINE

An IBM 407 Accounting Machine is shown in Figure 4-4. This machine provides reports in the form of printed lines. Each line has a capacity of 120 characters. In the process of preparing a line to be printed, the machine can do some elementary computations such as adding, subtracting, multiplying, and dividing, and it can accumulate sums. The machine obtains its input from punched data cards and is able to process those cards at a rate of 150 cards per minute.

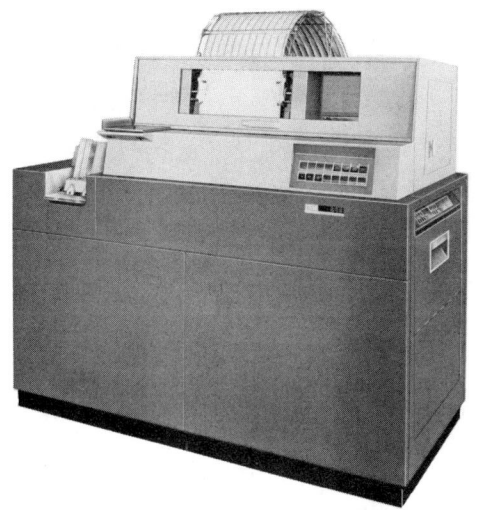

FIGURE 4-4. An IBM 407 Accounting Machine

REPRODUCER

Although the reproducer is capable of performing a number of related functions, it is best known for its ability to reproduce a deck of punched data cards. If a person has a deck that is beginning to show signs of wear, he may make an exact copy of it. Or, if he wishes to make a copy of a data deck for every person in a FORTRAN class, he may make several copies of the original.

The IBM 519 punches cards at a rate of 100 cards per minute.

The machines described above are termed EAM equipment, but the term *unit record equipment* applies to them, too. When we discuss files and records in the next chapter, we shall come back to unit record machines to see why they have that designation.

Several of the machines we have briefly described may be employed to accomplish varied tasks. The exact nature of a task that a machine is to accomplish is hand-wired upon a control panel (also called a plug board or a wire board).

CONTROL PANEL

Figure 4-5 shows an example of the control panel on an IBM 407 Accounting Machine.

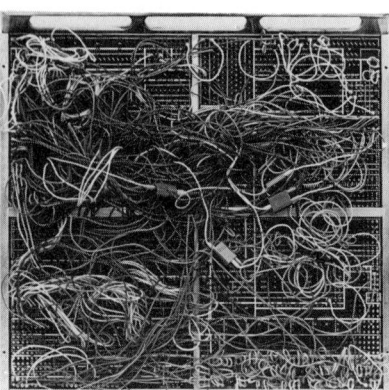

FIGURE 4-5. A Control Panel

Control panels are used on interpreters, accounting machines, reproducers, and collators. A person who really understands the wiring of control panels can almost make some machines act like electronic computers. This remark is especially true of the IBM 407.

We should emphasize again before leaving this chapter that many small companies do not need computers. To obtain them would be an extravagance and would actually cost the company money rather than save it. Properly used, EAM equipment is all the data processing machinery that some companies need. By its use companies can keep records, write reports, and even process payrolls.

SUMMARY

Dr. Herman Hollerith had a profound influence upon the development of data processing methods and equipment. His work in processing the census of 1890 resulted in the invention of the keypunch machine, the sorter, the reproducer, and other card-handling devices.

The punched card is almost universally used in the business world. Capable of recording up to 96 characters of data, it provides input not only to EAM equipment but also to electronic computers.

EAM Equipment

Important EAM devices used today are the keypunch, the sorter, the collator, the interpreter, and the reproducer. Often only EAM equipment is required in business concerns. The use of more sophisticated and expensive devices is not usually in the small company's interest.

QUESTIONS

1. Why is the census of 1890 important in the history of data processing?
2. What was the role of Dr. Herman Hollerith in connection with the census?
3. How many columns and rows does the most commonly used data processing card contain?
4. On an 80-column card, how many punches are needed in a column to represent a letter of the alphabet? A digit? A special symbol, such as comma or period?
5. How many characters may be punched on the data processing card used on IBM's System/3?
6. What is the function of a keypunch machine? Name some models in use today.
7. What is the function of a sorter?
8. When one is using a sorter, how many passes are required for a deck of cards if it is desired to sequence the cards numerically upon columns 1 through 9?
9. What is the function of a collator?
10. What is the function of an interpreter?
11. What is the function of an accounting machine?
12. What is the function of a reproducer?
13. What is meant by the term "unit record" device?
14. What is a control panel? How is it used in EAM devices?

5 | File Processing

FILES

A file is a collection of related data organized upon some key. Though the word "file" is extensively used in data processing, there is nothing mysterious about the term. You encounter files every day and indeed probably maintain some of your own.

For example, you may have a file of recipe cards. The cards are probably organized in such a way that you can easily find a needed card. The recipes may be alphabetized by dish name, such as "apple pie," "butter cookies," etc. Or they may be organized by food category, such as "meat dishes," "desserts," etc.

You may have a file of most-needed phone numbers. If there are a hundred or so of these numbers, you probably have them alphabetized by the persons' last names.

Files that one keeps at school or in the home tend to be small—there may be only one or two hundred units in them. (In data processing parlance, one of these units is called a "record," as we shall see.) The file units may be recorded in a notebook, or they may be individually written upon 3 × 5 in. cards. These small files may be stored in a drawer of your desk.

Files used in the business world tend to be much more voluminous. For example, a company may have a file of stockholders. That file may contain several hundred thousand entries. Since it is such a huge file, it cannot be stored conventionally, say, in notebooks or on 3 × 5 in. cards. It has to be stored on a more practical device, such as magnetic tape or magnetic disk. (We shall discuss these devices later.) If the file is not so large—if, say, it contains only a few thousand items—the file may be recorded on punched cards.

There are many kinds of files used in the business world. We have mentioned stockholder files. Some of the others in common use are pensioner files, accounts receivable and accounts payable files, inventory files, customer and vendor files, personnel files, and many more.

RECORDS, FIELDS, AND CHARACTERS

Files are broken down into units called "records." A record gives all of the information concerning a person or thing. For example, if we have a personnel file that contains 10,000 entries, each entry is a record. The record contains all of the information concerning a person: the person's social security number, name, pay rate, job description, number of dependents, taxes paid to date, earnings to date, and much more.

An inventory file would also be broken down into records. Each record would concern an individual part and might give its part number, the cost to produce it, its selling price, its bin location, and other information.

Suppose a file has been punched on cards. The individual parts of the file are shown in Fig. 5-1. In this illustration, the entire deck of cards constitutes the file. The file is broken down into records. When cards are used, a single record is usually (but not always) recorded on a single card. Each record of the file is broken down further into units called "fields." A field gives a unit of information, such as social security number, pay rate, year-to-date earnings, job code, etc.

UNIT RECORD PRINCIPLE

In a small company, the records of a file are often recorded upon punched cards. Those records are processed by EAM equipment. When records on punched cards are processed by EAM equipment, it is said that records are processed in "unit record mode." The term "unit record principle" refers to a mode of processing records. It means that, as far as possible, complete records are recorded upon

32   File Processing

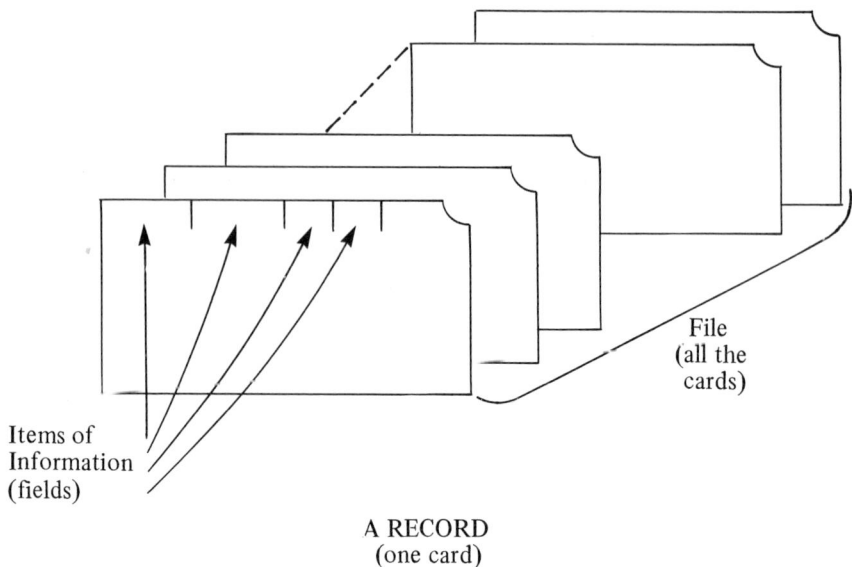

FIGURE 5-1. Parts of a File

single punched cards and these single cards are processed by machines especially suited to work in that mode. Such machines as collators, accounting machines, and others are often called unit record machines as well as EAM devices.

In order to fit all of the required information on a unit record card, a great deal of compacting and coding may have to be done. Each field of the card may have to be kept down to the minimum size that does the job. Social security number fields will have to allow for nine characters—no more, no less; last-name fields may be restricted to ten characters; job descriptions may have to be coded so that A may mean carpenter; B, pipe fitter; C, photographer, etc. If a one-character code is not sufficient to give all the job descriptions of the company, then perhaps two will have to be allocated.

MAGNETIC TAPE

When larger companies are concerned, the pressure to keep records restricted to a single card is not so severe. Files may be stored on magnetic tape, where records may be any required size and are processed by computers. Consider the personnel file of a larger company (see Fig. 5-2).

File Processing 33

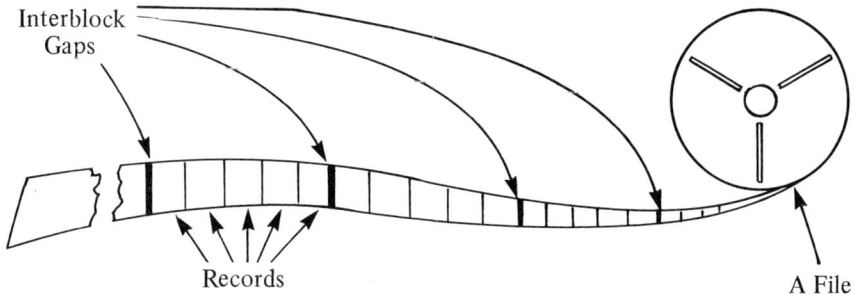

FIGURE 5-2. Magnetic Tape File

Magnetic tape may be used as file storage devices. A reel of tape is 1/2 in. wide and mounted on a 10 in. reel; its length is about 2,400 feet. Information may be recorded on tape with a density of 800 characters per inch (1,600 characters per inch is gradually replacing this density in the industry.). At a density of 800 characters per inch, you can easily calculate the maximum capacity of a reel of magnetic tape:

$$800 \times 12 \times 2,400 = 23,040,000$$

A reel of tape, when loaded to full capacity, stores the same amount of data that may be found upon 288,000 fully loaded 80-column punched cards.

The illustration shows that data may be magnetically recorded upon tape. The major breakdowns on a tape are

1. Blocks
2. Records
3. Fields
4. Characters

BLOCKS

A block is a grouping of records. There may be five records per block, as shown in Fig. 5-2, 10 records, 20, etc. Any grouping that the file designer deems appropriate may be used for the blocking of records. Observe that there is an "interblock gap" (sometimes called "interrecord gap") between each block of records. That gap is a blank space on the tape and may be 5/8 or 3/4 in. wide. We shall discuss the reason for blocking and for providing interblock gaps soon.

Within a block are the various data records, not separated by gaps. One record begins at the point where the previous record terminates. A record may be small or large. If it is a small record, it may occupy only 50 character positions on the tape (1/16 in); if it is a large record, it may occupy 5,000 character positions on the tape (6-1/4 in.). In general, the smaller a record is, the more records there are per block; the larger the record, the fewer per block.

Each record is broken down into fields. A field is a number of character positions that have been set aside to give some desired item of data. For example, a field of 40 characters may be needed to give an employee's home address.

Fields are broken down into the smallest unit found in files—character positions. A field may require only one character position, or it may require 20 or 30 character positions.

TAPE HANDLERS

Reels of magnetic tapes are mounted on devices called tape handlers. Figure 5-3 shows an IBM-401 tape handler. A tape handler is a device that is a part of a computer system. It is used to supply the data that a computer is to work with. Several tapes may be required to feed the data that a computer requires. Some computer systems employ over 20 reels of tape to supply input data.

As you can see in the figure, a file reel is mounted upon the left spindle and is "read" by the computer. When tape is "read," portions of the data on the file are transferred from the file reel to the machine reel. The machine reel is mounted upon the right spindle.

Tapes are read from interblock gap to interblock gap. That is, when a command is issued to the tape handler to supply records, the tape handler transfers to the computer's memory all of the records within a block of tape. If the block is small, few records are transferred; if the block is long, more are transferred.

BUFFERS

In the memory of the computer, sufficient memory space has been reserved to permit the storage of a complete block of records. This space is called a "buffer." The size of a buffer for a file must,

File Processing

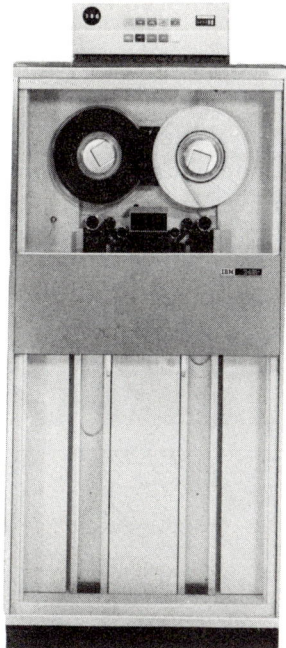

FIGURE 5-3. A Tape Handler

therefore, be the same size as a block in memory.

When the computer processes records, it does so from the buffer. Each record in the buffer is processed until all the records in the buffer have been taken care of. Then the computer sends another signal to the tape handler to bring in more records. Obeying this signal, the tape handler sends another block of records to the buffer. These new records overlie the records already in the memory, thus wiping out the ones in memory. The wiping out of old records should cause you no concern, since they have already been processed.

Not all records of a file can be brought into the memory of a computer at one time. Despite the fact that computer memories may have up to two million character positions available, data processing files are usually much larger than two million characters and therefore cannot fit in the memory all at the same time.

Further, a specific application may require the obtaining of input from two or more files. It is impossible to read into memory these complete files, but it is possible to read them in a little at a time.

CENTRAL PROCESSING UNIT

Two of the major components of computers are the memory and the central processing unit, or CPU. This is the module of a computer which actually computes. Figure 5-4 shows how information is read into the memory of a computer, how the information is transmitted to the CPU for processing, how results are returned to other portions of the memory, and how results are output.

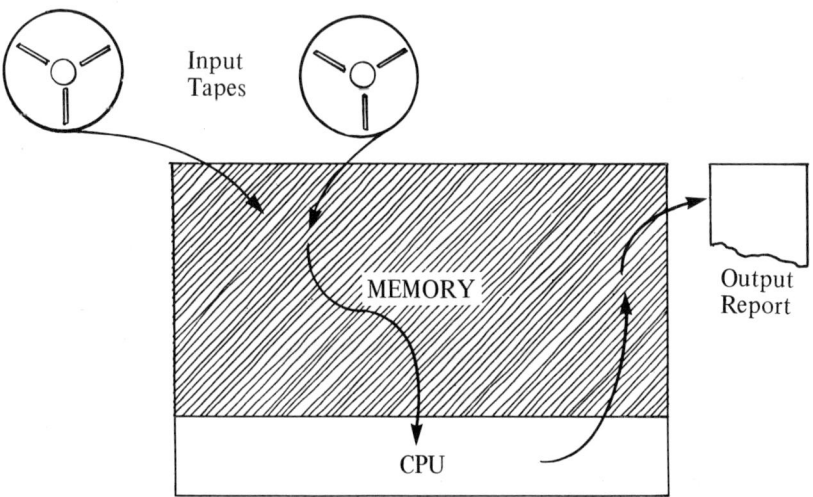

FIGURE 5-4. Records Being Processed

The figure shows that some records are read into the memory of the computer. They are then processed and results are returned to the memory. Output from memory may be on punched cards, magnetic tape, magnetic disk, high-speed printer paper, and others. In Fig. 5-4, output is being given on high-speed printer paper.

The figure does not show that the cycle shown here repeats over and over again, thousands of times if necessary, until all records on all input tapes have been processed.

BASIC DATA PROCESSING CYCLE

The flowchart in Fig. 5-5 shows the basic data processing cycle. The cycle goes from the "read data" step to the "process data" and "give some output" steps and back to the "read data" step. The process continues until there are no more input data. At the "end of file" (EOF), the program stops.

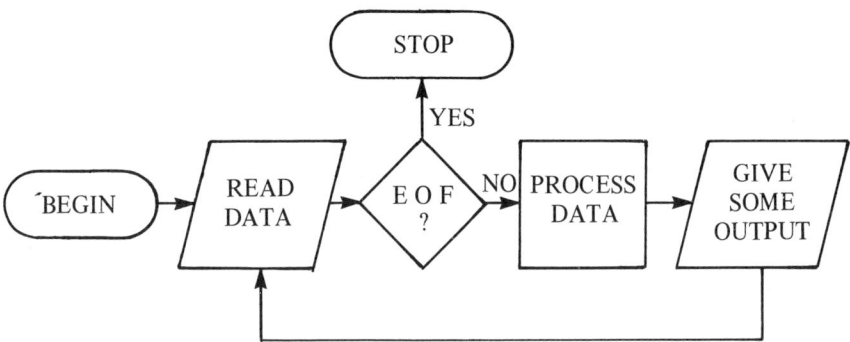

FIGURE 5-5. Basic Data Processing Cycle

SUMMARY

A file is a collection of related data organized around specific fields called its key. Files are often recorded on magnetic tape, but they may also be recorded on disks, drums, data cells, and cards. (We shall cover these devices in detail later.)

Files are constructed of blocks and records. Records are broken down into fields. Fields are further broken down into characters.

Small businesses often record complete files on data processing cards, one record per card. These cards are processed by unit record (EAM) equipment. The devices are called unit record machines because they process one card at a time, each card containing one record.

Magnetic tapes provide a very popular means for recording files. Recorded with a density of up to 1,600 characters per inch, enormous amounts of data or information can be recorded on tape. Records are stored in groups called blocks. Whenever the tape handler is requested to bring into memory some information, the handler brings in a whole block of records. These records are stored into memory areas called buffers, from which they are processed.

QUESTIONS

1. Define the term *file*.
2. Name several kinds of files that may be used in the business world.

File Processing

3. Define the term *record*.
4. Define the term *field*.
5. Define the term *character*.
6. What is meant by the term *unit record principle*? Name some unit record devices.
7. Why is the extensive use of codes needed when one is employing the unit record principle?
8. What is meant by the term *recording density on tape*? What are some typical densities?
9. What is an interblock gap? Why is it used?
10. What is a buffer? Why is it used?
11. What is a computer's CPU?
12. Describe the basic data processing cycle.

6 | Converting from EAM Equipment to a Computer

We have seen that a small company may well be able to do all of its data processing using only EAM equipment. Some items of EAM or unit record equipments take the form of card punch machines, interpreters, collators, sorters, duplicators, and accounting machines.

When a company grows and advances to the point where computers should be used, it may at first obtain a small computer. This computer may either be leased at, say, $4,000 each month or bought outright for, say, $80,000. At first, the company may find that the computer is used for only a short period of time each day. Much of the company's work may still be done on EAM equipment.

CONVERSION

Gradually a conversion effort begins, and applications currently on EAM equipment are transferred to the computer. In the process of making conversions, the applications involved may be expanded and improved. The company thereby gets more information from its data, since a computer has far more capacity to produce than does EAM equipment.

With a computer "in house," managers and scientists will have no difficulty in thinking of projects to be computerized. Those in charge of the computer make little effort to restrict these applications, since so much capacity is available that almost any project seems like a good idea.

Within a year or so, the computer is found to be fully utilized. A second or third shift for computer operations may be seriously considered. Already, the less timid persons in the computer section begin agitating for a larger and better machine.

The higher levels of management in the company will have to wrestle with a couple of nagging questions. First, after a year's experience with the machine, has the company's financial health improved or deteriorated? True, the EAM equipment has almost completely been phased out, and several clerks who used to operate the equipment have been transferred to other jobs. True, the company is getting more and faster reports. True, also, the scientists are elated, since they now have the time to make in-depth investigations that were earlier impossible. But what is the other side of the story?

This year there are additional costs involving computer operations. There are the lease charges and/or maintenance charges. There are extra costs for blank data processing cards, computer paper, and added air-conditioning costs. (Computers must be kept cool.)

THE COMPUTER BECOMES ENTRENCHED

There is also an expensive computer staff including a data processing manager, a couple of programmers, and a couple of computer operators. The programmers and operators were recruited from the ranks of the EAM operators. In fact, all the former EAM personnel are now working with the computers and making more money. And the data processing manager is now asking for a larger computer and more people to operate it.

The happy scientists are turning out volumes of reports concerning dozens of interesting studies, but to date it is difficult to identify any significant product "breakthroughs" that have come about because of the computer's existence. If one did not know better, he might almost believe that there was better research and development being done before the computer arrived.

There is a serious question of whether the new computer is earning its keep. After a year almost every person interrogated claims that the computer is a necessity—that it is a wonder that the company was able to survive for so long without one.

Not convinced, higher management may commission a study conducted by an outside consulting firm. After several months, the outside concern advises that the computer is indeed providing a valuable service and that the company needs a larger one. (The computer itself was utilized to help come up with that conclusion.) The computer vendor agrees. He recommends that the company convert to a larger machine in the same computer series.

So the larger machine is ordered, and it arrives a few months later. The old computer, which by the time the new one arrives is greatly overloaded, is removed, and the new one takes its place. The data processing manager is permitted to hire two new programmers. Everyone is now convinced that the company does indeed need a computer to do its data processing and that the larger it is, the better.

INCREASING CAPACITY

The growth cycle begins all over again. At first the new computer, which has five times the capacity of the old one, is utilized for only a small percentage of that capacity. But new projects begin to pour in, conversion efforts from old computer to new consume a great deal of computer time (the vendor said conversion would be a trivial problem), and recently developed projects are expanded and improved. Two years later, the new computer is heavily loaded and higher management begins asking questions again.

As time passes, the computer department gains greatly in importance. It becomes the heart of the company and increasingly has a large impact in whatever the company does. The data processing manager is permitted to reorganize his group. He breaks up his department into two portions; the first deals with computer programming and the second with computer operations. New people are added to both groups. Involved procedures are developed so that company personnel may efficiently utilize the services of the two groups.

The company prospers, but few bother to inquire whether the company prospers because of its computer or despite it. The existence of the computer is taken for granted, and no one questions whether it pays its own way. It has become a prestigious symbol, anyway, and higher management is confident that the company will be prosperous enough to be able to afford it.

This story about how a company acquires a computer and how the computer entrenches itself has been recounted almost with tongue in cheek. Certainly, not all computers have been installed under such vague conditions. But many have. The managers of these latter companies should indeed hope that the companies will prosper sufficiently to be able to afford them.

SUMMARY

This chapter points out that once a business graduates to a computer, there is usually no looking backward. The computer becomes entrenched in the organization, and there are soon demands that it be replaced with a larger one.

There is no question that computers are ideal for the processing of certain applications, such as payroll or inventory control. It is also true that much computer capacity is wasted. Computers tend to be symbols of success, and companies obtain computers just to display them. Further, much work done on computers is needless. Reports are issued which few people read; studies are conducted upon which no action is taken.

A business concern contemplating the installation of a computer to replace EAM equipment should take the step after only the most thorough of feasibility studies.

QUESTIONS

1. What are some of the reasons that a business concern installs a computer system? Which are valid? Which are not?
2. Typically, what is a computer's level of utilization when it is first installed? What is it, say, a year later?
3. What are some of the costs connected with having an on-site computer center?
4. Assuming that you are a data processing expert, what are some of the cautions and items of advice that you would give to a manager who is thinking of installing a computer?

7 | Computer Input/Output Devices

Just as there are EAM input and output devices, there are also input and output devices used with computer systems. Figure 7-1 shows some of those devices and identifies them as input, output, or both:

In addition to these widely used devices, there are other devices that are not used so extensively. We shall mention these devices later in this chapter.

CARD READER

Let us consider the card reader first (see Fig. 7-2). A card reader is an item of computer hardware which accepts a deck of punched cards and senses what is on each card (reads it). Then the data punched on the cards are transmitted to the memory of the computer.

Card readers are of two basic types: mechanical and optical. Mechanical card readers use metal brushes, which feel for holes. Once the holes have been found, electrical circuits are established which enable the card reader to transmit data, in the form of characters, to the computer's memory. Optical card readers operate similarly to mechanical ones, except that light beams detect the holes. Electrical circuits are established, and information is transmitted.

Mechanical card readers read cards at about the rate of 250 cards

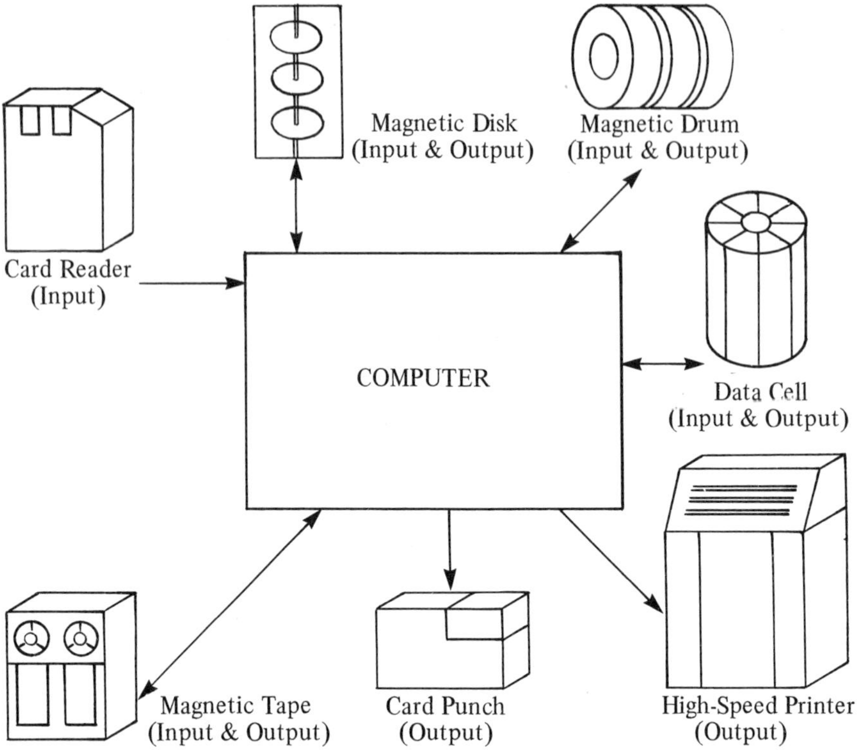

FIGURE 7-1. Input and Output Devices

FIGURE 7-2. A Card Reader

per minute. Optical card readers read cards at rates of up to 2,000 cards per minute. At the fastest speeds, card readers supply data to a computer's memory at a rate of over 2,500 characters per second.

MAGNETIC TAPE

Figure 7-3 is a photo of a tape handler.

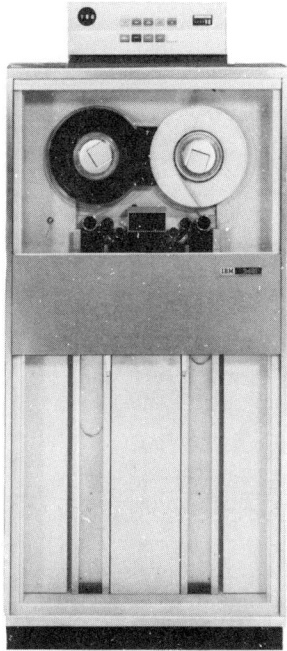

FIGURE 7-3. A Tape Handler

Earlier in this text, you saw that over 23 million characters of data may be stored upon a reel of tape. You saw also that tape transmission rates may easily exceed 100,000 characters per second. This speed, which is about 40 times faster than a fast card reader, makes tape handlers an attractive alternative to the use of card readers. Often, cards are punched, and then the information is recorded on tape, an item of hardware called a card-to-tape converter being used. The tape may then be used for providing input to a computer. Magnetic tape is reusable many times for many applications. As in a home tape recorder, recording over a used portion of tape erases what was there and replaces it with new data. Tape may also be used for output, as we shall see when we discuss high-speed printers later in this chapter.

DISK

Figure 7-4 shows a magnetic disk unit. Magnetic disk units consist of circular rotating platters upon which data may be recorded magnetically in tightly packed form. The data may be recorded on both the top and bottom surfaces. There may be as few as four surfaces to a unit, or as many as 32. Looking down at the top surface of a platter, we might see as many as 200 tracks per surface, if they were visible (see Fig. 7-5).

FIGURE 7-4. A Magnetic Disk Unit

Data are recorded upon the tracks. Disk units employ arms that move read/write heads across the tracks, either writing upon the surfaces of the platters or reading from them.

Disks are available in either small, medium, or large sizes. Small disks are portable and may be transported, stored, and mounted in much the same way that magnetic tapes are transported, stored, and mounted. Larger disks usually remain in one position.

Like tape, data recorded magnetically upon disks may be replaced

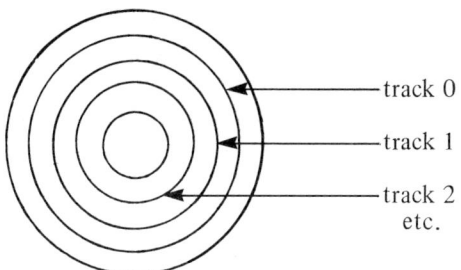

FIGURE 7-5. Top Surface of a Platter

with new data. When this happens, the old data are automatically erased.

The amount of information that may be recorded upon a complete disk unit ranges from 2 million characters to 20 million. Transfer rates of information to the memory of a computer or from the memory may range from a quarter million characters per second to about one million characters per second.

Disks are much faster than magnetic tapes, but are also more costly to install, use, and maintain. They should be used only where great rates of transmission speeds are required, or, as we shall see, where file records must be accessed in random sequence.

DRUM

Similar in operation to disks but different in appearance are magnetic drums (see Fig. 7-6). Drums are devices that have a barrel shape. Data may be magnetically recorded in tightly packed form upon the surfaces of the units. The units rotate and permit data to pass under read/write heads. The costs, speeds, and capacities of magnetic drums are similar to those of magnetic disks. The two devices may often be used interchangeably for the performance of various tasks. The capacity of a drum may be only about one-fourth the capacity of a disk, however.

DATA CELL

Figure 7-7 shows an IBM 2321 Data Cell. A data cell is a cylindrical device that positions thousands of short strips of magnetic tape in easily accessible form. When a strip of tape is required, the

48 Computer Input/Output Devices

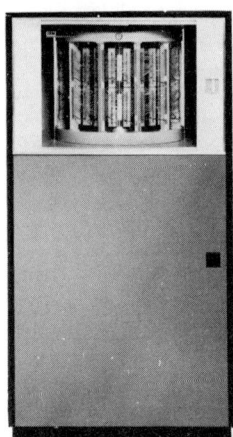

FIGURE 7-6. A Magnetic Drum

computer sends a signal to the data cell. The cell releases a selected strip of tape and causes it to be wound tightly around a drum. The tape is now read from or written upon.

FIGURE 7-7. An IBM 2321 Data Cell

Data cells permit immensely large quantities of information to be stored and retrieved. But mechanically removing a strip from its storage location in the cell and winding it upon a drum takes time.

The capacity of a data cell unit may be up to 400 million characters. Its transmission rate is about 60,000 characters per second. The cost of storing information in data cells is relatively low and would be chosen as the storage medium for applications where large volumes of data must be stored and retrieved at moderately fast rates of speed.

HIGH-SPEED PRINTER

A high-speed printer is shown in Fig. 7-8. This device is strictly an output device. It provides output in the form of reports. The unit is capable of printing up to 1,500 lines of printed matter per minute. Each line may typically contain 120 or 132 characters of information.

FIGURE 7-8. A High-Speed Printer

The printer prints upon continuous forms, which are stacked accordion-style (see Fig. 7-9). Each page contains up to 66 lines of information. When printed, the output sheets may or may not be torn along the perforated edges as required by programmers.

Despite their name, high-speed printers are relatively slow, providing only about 2,500 characters of output per second. Because printers are slow, output is often written upon magnetic tape, and then the tape is taken to a tape-to-printer device after the computer operation has been completed. As you have seen, information can be written upon tape at a typical rate of 120,000 characters per second.

The tape-to-printer operation is called an "off-line" operation, since it does not require the use of a computer. Off-line operations such as card-to-tape and tape-to-printer may be done at the convenience of the computer center. Since computers are not used during these conversions, the final costs are lower than if the complete operations had been done "on-line."

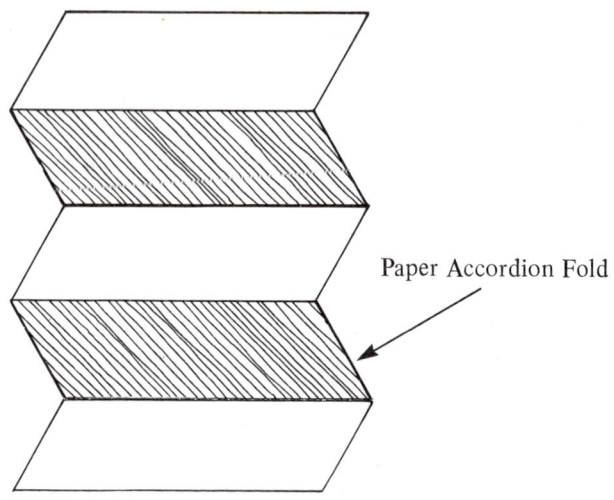

FIGURE 7-9. A Printed Report

OPTICAL SCANNER

Several other types of devices are used for providing input and output to a computer system. One type is the optical scanner (see Fig. 7-10). This type optically examines a document and transfers pertinent information to the memory of the computer.

Although optical scanners are being used today, a good deal of development work may have to be done before they can be truly effective. For example, optical scanners are not good at reading poorly handwritten material.

When these machines are improved, much of the preparatory work now required in order to provide data for a computer will be eliminated.

MICR

Another type of character recognition is the MICR system. MICR stands for magnetic ink character recognition. In use, characters are

FIGURE 7-10. An Optical Scanner

printed with magnetic ink on paper in a special configuration. MICR equipment is able to recognize these characters from the shapes and magnetic properties.

TYPEWRITER

This kind of equipment is widely used by banks in the automatic handling of checks and other documents.

The typewriter found at the console of almost all computers being built today permits humans to communicate with a computer. A computer operator may type a code that asks a computer a question such as "What program are you working on now?" The computer responds, giving the information. Later the computer may type a message directing a computer operator to mount a certain tape reel. The operator performs the task and tells the computer that he has done so.

Since typewriters are very slow devices, they should be used only for the most essential of communications between computer and human.

PRINTERS

Special printers have been developed for obtaining printed material. One type, the electrostatic, operates at the rate of about 5,000 lines per minute. In operation this device first charges a sheet of paper at selected points, then fogs the paper with an inky mist. Ink is attracted to the charged portions of the paper and sticks there. By the use of heat, the ink is fused into place.

The actions described above take place at high rates of speed, thus giving a great quantity of printed material in a short time. The process is expensive, though, and only one copy may be obtained at one time from the printer.

PHOTOGRAPHY

Another method of obtaining fast output is through the use of photography. When the computer has generated a report page image in its memory, that image is flashed on a CRT (cathode ray tube). A CRT is a screen similar to those seen on television sets. When the page image is placed on the screen, a microfilm camera takes its picture. The picture is later developed. An engineer or manager wanting to study the page must do so with the aid of a microfilm viewer.

COMPUTER OUTPUT MICROFILM (COM)

For certain types of output, filmed reports are ideal. As many as 8,000 lines of information per minute may be obtained from the computer. This is about six to eight times as fast as the speed available from the ordinary high-speed printer. The next chapter in this book explains COM in more detail.

VOICE

Even voice is being used for both input and output in connection with certain devices. A person may slowly and carefully speak certain words into a device, and then obtain the answer in spoken form.

For example, a broker might inquire

QUOTE IBM

and the device will respond

FOUR THIRTY FIVE BID FOUR FIFTY ASKED

Though voice devices are, at present, primitive, they will undoubtedly improve with time.

CARD PUNCH

The card punch is another form of output device. This item punches output on standard data processing cards. Since there is no printing on these cards, some of them must be interpreted by using the EAM device called the interpreter.

SUMMARY

In order to be able to process data, computers must obtain them from external sources. Devices that are capable of holding data are punched cards, magnetic tapes, magnetic disks, magnetic drums, and others. Characters may be transferred from these devices to the computer's memory at various rates of speed.

Information in the computer's memory may be written upon external devices. Some of the external devices in common use are high-speed printer, magnetic tape, magnetic disk, and others. The computer can, if desired, be requested to punch its output upon data processing cards.

Since most methods of giving a computer input data and of receiving information from a computer are relatively slow, devices have been developed to transmit data more rapidly. One of those devices for output is COM (Computer Output Microfilm). Output is flashed page by page upon the screen of a cathode ray tube, then photographed. Output is placed upon microfilm in special formats. We give more details concerning COM in the next chapter.

QUESTIONS

1. Name the major devices that may be used to provide input to a computer. Rank them in order of transmission speeds.
2. Name the major devices that may be used to provide output from a computer. Rank them in order of transmission speeds.
3. What are the two kinds of card readers insofar as the punched holes are detected?
4. What is the function of a card-to-tape converter?
5. On disks, what are *tracks*?

6. What is a read/write head and what devices use it?
7. What are the advantages and disadvantages of data cells?
8. What is meant by "off-line" operation?
9. How does an electrostatic printer operate?
10. Is voice an effective way to communicate with a computer at this time? Explain.

8 | Computer Output Microfilm

With the increasing calculating speeds of computers, a problem has developed in obtaining output from a computer. Printers have become faster but are still slow in comparison with the speeds at which computers may generate output.

A typical high-speed printer is capable of printing at a rate of 1,000 to 1,200 lines of output per minute. Each line of output may contain up to 132 characters of information.

True, electrostatic printers are available which print at rates of up to 15,000 lines per minute, but such printers operate under rather sophisticated conditions. Paper is charged with line images and is passed through an ink fog. Ink adheres to the charged portions of the paper. Then heat is used to fix the line images.

The electrostatic systems are expensive to use and give only one copy of printed pages, but they do provide an alternative to conventional printers.

COM (Computer Output Microfilm) has recently come of age. COM does not solve all problems associated with computer output, but it provides an additional option that system designers may consider. Figure 8-1 shows how COM operates.

Instead of printing pages on the computer's high-speed printer, the computer generates an output tape. The information on this tape may be transformed to output pages off-line if desired, but the very same tape may be fed as input to a COM microfilmer. (An example

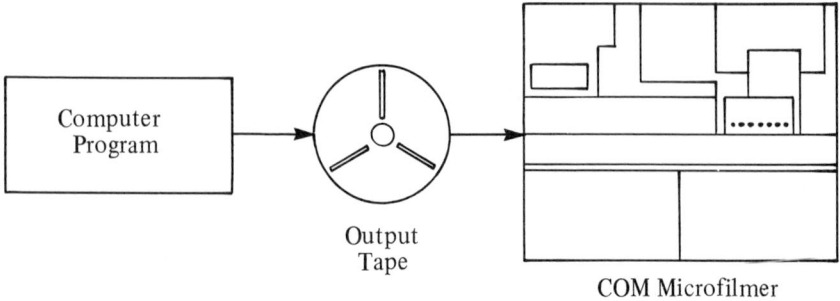
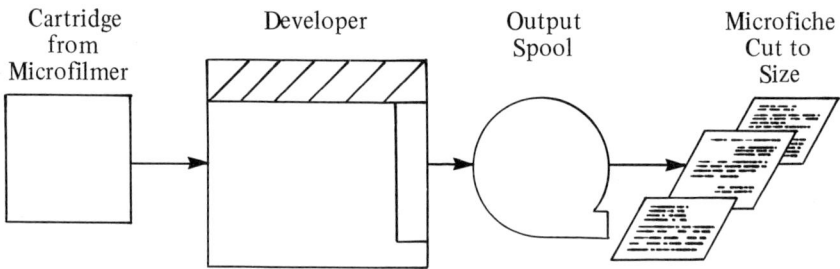

FIGURE 8-1. COM Operation

of a COM microfilmer is Kodak's KOM-80.) Installed on a tape handler used in association with the microfilmer, the machine can produce page images on a CRT (cathode ray tube) and photograph them at a rate that varies from 150 to 500 pages per minute. As a rough rule of thumb, producing film output from the tape is roughly twenty times as fast as printing out output on paper. The output is available in a small cartridge weighing less than a pound.

ADVANTAGES OF COM

At this point, three of the advantages of COM become crystal clear. First, speed. With a speed advantage of about twenty times printing speed, COM frees output operators to perform other functions in an output processing area. Second, the sheer volume of output is reduced. The output from COM requires only about 2 percent of the space that printed output requires. Third, the cost of the output is greatly reduced. The cost of COM is only about 5 percent of that of the corresponding printed output.

APPLICATIONS OF COM

Once the film has been exposed, the cartridge in which it resides may be inserted in a developing device. The device develops and dries the film in a total time of about two minutes. The film may then be cut to size or retained in spools.

One popular form of microfilm output is "microfiche." A microfiche is a sheet of film about 4 × 6 in. (105 mm × 148.75 mm). On the sheet are recorded up to 270 pages of computer output. These pages are recorded in a grid of 15 rows by 18 columns. The output is photo reduced by a factor of 48 to 1. Other reducing ratios are available, but this one may become the standard in the industry.

Obviously, pages on microfiche are too small be to viewed with the naked eye. There are several types of viewers that can be used for examining selected sheets of film.

In producing microfiche, the COM microfilmer may be directed to place indexes and legends upon the microfiches so that desired information may readily be found. For instance, fiches have printed headings upon them that may be easily read with the naked eye. A person can, therefore, readily select the microfiche he wishes to place in a viewer. In the viewer, the user can position it so that a special index page is in view. The index page gives a cross reference to the content of the other pages upon the fiche. Having found a reference to the page he wants to examine, the user may then position the viewer to the page.

Copies of microfiche may easily be made by using a special exposer and a developer. The entire process requires about a minute.

As we said, microfilm may not be the answer to all output problems, but it is the ideal answer for many of them. Many reports are required, not for page-by-page study, but for historical reference. It makes a great deal of sense to place those kinds of reports in a form that allows infrequent reference yet does not take up a great deal of storage space nor require a great deal of expense to produce.

SUMMARY

COM (Computer Output Microfilm) offers three advantages. It permits computer output to be processed faster, less expensively, and with less bulk.

Output is written on magnetic tape in page format. Then, rather than being printed off-line at the rate of 1,000 to 1,200 lines per minute, it is photographed and placed on film at a rate that is approximately twenty times as fast. The resulting film in either roll or microfiche form takes up only a fraction of the space that printed material requries and is much less expensive to produce.

Although not all output is an ideal candidate for microfilm, a great deal of it is. Reports which must be generated for various reasons but which need to be looked at infrequently can advantageously be recorded on film. If viewers are used, selected pages of the reports may be easily studied. Copies may be easily made of these reports.

QUESTIONS

1. What is COM? what are *three* advantages that it offers?
2. Describe microfiche.
3. For what types of reports can COM be most advantageously used?

9 | Binary Bits

In the chapters that follow we shall describe how a computer functions. In order for you to be able to follow the discussion, you should know how a computer stores data and how it computes.

A computer stores data in the form of zeroes and ones. As an example, the integer value of 25 is represented this way in many computers:

      000...00011001

and the number 2,049 is represented this way:

      000...00100000000001

In the examples shown, the series of dots indicates additional zeroes that are not shown. We shall see presently how many zeroes are actually represented.

DECIMAL NUMBERS

In the pages that follow, there will sometimes be some confusion regarding what numeric value a series of digits represents. To clarify ambiguous numbers, we shall sometimes give a subscript in connection with a number. For example, the number

8567_{10}

represents the value 8,567 in the decimal (base 10) numbering system. The decimal numbering system is the system we use every day. In this system ten different digits are used (hence the term base 10). The ten digits are

0 1 2 3 4 5 6 7 8 9

Numbers in the decimal system mean exactly what they say. At least, you have a clear mental idea of what the numbers mean. The number

324_{10}

represents three groups of hundreds, two groups of tens, and four groups of singles.

BINARY NUMBERS

A number written in some other base may not give you an instant feel for what it really represents. For example, the number

$000\ldots00100110_2$

may appear to be a relatively large value, but it is not. In decimal terms, the number shown is equivalent to 38_{10}.

The number shown above is in the base 2 numbering system, the system that most computers employ. The base 2 numbering system uses only two digits, 0 and 1.

The digits in a base 2 number have various equivalent values in the decimal system depending upon the positions of the base 2 digits within the entire number.

Consider this next number.

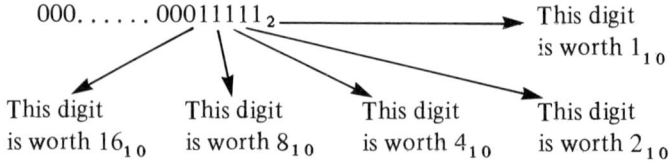

Binary Bits

The five 1's have different values, depending upon their positions. To determine the value of the entire number, all you have to do is add together the various positional values. Thus, $16 + 8 + 4 + 2 + 1$ equals 31_{10}.

The model number suggests that the value of the digit 1 doubles and redoubles as the 1 is found further left in a value.

In determining the decimal equivalent of a value, one adds together all the positional values associated with any 1's shown in a value. In this next example,

$$000...0010011_2$$

the decimal equivalent of the binary value is 19_{10}. The values of the 1's in the example are 16_{10}, 2_{10}, and 1_{10}, respectively, reading from left to right.

The following chart should be helpful when you establish the base 2 (binary) equivalent of a decimal value:

	2^7	2^6	2^5	2^4	2^3	2^2	2^1	2^0
Powers of 2 corresponding values	128_{10}	64_{10}	32_{10}	16_{10}	8_{10}	4_{10}	2_{10}	1_{10}

Suppose that you are required to establish the base 2 equivalent of 105_{10}. You should select the values to make up 105_{10}, examining the values in the chart from left to right.

The number 128_{10} cannot be used to help establish 105_{10}, but 64_{10} can be used. Therefore, place a zero in the box shown under 128_{10} and a one in the box shown under 64_{10}. You now have this:

	2^7	2^6	2^5	2^4	2^3	2^2	2^1	2^0
Powers of 2 corresponding values	128_{10}	64_{10}	32_{10}	16_{10}	8_{10}	4_{10}	2_{10}	1_{10}
	0	1						

Now if you subtract 64_{10} from 105_{10}, the result is 41_{10}. Now you select 32_{10} as being required to make up 41_{10}. You place a 1 in the box under 32_{10}.

Subtracting again $41_{10} - 32_{10}$, you see that the difference is 9_{10}. The 8_{10} and the 1_{10} are selected, and the value 105_{10} has been established. The final result in the chart is this:

	2^7	2^6	2^5	2^4	2^3	2^2	2^1	2^0
Powers of 2 corresponding values	128_{10}	64_{10}	32_{10}	16_{10}	8_{10}	4_{10}	2_{10}	1_{10}
	0	1	1	0	1	0	0	1

We may write now that

$$105_{10} = 000\ldots0001101001_2$$

The actual binary value is composed of 32 zeroes and ones. In the above value, therefore, the series of dots in the number represents 19 zeroes.

WORDS

Not all computers use 32 zeroes and ones to represent an integer value. Some computers use 20, some 36, some 48. In this text we shall use 32, since most series of popular computers being used today use that number of digits. A group of bits representing some data value is called a "word."

Binary digits are known as "bits." The word "bit" is a contraction of the two words *bi*nary digi*t*. Whenever we mention "bits," therefore, you should visualize a binary digit, either zero or one.

A computer's memory often has the capacity of storing about ten million bits of information. The exact number of memory bits depends upon the computer being discussed. A computer that has a capacity of ten million bits is today considered a large computer.

CORES

Each mathematical bit has a hardware partner in the computer's memory. That partner is called a core. If a computer has the ability to store ten million bits of data, then the memory has ten million cores. Each core, greatly magnified, looks like Fig. 9-1.

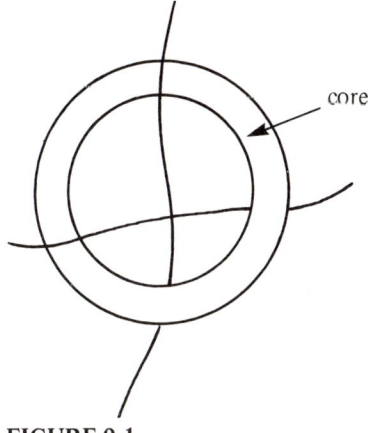

FIGURE 9-1

A core is very tiny. It is a little larger than the period shown at the end of this sentence. Wires pass through these cores linking various sets of cores together.

A core is made of metal and may be magnetized in one of two directions. The directions are shown in Fig. 9-2 by the arrows.

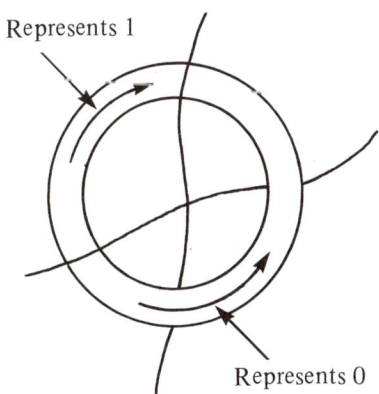

FIGURE 9-2

If a core is magnetized in one direction, the direction is arbitrarily defined to represent the binary value 1; if it is magnetized in the other direction, it represents 0. The wires shown in the illustration supply the current that magnetizes the cores in one way or the other.

When an integer value is to be represented, the computer utilizes a set of 32 cores. It magnetizes some of them to represent ones, and some to represent zeroes. Those settings can be entirely changed in one microsecond. (A microsecond is one millionth of a second.) Thus a set of 32 cores (a word) may represent one value at some given time and an entirely different value only one microsecond later.

The first few decimal values expressed in binary notation are these:

$$0000...0000001 = 1_{10}$$
$$0000...0000010 = 2_{10}$$
$$0000...0000011 = 3_{10}$$
$$0000...0000100 = 4_{10}$$
$$0000...0000101 = 5_{10}$$
$$0000...0000110 = 6_{10}$$
$$0000...0000111 = 7_{10}$$
$$0000...0001000 = 8_{10}, \text{etc.}$$

The largest integer that may be represented with 32 bits is

$$01111...11111_2$$

The dots indicate the presence of 22 additional 1's. This value is $2^{31} - 1$, a value that is in excess of two billion. (The exact value is 2,147,483,647.)

In passing, it should be pointed out that other main storage mediums exist besides magnetic cores. Some other devices are thin films, plated wires, monolithic storage, and others. Cores are still widely used, but are gradually being replaced by these more sophisticated devices.

SUMMARY

Computers employ numbers that are constructed according to base 2 principles. In the base 2, or binary, numbering system, only two digits are used—zero and one.

In the memory of a computer, data are represented as a series of zeroes and ones. Each binary digit (bit) comes from the state of a magnetic core. If the core has been magnetized to represent a 1, then the corresponding bit is 1; if the core has been magnetized to represent 0, then the corresponding bit is 0.

In a computer, several million cores may be used to represent both zeroes and ones. These bits are often organized into groups of 32, each group being called a "word." The contents of words can be changed in as little time as one microsecond.

QUESTIONS

1. What is the name of the numbering system employed by computers?
2. What is a core, and what are the two states that it may attain?
3. What is a *bit*?
4. What is a *word*? Of how many bits is it typically composed?
5. What is the decimal numbering system? How many digits does it employ?
6. What are the decimal values of the individual one bits in the word shown below?

    $000...00111011_2$

7. What is the decimal value of the following binary number?

    $000...0010111011_2$

8. How does the decimal value of a binary number change as a zero is appended at the right? Example:

    $000...0010100_2$

    $000...0101000_2$

9. What is the decimal value of the following binary number? (Assume 32 bits.)

    $01111...111_2$

    (Express the answer as a power of two.)
10. How long does it it take to change the state of a core from representing a zero to representing a one?

10 | Integers

POSITIVE INTEGERS

In expressing numeric values, a computer works with powers of 2. To express integer 1, it uses 2^0; to express integer 2, 2^1; integer 3, $2^1 + 2^0$; etc. This table shows the positional values in an integer number:

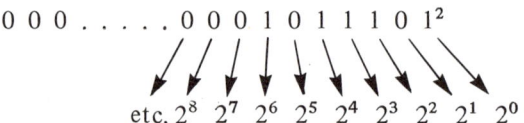

$$0\ 0\ 0\ \ldots\ \ldots\ 0\ 0\ 1\ 0\ 1\ 1\ 1\ 0\ 1^2$$

etc. $2^8\ 2^7\ 2^6\ 2^5\ 2^4\ 2^3\ 2^2\ 2^1\ 2^0$

The decimal equivalent of the integer value shown above is

$$2^6 + 2^4 + 2^3 + 2^2 + 2^0$$

or

$$64 + 16 + 8 + 4 + 1$$

or 93_{10}

Integers

TWO'S COMPLEMENT

So far we have discussed only positive values. Negative integer values are expressed in a mode called "two's complement." In two's complement arithmetic, -1_{10} looks like this:

$1111\ldots1111_2$

Negative 12_{10} looks like this:

$1111\ldots110100_2$

In the examples, the dots indicate a string of 1's that are not shown. Negative numbers use 32 bits just as positive numbers do.

NEGATIVE INTEGERS

To convert a positive number to its negative form, one uses a simple procedure. We shall illustrate the procedure on several positive numbers. The number shown below is 140_{10}.

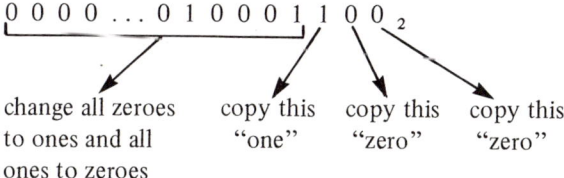

$0\ 0\ 0\ 0\ \ldots\ 0\ 1\ 0\ 0\ 0\ 1\ 1\ 0\ 0_2$

change all zeroes to ones and all ones to zeroes | copy this "one" | copy this "zero" | copy this "zero"

Scanning the positive number from right to left, you copy any zeroes that might be found. Then you copy the very first 1 you find as you move toward the left. Having copied the 1, you then change all the ones to zeroes and all the zeroes to ones.

Here are some examples:

$0\ 0\ 0\ \ldots\ 0\ 0\ 1\ 1\ 0\ 0\ 1_2\ =\ 25_{10}$

$1\ 1\ 1\ \ldots\ 1\ 1\ 0\ 0\ 1\ 1\ 1_2\ =\ -25_{10}$

$0\ 0\ 0\ \ldots\ 0\ 0\ 1\ 0\ 0\ 0\ 0\ 0_2\ =\ 32_{10}$

$1\ 1\ 1\ \ldots\ 1\ 1\ 1\ 0\ 0\ 0\ 0\ 0_2\ =\ -32_{10}$

Exactly the same procedure is employed to convert any negative number to its positive form. Examples are

$$1\ 1\ 1\ \ldots\ 1\ 1\ 0\ 0\ 0\ 1\ 0_2 = -30_{10}$$
$$0\ 0\ 0\ 0\ \ldots\ 0\ 0\ 1\ 1\ 1\ 1\ 0_2 = 30_{10}$$
$$1\ 1\ 1\ 1\ \ldots\ 1\ 1\ 1\ 1\ 1\ 1\ 1\ = -1_{10}$$
$$0\ 0\ 0\ 0\ \ldots\ 0\ 0\ 0\ 0\ 0\ 0\ 1\ = 1_{10}$$

One can always tell at a glance whether a given binary number is positive or negative. If the leftmost bit is zero, the number is positive. If it is 1, the number is negative. These numbers are positive:

$$0\ 0\ 0\ \ldots\ 0\ 0\ 1\ 1\ 0\ 0\ 0_2$$
$$0\ 0\ 0\ \ldots\ 0\ 1\ 0\ 0\ 0\ 0\ 0_2$$
$$0\ 1\ 1\ \ldots\ 1\ 1\ 1\ 1\ 1\ 1\ 1_2$$

These numbers are negative:

$$1\ 1\ 1\ \ldots\ 1\ 1\ 1\ 1\ 1\ 1\ 1_2$$
$$1\ 1\ 1\ \ldots\ 1\ 1\ 0\ 0\ 0\ 0\ 0_2$$
$$1\ 0\ 0\ \ldots\ 0\ 0\ 0\ 0\ 0\ 0\ 0_2$$

In a 32-bit configuration the largest positive number, as we have seen, is

$$0\ 1\ 1\ 1\ 1\ \ldots\ 1\ 1\ 1\ 1_2$$

and is equivalent to $2^{31} - 1$ (2,147,483,647).

The largest negative number is

$$1\ 0\ 0\ 0\ \ldots\ 0\ 0\ 0\ 0_2$$

and is equivalent to 2^{31} (2,147,483,648). The largest negative value is greater in magnitude by 1 than the largest positive number.

ADDING IN BINARY

When the computer adds binary integers, it uses a very simple addition table. The table includes only these four entries:

Integers

```
   0       0       1       1
  +0      +1      +0      +1
  ──      ──      ──      ──
   0       1       1      10
```

Let us try adding a few binary values in the way that a computer would do it. Suppose that the values and the sum are

$$0\ 0\ 0\ \ldots\ 0\ 0\ 0\ 0\ 1\ 1\ 1\ 0\ 0\ 1\ 1\ 0_2 = 230_{10}$$
$$0\ 0\ 0\ \ldots\ 0\ 0\ 0\ 0\ 0\ 1\ 1\ 1\ 0\ 1\ 1\ 1_2 = 119_{10}$$
$$\overline{0\ 0\ 0\ \ldots\ 0\ 0\ 0\ 1\ 0\ 1\ 0\ 1\ 1\ 1\ 0\ 1_2} = 349_{10}$$

Beginning at the right, we find that 0 + 1 gives 1. Then 1 + 1 gives 10. This translates to 0 with a 1 "carry." Next, 1 + 1 gives 10. Adding the carry, we get 11. This translates to 1 with a 1 "carry." In the next column to the left, 0 + 0 gives 0, but the carry gives 1 as the final result for the column. The remainder of the problem should be straightforward. The decimal equivalents of the three numbers shown in the example are given so that we can check our work.

If one adds a positive number and a negative one, the answer will be algebraically correct. Example:

$$0\ 0\ 0\ \ldots\ 0\ 0\ 0\ 0\ 0\ 0\ 1_2 = 1_{10}$$
$$1\ 1\ 1\ \ldots\ 1\ 0\ 1\ 1\ 1\ 1\ 1_2 = -33_{10}$$
$$\overline{1\ 1\ 1\ \ldots\ 1\ 1\ 0\ 0\ 0\ 0\ 0_2} = -32_{10}$$

Another example:

$$0\ 0\ 0\ \ldots\ 0\ 0\ 1\ 1\ 0\ 0\ 0_2 = 24_{10}$$
$$1\ 1\ 1\ \ldots\ 1\ 1\ 1\ 1\ 1\ 1\ 0_2 = -2_{10}$$
$$\overline{1\ 0\ 0\ 0\ \ldots\ 0\ 0\ 1\ 0\ 1\ 1\ 0_2} = 22_{10}$$

↑ This bit is ignored because it falls outside of the 32-bit configuration.

To determine by inspection what the value of a negative number is, apply positional values to the digits of a negative number, then add the values represented by the *zeroes* only. Add 1 to the result and affix a minus sign. Example:

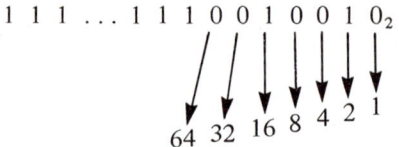

The sum of the values represented by zeroes is $64 + 32 + 8 + 4 + 1 = 109_{10}$. Adding 1 gives 110_{10}. Affixing a minus sign gives -110_{10}.

To check, we convert

$$1\ 1\ 1\ \ldots\ 1\ 1\ 1\ 0\ 0\ 1\ 0\ 0\ 1\ 0_2$$

to its positive form. The conversion gives

$$0\ 0\ 0\ \ldots\ 0\ 0\ 0\ 1\ 1\ 0\ 1\ 1\ 1\ 0_2 = 110$$

so our answer checks.

A computer can add, subtract, multiply, and divide in binary. We shall not discuss the operations other than addition in this text.

Here is a final example of adding in binary:

$$000\ldots0011111_2 = 31_{10}$$
$$000\ldots0011001_2 = 25_{10}$$
$$\overline{000\ldots0111000_2 = 56_{10}}$$

This example shows that adding $1_2 + 1_2 + 1_2$ gives a result of 1_2 with a 1_2 carry.

SUMMARY

In binary, integers (whole numbers) may be formed by applying the positional values of base 2 digits. Those positional values are 2^0, 2^1, 2^2, etc. Example:

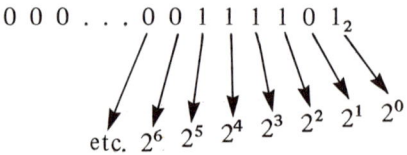

Integers

Negative binary numbers are obtained by employment of the two's complement number form. The procedure given in the text, in effect, changes all zeroes to ones and all ones to zero; then it adds one. Example:

$$
\begin{array}{r}
0\ 0\ 0\ \ldots\ 0\ 0\ 0\ 1\ 1\ 0\ 1\ 1_2 \\
1\ 1\ 1\ \ldots\ 1\ 1\ 1\ 0\ 0\ 1\ 0\ 0_2 \\
+\ \hspace{8em} 1 \\
\hline
1\ 1\ 1\ \ldots\ 1\ 1\ 1\ 0\ 0\ 1\ 0\ 1_2
\end{array}
$$

change all zeroes to ones and all ones to zeroes, then add one.

The procedure for changing positive numbers to negative is exactly the same as that for changing negative numbers to positive.

When the computer adds two numbers, it does not matter whether the numbers are negative or positive; the end result is algebraically correct.

The addition table in the binary numbering system is very simple. The only four possible combinations are

$$0 + 0 = 0$$
$$0 + 1 = 1$$
$$1 + 0 = 1$$
$$1 + 1 = 10$$

QUESTIONS

1. What is an integer?
2. What is meant by the term *two's complement*?
3. How can one determine at a glance whether an integer value is negative or positive?
4. What is the decimal value of the following negative number?

   $111\ldots110011_2$

5. Convert the following positive number to negative.

   $000\ldots00111 0010_2$

6. Convert the following negative number to positive.

   $111\ldots110001110_2$

72   Integers

7. Add the following two binary numbers.

$$000\ldots001110010_2$$
$$\underline{111\ldots110001110_2}$$

8. Is the result of Problem 7 reasonable? Why?
9. In binary, what are the sums of

$$1 + 1 + 1 \quad\quad = \ ?$$
$$1 + 1 + 1 + 1 \quad = \ ?$$
$$1 + 1 + 1 + 1 + 1 = \ ?$$

10. Add these binary numbers:

$$000\ldots001110_2$$
$$000\ldots000111_2$$
$$000\ldots001010_2$$
$$\underline{000\ldots000011_2}$$

11 | Floating Point

Most computers being built today are capable of storing numeric values in two ways: integer and floating-point. In the last chapter we discussed how a computer stores integer values in 32-bit formats. Both positive and negative numbers may be represented in integer form. As you remember, the largest value that can be expressed in integer format is $2^{31} - 1$, and the smallest is -2^{31}. (These values are 2,147,483,647 and −2,147,483,648, respectively.) As the name of the format indicates, integer numbers are always whole numbers.

MIXED NUMBERS

In data processing we must often work with mixed numbers. For example, hours worked must sometimes be expressed in whole and parts of hours; pay rates must be expressed in dollars and cents; the nation's unemployment rate is usually expressed as a percentage. To store a numeric value having a whole part and a fractional part, computers use a method called "floating point."

FLOATING POINT

To store a number in floating-point format, the computer uses 32 bits. It divides those bits into two groups. One group, having eight bits, is termed the *characteristic*; the other group, having 24 bits, is called the *mantissa*. Study Fig. 11-1.

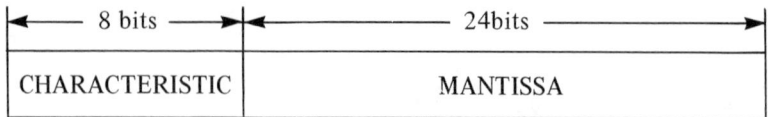

FIGURE 11-1

Characteristic

Both portions of a floating-point format must be evaluated in order to determine what the value of a mixed number is. To find out what value the characteristic alone is representing at any given time, simply treat the rightmost 7 bits of that number as an integer, then subtract 64. Thus a characteristic of

0 0 0 0 0 1 1

represents -61_{10} (3 − 64 = −61).
A characteristic of

0 1 1 1 1 1 1 1

represents 63_{10} (127 − 64 = 63).
The largest characteristic possible is the one given above, 63.
The leftmost bit of the characteristic has a special use, which we shall give shortly.

Mantissa

Now to compute the value of the mantissa, apply positional values beginning with 0.5 at the left and halving the values while moving to the right. This way:

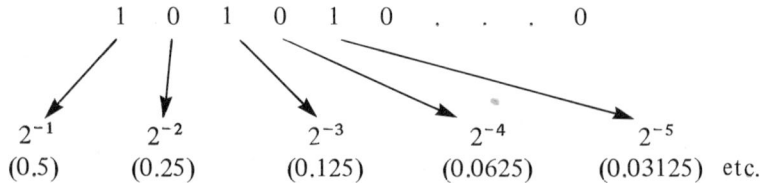

Floating Point

The value of the mantissa is determined by summing the fractional values represented by a 1. The fractional values to be summed in this example are

$$\begin{array}{r} 0.5 \\ 0.125 \\ \underline{0.03125} \\ \text{sum} = 0.65625 \end{array}$$

The value of the mantissa is 0.65625_{10}.

COMBINING THE CHARACTERISTIC AND MANTISSA

Knowing the values of both characteristic and mantissa, we can determine the value of the floating-point number by multiplying the characteristic, used as a power of 16, by the mantissa. Suppose, for example, that a characteristic is 3 and the mantissa is 0.5. We may determine the value of the number by multiplying 16^3 by 0.5. The value of 16^3 is 4,096; therefore, the computation 4,096 × 0.5 gives 2,048.

REPRESENTING WHOLE AND MIXED NUMBERS

The number 2048 can be represented both as an integer or as a floating-point number. *All* whole numbers may be represented both ways. Mixed numbers, though, may be represented only as floating-point numbers. Consider this example:

CHARACTERISTIC	MANTISSA
01000001	010010....000

The characteristic is

01000001_2

which has a value of 1_{10}. (65 − 64 = 1).
 The mantissa is

$010010\ldots000_2$

Its value is 0.28125_{10} $(0.25 + 0.03125)$.
The parts to be multiplied are

$$16^1 \times 0.28125 \quad \text{or} \quad 16 \times 0.28125 = 4.5$$

The floating-point number represented is 4.5_{10}.

EXCESS-64 METHOD

There are several floating-point methods used in various computers. The method that we have just described is called the excess-64 method. The name of the method arises from the fact that the characteristic is first evaluated as an integer, and then 64 is subtracted from it. The largest characteristic that may be obtained, therefore, is 63_{10}, and the smallest is -64_{10}. Characteristics, once determined, are used as powers of 16. Table 11-1 shows how the characteristic is determined once the integer value of the 8 characteristic bits has been evaluated.

Table 11-1

Value of Integer	Value of Characteristic	Notes
0	−64	0 − 64 = −64
1	−63	1 − 64 = −63
2	−62	2 − 64 = −62
.	.	.
.	.	.
.	.	.
63	−1	63 − 64 = −1
64	0	64 − 64 = 0
65	1	65 − 64 = 1
.	.	.
.	.	.
.	.	.
125	61	125 − 64 = 61
126	62	126 − 64 = 62
127	63	127 − 64 = 63

Floating Point

The leftmost bit of the 8-bit characteristic tells whether the entire number (not the characteristic) is negative. Thus, if a characteristic is

1 1 0 0 0 0 0 1

its value is 1_{10} (65 − 64), and the sign of the number being represented is negative.

Let us go through the steps of converting a decimal value to floating point. Suppose that value is 262.144_{10}. The first step is to select a power of 16 that gives a number *greater than* 262.144.

16^0 gives the value 1_{10}. Therefore, zero is not the number we are looking for. 16^1 gives the value 16_{10}, so 1 is not it. 16^2 gives 256_{10}. This is close but not greater than 262.144_{10}. 16^3 gives 4096_{10}. Since 4096_{10} is greater than 262.144_{10}, we have found the number to use to establish the characteristic. That number is 3, since it is the power of 16. Adding 64_{10} to 3_{10}, we get 67_{10}. This number, expressed as an integer, is the characteristic. It is written thus:

0 1 0 0 0 0 1 1

Now for the mantissa. First, divide $4,096_{10}$ into 262.144_{10}. This calculation gives the mantissa to be established. The result of the calculation is 0.064.

The next step is to select positional values in the mantissa which, when added together, give 0.064_{10}. Here are the available mantissa values:

| 0.5 | 0.25 | 0.125 | 0.0625 | 0.03125 | 0.015625 | , etc. |

To establish the value 0.064_{10}, we do not require 0.5_{10}, so we place a zero over the square containing that value. We do not need 0.25_{10} or 0.125. Therefore, zeroes are placed above those squares. The value 0.0625_{10} can be used to establish 0.064_{10}, so a 1 is placed above the square holding that value. The mantissa now looks like this:

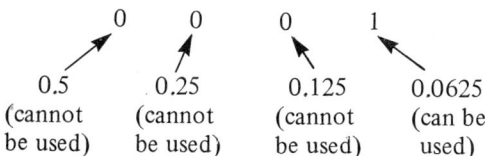

78   Floating Point

Subtracting 0.0625_{10} from 0.064_{10}, we get 0.0015_{10}. This value is to be established by using the 20 bits of the mantissa that have not yet been used. Working out by hand the correct zeroes and ones needed is a tedious task, and a person would not like to do it more than once. A computer is very fast, though, and it has no difficulty coming up with the correct mantissa:

$$0\ 0\ 0\ 1\ 0\ 0\ 0\ 0\ 0\ 1\ 1\ 0\ 0\ 0\ 1\ 0\ 0\ 1\ 0\ 0\ 1\ 1\ 0\ 1_2$$

This mantissa is not an *exact* binary replacement for decimal 0.064_{10}. It comes very close, as Table 11-2 shows.

Table 11-2

Power of 2	Decimal Value	Bits needed to establish 0.064_{10}
2^{-1}	0.5	
2^{-2}	0.25	
2^{-3}	0.125	
2^{-4}	0.0625	X
2^{-5}	0.03125	
2^{-6}	0.015625	
2^{-7}	0.0078125	
2^{-8}	0.00390625	
2^{-9}	0.001953125	
2^{-10}	0.0009765625	X
2^{-11}	0.00048828125	X
2^{-12}	0.000244140625	
2^{-13}	0.0001220703125	
2^{-14}	0.00006103515625	
2^{-15}	0.000030517578125	X
2^{-16}	0.0000152587890625	
2^{-17}	0.00000762939453125	
2^{-18}	0.000003814697265625	X
2^{-19}	0.0000019073486328125	
2^{-20}	0.00000095367431640625	
2^{-21}	0.000000476837158203125	X
2^{-22}	0.0000002384185791015625	X
2^{-23}	0.00000011920928955078125	
2^{-24}	0.000000059604644775390625	X

Adding the various values required to establish 0.064_{10}, we find that the closest we can get to this value is

Table 11-3. Powers of 2 Table

2^n	n	2^{-n}
1	0	1.0
2	1	0.5
4	2	0.25
8	3	0.125
16	4	0.062 5
32	5	0.031 25
64	6	0.015 625
128	7	0.007 812 5
256	8	0.003 906 25
512	9	0.001 953 125
1 024	10	0.000 976 562 5
2 048	11	0.000 488 281 25
4 096	12	0.000 244 140 625
8 192	13	0.000 122 070 312 5
16 384	14	0.000 061 035 156 25
32 768	15	0.000 030 517 578 125
65 536	16	0.000 015 258 789 062 5
131 072	17	0.000 007 629 394 531 25
262 144	18	0.000 003 814 697 265 625
524 288	19	0.000 001 907 348 632 812 5
1 048 576	20	0.000 000 953 674 316 406 25
2 097 152	21	0.000 000 476 837 158 203 125
4 194 304	22	0.000 000 238 418 579 101 562 5
8 388 608	23	0.000 000 119 209 289 550 781 25
16 777 216	24	0.000 000 059 604 644 775 390 625
33 554 432	25	0.000 000 029 802 322 387 695 312 5
67 108 864	26	0.000 000 014 901 161 193 847 656 25
134 217 728	27	0.000 000 007 450 580 596 923 828 125
268 435 456	28	0.000 000 003 725 290 298 461 914 062 5
536 870 912	29	0.000 000 001 862 645 149 230 957 031 25
1 073 741 824	30	0.000 000 000 931 322 574 615 478 515 625
2 147 483 648	31	0.000 000 000 465 661 287 307 739 257 812 5
4 294 967 296	32	0.000 000 000 232 830 643 653 869 628 906 25
8 589 934 592	33	0.000 000 000 116 415 321 826 934 814 453 125
17 179 869 184	34	0.000 000 000 058 207 660 913 467 407 226 562 5
34 359 738 368	35	0.000 000 000 029 103 830 456 733 703 613 281 25
68 719 476 736	36	0.000 000 000 014 551 915 228 366 851 806 640 625
137 438 953 472	37	0.000 000 000 007 275 957 614 183 425 903 320 312 5
274 877 906 944	38	0.000 000 000 003 637 978 807 091 712 951 660 156 25
549 755 813 888	39	0.000 000 000 001 818 989 403 545 856 475 830 078 125

$0.06399995088577270507812_{10}$. For most practical purposes, this is close enough.

Now let us put characteristic and mantissa together to obtain the floating-point equivalent of 262.144_{10}.

0 1 0 0 0 0 1 1	000100000110001001001101
Characteristic	Mantissa

If the value had been negative (−262.444), the only change in the above configuration would be a 1 replacing the leftmost zero of the characteristic.

For practice let us evaluate one more number. Tell what is the value of this floating-point number.

1 0 1 1 1 1 1 1	0 1 0 0 ... 0 0 0
Characteristic	Mantissa

We can see that the number is negative. (Examine the leftmost bit of the characteristic.) The characteristic itself is -1_{10} ($63 - 64 = -1$). The power by which to multiply the mantissa is 16^{-1} or 0.0625_{10} (1/16).

The mantissa is 0.25_{10}. So $0.0625_{10} \times 0.25_{10}$ gives 0.015625_{10}. This is the decimal value represented by the floating-point configuration shown above. Note that this time the binary and decimal values are precisely equivalent.

SUMMARY

Integer numeric values are expressed in a "fixed-point" format. This means that the decimal point is assumed to be at the right-hand end of a string of bits. Not all numbers used in data processing are whole numbers. Mixed values are expressed by a string of bits having both a characteristic and mantissa portion.

The characteristic is a whole number that is used as a power of 16. The mantissa is a fraction that lies between 1/16 (0.0625) and 1. (The fraction 1/16 is permissible at the lower end, but 1 is not permissible at the upper end.)

In making calculations, computers may have to adjust (normalize) a floating-point number before storing a result. For example, the value 2 is expressed as 16^1 (characteristic) × 1/8 (mantissa). If the calculation 2 × 2 is performed, the computer gives the temporary result 16^2 × 1/64. To store the result, the computer converts it to 16^1 × ¼. Normalizing values before storing them conserves accuracy.

One floating-point scheme in common use is called excess-64. The raw characteristic may range from 0 through 127. When adjusted by subtracting 64, the range becomes 63 through −64. A value may be indicated as negative by installing a 1 bit as the leftmost of the bits representing the floating-point number.

QUESTIONS

1. Name the two portions of a floating-point number.
2. What is the function of the characteristic in a floating-point number?
3. What is the function of the mantissa in a floating-point number?
4. What is meant by excess-64 as the name of a floating-point format?
5. Are all mixed values precisely expressible in floating point? Explain.
6. How is a negative number indicated in a floating-point format?
7. What is the value of the following number expressed in floating-point format?

    $0\ 1\ 0\ 0\ 0\ 0\ 1\ 0\ 1\ 0\ 0\ \ldots\ 0\ 0_2$

8. What is the value of the following number expressed in floating-point format?

    $1\ 1\ 0\ 0\ 0\ 0\ 0\ 1\ 0\ 1\ 0\ 0\ \ldots\ 0\ 0_2$

9. How does the computer express the value 0.25_{10} in floating point?
10. What is meant by the term *normalize*? Why is it used?

12 | Hexadecimal and Octal Codes

USING INTEGERS AND FLOATING-POINT NUMBERS

Integer and floating-point numbers are used when a computer needs to perform calculations. Hardware in most computers enables them to perform calculations in either mode. Since it is easier and faster for a computer to do work in integer mode, it should be given integers to work with whenever possible. Suppose, for example, that a program deals with the number of checkout lines needed in a department store. Numbers representing checkout lines and customers should be in integer format, since it makes no sense to think in terms of portions of checkout lines and portions of persons.

If numbers can represent mixed values such as the depreciating worth of an apartment house over a period of time, then floating-point numbers should be used because dollars and cents are involved. True, the dollar figures will sometimes be whole numbers, but floating-point numbers must still be used, because most of the time the figures are not whole numbers.

Integer values and floating-point numbers both require 32-bit formats. Since bits are merely zeroes and ones, there is little or no information within a number which tells what format it is in. For example, suppose we know that these next 32 bits represent a numeric value:

0 0 0 1 1 1 1 0 0 0 1 1 0 0 0 ... 0 0 0

Hexadecimal and Octal Codes

Does the configuration represent a floating-point number ($16^{-34} \times 0.1875$) or an integer value ($2^{28} + 2^{27} + 2^{26} + 2^{25} + 2^{21} + 2^{20}$)? There is no way to tell for sure by simply looking at the number. Fortunately, when a programmer tells the computer to establish a numeric value and gives that number a name, he may write a simple command like

$$P = 8.5$$

or

$$JAQ = -64$$

The computer will establish the correct values in either floating-point or integer format as the programmer has requested, then store the values in memory cells. The computer stores the first number (floating-point 8.5) in a memory cell called P, and it stores the second number (integer −64) in another memory cell called JAQ. The two configurations look like this:

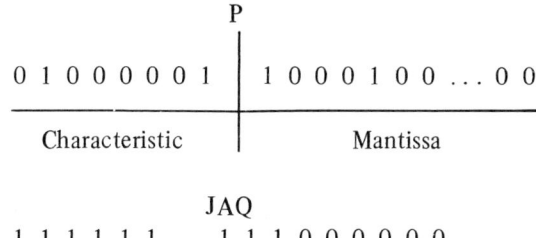

In storing these values, the programmer tells the computer whether the numbers are floating-point or integer. When he stores P, the programmer tells the computer that the number is stored in floating-point format. When he stores JAQ, he tells the computer that the number is stored in integer format. Later, when we discuss programming languages, we shall see exactly how this information is given to the computer.

Later, when the programmer wishes to have the computer work with the values, he calls for the use of those values by their names. He may instruct the computer this way, for example:

$$A = P + 4.6$$

He is telling the computer to take the value currently stored in P, add 4.6 to it, and store the result in A. The computer will do the work in floating-point mode, because it has already been told that P and A are floating-point numbers and it can see that 4.6 is a floating-point number. Computers remember the modes of the values that have been fed to them.

Later the programmer may instruct the computer to obey this command:

$$KIB = JAQ - LF$$

The computer does all this work in integer mode, because it has been told that all data names represent integer values.

Some computer systems forbid mixing of modes. That is, a command like

$$A = P + 6$$

is forbidden, because P represents a floating-point number and 6 is an integer number. If mixing modes is not forbidden, the computer converts numbers so that all numbers are in the same mode—usually floating-point.

When making calculations, computers keep track of decimal points. Thus, if you instruct a computer to multiply 4.6 by 2.5, the result will be stored as the floating-point number, 11.50. The computer remembers the name of the value and where it has been stored so that a subsequent use of the value may be made.

HEXADECIMAL CODE

So that programmers may more easily deal with numbers and other data stored in the form of bits, the hexadecimal and octal nomenclature systems have been developed. A string of 32 bits can be expressed as a group of 8 hexadecimal characters. Suppose we have this 32-bit binary number:

$$01100101100010100111001100001001_2$$

The 32 bits are difficult to deal with. If we copy the digits from one sheet of paper to another, the chances for making a mistake are not remote. If we read this string of digits into a phone receiver, the person on the other end may well copy one or two digits incorrectly.

Hexadecimal and Octal Codes 85

If we break the 32 bits into eight groups of four bits, we will have this:

0110 0101 1000 1010 0111 0011 0000 1001

Now we can assign a character to each of these groups. Characters are selected from Table 12-1.

Table 12-1. Hexadecimal Table

Group of four bits	Hexadecimal character
0000	0
0001	1
0010	2
0011	3
0100	4
0101	5
0110	6
0111	7
1000	8
1001	9
1010	A
1011	B
1100	C
1101	D
1110	E
1111	F

The assigned characters, therefore, are

0110 0101 1000 1010 0111 0011 0000 1001
  6   5   8   A   7   3   0   9

The hexadecimal system is really a base 16 numbering system. Base 16 numbers and base 2 numbers can be used in several capacities. For example, suppose that we wish to determine what the decimal equivalent is of the base 2 integer number:

$00000000000110001001000010000111_2$

We can first determine the hexadecimal version of this number:

00189087_{16}

The subscript 16 indicates that the number is a base 16 (hexadecimal) value. We can calculate the value of the number by applying base 16 positional values. This way:

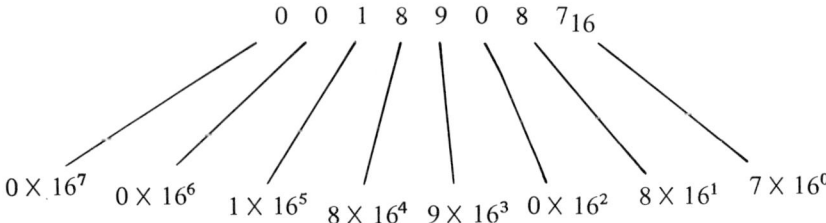

Summing the indicated portions, we get

$$
\begin{aligned}
7 \times 16^0 &= 7 \times 1 &&= &&7 \\
8 \times 16^1 &= 8 \times 16 &&= &&128 \\
9 \times 16^3 &= 9 \times 4096 &&= &&36{,}864 \\
8 \times 16^4 &= 8 \times 65{,}536 &&= &&524{,}288 \\
1 \times 16^5 &= 1 \times 1{,}048{,}576 &&= &&1{,}048{,}576 \\
& & & & &\overline{1{,}609{,}863}
\end{aligned}
$$

This value can be verified by evaluating the binary number independently.

A decimal number may be converted to its base 16 equivalent by dividing the number repeatedly by 16. Suppose we need to convert $5{,}634_{10}$ to base 16.

Divide the number by 16_{10}.

```
       352
   16 ⟌ 5634
        48
        ──
        83
        80
        ──
         34
         32
         ──
          2   Remainder
```

Save the remainder (2), then divide 352_{10} by 16_{10}.

$$\begin{array}{r} 22 \\ 16\overline{)352} \\ \underline{32} \\ 32 \\ \underline{32} \\ 0 \quad \text{Remainder} \end{array}$$

Save the remainder (0), then divide 22_{10} by 16_{10}.

$$\begin{array}{r} 1 \\ 16\overline{)22} \\ \underline{16} \\ 6 \quad \text{Remainder} \end{array}$$

Save the remainder (6), then divide 1_{10} by 16_{10}.

$$\begin{array}{r} 0 \\ 16\overline{)1} \quad \text{Remainder} \end{array}$$

Now collect the remainders, last one first:

$1\ 6\ 0\ 2_{16}$

The result is the base 16 equivalent of $5,634_{10}$. We can check the result by summing the base 16 positional values found in $1,602_{16}$.

$$\begin{array}{lll} 2 \times 16^0 = 2 \times 1 & = & 2 \\ 6 \times 16^2 = 6 \times 256 & = & 1,536 \\ 1 \times 16^3 = 1 \times 4096 & = & 4,096 \\ \hline & & 5,634_{10} \end{array}$$

The value $1,602_{16}$ can now be converted to binary (base 2) by writing down the four bits that are associated with each of the base 16 characters. Thus,

$1,602_{16} = 0001011000000010_2$

The leading zeroes in the binary number contribute nothing to its value, so they may be deleted:

1011000000010_2

OCTAL CODE

It is not our intent to delve too deeply into hexadecimal and binary numbers and the uses to which these numbers may be put. A course in data processing mathematics would probably cover these topics.

Before leaving this chapter we do want to introduce the well-known octal numbering system. Consider a computer that employs 32 bits for an integer value. That integer value may look like this:

$$00010110001111001010011001001001_2$$

Breaking up the number into groups of 3 bits (working from right to left), and selecting bits from Table 12-2, we transform the 32 bit number to an octal (base 8) value.

Table 12-2. Octal Table

Group of 3 bits	Octal digit
000	0
001	1
010	2
011	3
100	4
101	5
110	6
111	7

$$00010110001111001010011001001001_2$$

converts to

000 010 110 001 111 001 010 011 001 001 001

The leftmost zero is added to fill out the group of three bits.
The octal number is, therefore,

$$02617123111_8$$

Hexadecimal and Octal Codes

INTERRELATIONSHIPS OF NUMBER SYSTEMS

Conversions between binary, octal, and hexadecimal numbers may easily be made once it is understood how intimately the three numbering systems are related. For example,

$$0000000 1234_8$$

is equivalent to 668_{10}. Proof:

$$
\begin{aligned}
4 \times 8^0 &= 4 \times 1 = 4 \\
3 \times 8^1 &= 3 \times 8 = 24 \\
2 \times 8^2 &= 2 \times 64 = 128 \\
1 \times 8^3 &= 1 \times 512 = \underline{512} \\
& \qquad\qquad\qquad 668_{10}
\end{aligned}
$$

This value is

$$000000000000000000000010100111 00_2$$

which is equivalent to

$$0000029C_{16}$$

which again is 668_{10}. Proof:

$$
\begin{aligned}
C \times 16^0 &= 12 \times 1 = 12 \\
9 \times 16^1 &= 9 \times 16 = 144 \\
2 \times 16^2 &= 2 \times 256 = \underline{512} \\
& \qquad\qquad\qquad 668_{10}
\end{aligned}
$$

A decimal value may easily be converted to base 8 by dividing it repeatedly by 8_{10}. Example:

```
            0   1   Remainders
         8 ⌐1    2
         8 ⌐10   3
         8 ⌐83   4
       8₁₀ ⌐668₁₀
```

The remainder gives the octal equivalent of the decimal value. Thus

$$668_{10} = 1234_8 = 29C_{16}$$

SUMMARY

In using a computer, one may employ both integer and floating-point numbers. Computers are able to work more efficiently with integer values; therefore, integers should be called for wherever possible.

Working with a string of 32, 36, or more bits can be difficult for people. Codes have been developed that permit easier communications between people or between people and machines. Two prominent codes are hexadecimal and octal.

The hexadecimal system employs 16 characters, each character representing 4 bits. The octal system employs 8 characters, each character representing 3 bits.

Numbers in the binary (base 2), octal (base 8), and hexadecimal (base 16) numbering systems are interrelated. A person wishing to convert a decimal number to binary may first convert it to octal or hexadecimal, then convert directly to binary, selecting bits from the octal or hexadecimal tables. A person wishing to convert from binary to decimal may first convert to octal or hexadecimal, then to decimal.

QUESTIONS

1. When should a computer be instructed to use integer values in the solution of a problem? When to use floating-point numbers?
2. What is meant by the term "mixing modes?" Do computers permit mixing modes?
3. How many digits are employed in the binary numbering system? Name them.
4. How many digits are employed in the octal numbering system? Name them.
5. How many digits are employed in the hexadecimal numbering system? Name them.
6. Convert the value 283_{10} to hexadecimal, octal, and binary.

7. Convert the following binary number to octal. (Assume that the number has 36 bits.)

    000...0110100110$_2$

8. Convert the following binary number to hexadecimal. (Assume that the number has 32 bits.)

    000...01011100010011$_2$

9. Convert the following octal number to hexadecimal. (Assume that the number has 36 bits.)

    000000011456$_8$

10. What is the decimal equivalent of the following hexadecimal number? (Assume a floating-point number.)

    C1400000$_{16}$

13 | Computer Memories

COMPUTER COMPONENTS

There are three major components in most computer systems (see Fig. 13-1).

MEMORY	
CPU	CONTROL

FIGURE 13-1

MEMORY CONFIGURATIONS

The memory of a computer holds the data that the computer is to work with. The CPU actually processes data by performing computations or otherwise modifying the data. The control acts as a coordinator between memory and CPU. (We shall see more about the control when we discuss machine-language programming in a later chapter.)

In this chapter we shall examine the memory of a computer in more detail than we have done in earlier chapters.

Computer memories fall into two major classifications: (1) variable word-length; (2) fixed word-length.

In the early days of computers (circa 1950), computer memories were made up of fixed word lengths. The memory of a computer could be thought of as appearing as shown in Fig. 13-2. A computer's memory consisted of several thousand units called memory cells. A typical memory might contain 8,192 cells. The first cell was Cell 0 and the last cell was Cell 8,191.

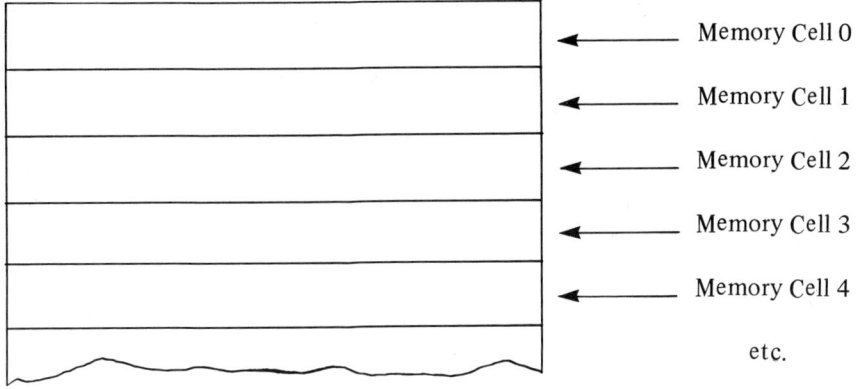

FIGURE 13-2

Each of these cells was further broken down into bits. (The word "bit" is a contraction of the two words *bi*nary digi*t*.) Typically, there were 36 bits to a memory cell. A memory cell could hold several kinds of data, and it could also hold instructions. Unless one knew what to look for in a memory cell, he would not know whether it contained an integer number, a floating-point number, alphanumeric information, or an instruction. Consider, for example, memory cell 2000, which at some time in the past might have contained these bits:

$$001000110010010011110101011000101110_2$$

You will recall that these bits hold values of either zero or one because there is a tiny ferrite (iron) core behind each bit. That core could be magnetized in one of two ways to represent either a zero or a one.

In the example, some of the cores have been magnetized to hold zeroes and some have been magnetized to hold ones. The magnetic states of cores can be changed at electronic speeds. When necessary, all the cores representing the example above could be changed in about a millisecond in slower computers or in about a microsecond in the faster computers. (A millisecond is 1/1,000 of a second, and a microsecond is 1/1,000,000 of a second.)

The question arises: What does the above memory cell contain? If it is an integer value, then it is a relatively large number, because there is a 1 bit in the position that represents 2^{33}.

If it is a floating-point number, then a portion of the number holds the characteristic and a portion holds the mantissa. Depending upon which floating-point system has been used (there are several), the value being represented could be determined.

If cell 2,000 holds alphanumeric information, then the content of that information could be discovered by applying the computer's alphanumeric codes to various groups of bits in the cell. For example, the 36 bits can be broken down into six groups of six bits. Like this:

001000 110010 010011 110101 011000 101110

Then each group can be looked up in a table and a character can be assigned. One table containing 64 entries (one entry for every possible combination of six zeroes and ones) gives these characters as the alphanumeric information represented by the 36 bits shown:

8 S C V H ;

If Cell 2000 holds a computer instruction, then the exact meaning of the instruction depends upon the instruction format of the computer being used. Some of the bits in the 36 would be considered an "operation"; other bits would be considered an "address"; remaining bits would be considered "index" information. Since instruction formats differ greatly from computer system to computer system, we shall not concentrate upon any one computer in this text, but give typical formats.

What a portion of memory holds at any one time depends upon that portion's relationship with the rest of memory. For example, at one moment a memory layout may appear as shown in Fig. 13-3. The computer is directed to the instructions portion of memory and told to expect only instructions in that area. If will also be told what area of memory holds data and what form those data have.

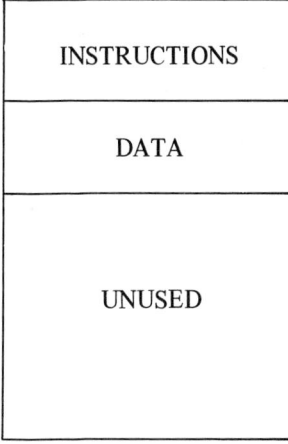

FIGURE 13-3

You can see that the information that a user gives to a computer must be accurate. If he tells the computer that the portion actually holding data is the portion containing instructions, the computer will become confused when it tries to execute data. Since it makes little sense to perform this kind of action, the computer will probably stop and type on the console typewriter some sort of an error message.

The memory cells that we have discussed so far have fixed lengths. The example cell has 36 bits, but there is nothing sacred about that number. Other computers have been built which have fixed cell lengths of 16 bits, 20 bits, 32 bits, 48 bits, 60 bits, and even more.

A memory cell is often called a memory location or a memory word. Thus, if you ask a programmer to describe his computer, he may say it has 8,192 memory cells, memory locations, or memory words. Then he might add that every cell (or location or word) contains 36 bits.

An alternate way that he might describe the memory would be for him to say that it has an 8K 36-bit memory. A K in computer parlance means 1,024. He is saying that the memory contains 8 × 1,024 memory cells and that each cell has a fixed length of 36 bits. The product 8 × 1,024 is 8,192, which is the number of computer cells in the computer.

Fixed-length memory sizes are usually constructed in powers of 2. It is not unusual, for example, to find computers that have 16K, 32K, 64K, even 256K fixed-length memory cells. A computer having 256K memory cells actually contains 262,144 cells. If the cell contains 36 bits, then the bit capacity of the machine is 36 × 262,144, or 9,437,184; a relatively large memory.

BYTES

The trend in recent years has been for computers to be built with variable-length memories. This means that cells containing 36 bits or 20 bits, etc. are giving way to smaller units called "bytes." The concept of a byte varies slightly from computer to computer, but the typical byte of today contains 8 bits.

Byte memories may be thought of as looking like Fig. 13-4.

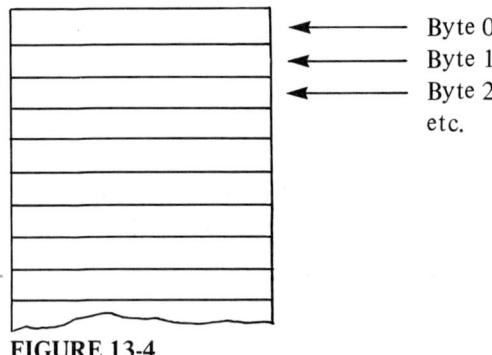

FIGURE 13-4

Memories are still measured in K's. That is, a memory may contain 16K bytes, or 64K bytes, etc. Since a byte contains only 8 bits, it is clear that a 16K-word machine has more capacity than a 16K-byte machine.

A byte is capable of holding a single character of information. That character may be a digit, or a letter of the alphabet, or some special symbol like ?, /, =, or #. There are 256 different ways that 8 bits may be combined. Since each way may be assigned as the code for an individual character, a byte position may contain any one of 256 different characters.

EBCDIC

The name of the code used to represent characters in bytes is called "Extended Binary Coded Decimal Interchange Code," or EBCDIC. A few of the entries in the EBCDIC table are given in Table 13-1.

Table 13-1. EBCDIC Table

Group of 8 bits	Character
11110000	0
11110001	1
11110010	2
11110011	3
.	.
.	.
.	.
11111000	8
11111001	9
11000001	A
11000010	B
11000011	C
.	.
.	.
.	.
11101000	Y
11101001	Z
01000000	Blank
01011011	$
01111011	#
.	.
.	.
.	.

#256

A variable-word-length computer may assign as many bytes as required for any required piece of information. For example, nine bytes may be used for social security numbers, 15 bytes for persons' last names, etc. Using just enough memory to hold various items of data contributes to more efficient memory utilization, and, therefore, to lower cost for work being done.

In byte machines, four bytes are often grouped to form words. Such words, of course, contain 32 bits.

SUMMARY

A typical computer consists of three major components: CPU, control, and memory.

Memories of computers are of two basic types—fixed word-length and variable word-length. The trend for memory organizations is toward the variable type with basic units called bytes.

Memory sizes are measured in K's. A memory of 16K could mean 16 × 1,024 fixed-length words or 16 × 1,024 bytes.

QUESTIONS

1. What are the three major components of a typical computer?
2. What is the function of a computer's central processing unit (CPU)?
3. What is the function of a computer's control?
4. What is the function of a computer's memory?
5. What are two forms of memory organizations?
6. What is a K and how does it designate the size of a memory?
7. What may be included with a memory cell besides data?
8. What is meant by the term *instruction format*?
9. Why should instructions and data be kept separated within a computer's memory?
10. What is a byte? Of how many bits is it usually constructed?
11. What is EBCDIC?
12. What is a word in fixed-word-length machines? In byte machines?

14 | Instructional Formats

MACHINE-LANGUAGE PROGRAMMING

In this chapter we shall take a quick look at machine-language programming. The intent here is not to make an expert machine-language programmer of you, but simply to give you an overview of the topic. Machine-language programming is not practiced much nowadays, so our discussion is intended to lead naturally into a study of assembly-language and compiler-language programming.

HYPOTHETICAL LEARNING COMPUTER (HLC)

To begin a discussion of machine-language programming, let us first imagine a hypothetical computer. (We shall call it HLC for Hypothetical Learning Computer.) This computer has a memory size of 64K bytes. This, of course, means that its exact size in bytes is 10000_{16} ($65,536_{10}$). The computer uses 4 bytes for every integer value and 4 bytes for every floating-point value. The formats for integers and for floating-point numbers are the ones we gave in the last chapters covering these topics.

The instruction format of the computer is shown in Fig. 14-1.

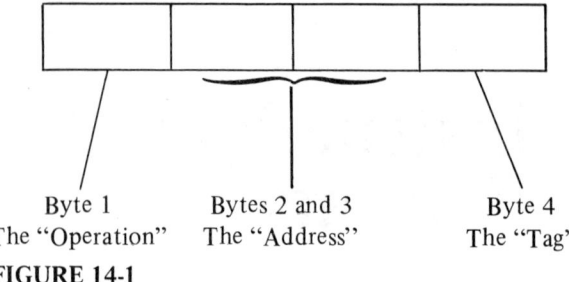

FIGURE 14-1

Four bytes are used for every instruction. When the computer is told that a certain series of 4 bytes contains an instruction, the computer first "decodes" the instruction, then executes it.

This is where the control module of a computer enters the picture. Do you recall the illustration in Fig. 14-2?

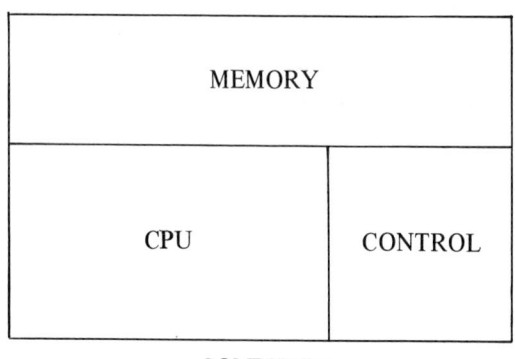

FIGURE 14-2

The memory receives data from input devices. The CPU processes the data. In processing the data, the control obtains instructions that are in the memory. Memory, therefore, contains not only data for the computer to work with but also instructions. When the control obtains an instruction, it "decodes" it. By decoding it is meant that the control determines what has to be done. It then directs the CPU to do what the instruction directs. After the CPU has executed the instruction, the control obtains another instruction from the next available set of 4 bytes in the memory.

Instruction Formats 101

PROGRAMS

HLC is called a "stored program computer" since, as is generally the practice, a program containing instructions to be executed is stored in the memory of the computer in much that same way that data values are stored there.

Let us assume that at some given moment, the memory of HLC looks like Fig. 14-3. The control must be told that the first instruction is located in the set of 4 bytes beginning with byte 0. From this point, the control has no difficulty in finding additional instructions. An automatic sequencer adds 4 to a special register called the instruction counter. The instruction counter tells where the beginning byte of the next instruction is to be found.

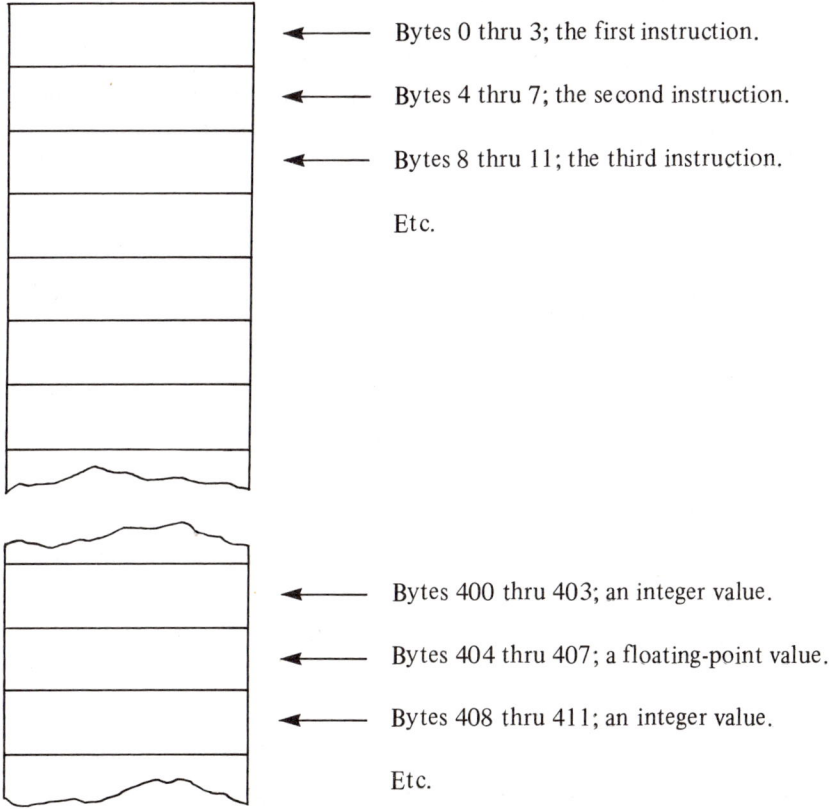

Bytes 0 thru 3; the first instruction.

Bytes 4 thru 7; the second instruction.

Bytes 8 thru 11; the third instruction.

Etc.

Bytes 400 thru 403; an integer value.

Bytes 404 thru 407; a floating-point value.

Bytes 408 thru 411; an integer value.

Etc.

FIGURE 14-3

It is the programmer's responsibility to make sure that instructions and data items do not interfere with each other. Therefore, if the instruction counter approaches 400 in the above example, the counter must be given a value that will cause it to jump around the three data values located at bytes 400, 404, and 408. (These numbers are in base 16 notation.)

A jump is given by an instruction called a transfer instruction. We shall see how transfers work soon.

A set of instructions given to a computer constitutes a "program." Programs may be written in machine language, such as those we are discussing in this chapter and the next, or they may be given in an assembly language such as BAL, which is used on IBM 360's and 370's, or they may be given in a compiler language such as FORTRAN, COBOL, or PL/I.

Not let us study the instruction format of HLC more closely. We have seen that one byte is assigned to the "operation" portion of the instruction (see Fig. 14-4). Since a byte contains 8 bits, there are 256 different ways that those bits may be arranged. Each of those ways may be assigned an operation, something that HLC is wired to do. For example, if the operation bits are

0 0 0 0 1 0 0 0

those bits may represent the computer's ability to add. If the bits are

0 0 0 0 1 0 0 1

the bits may represent subtraction, etc.

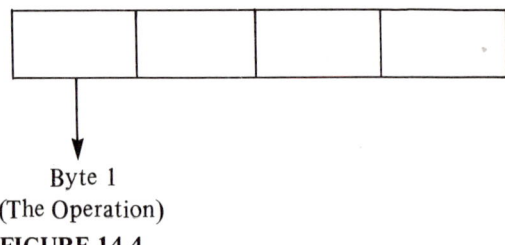

Byte 1
(The Operation)
FIGURE 14-4

When HLC was built, it was wired with the ability to perform 256 different kinds of operations. Some of these are

Clear and load accumulator

Instruction Formats

Add to accumulator

Subtract from accumulator

Shift accumulator left

Shift accumulator right

Store to memory from the accumulator, etc.

ACCUMULATOR

Many of the instructions that HLC can perform affect a register called an accumulator. The accumulator register is a 32-bit register found in the CPU. Being exactly the same size as a 32-bit integer or 32-bit floating-point number, it has the ability to hold a complete number. Numbers may be added to the accumulator, subtracted from it, etc.

In the next chapter we shall give some actual segments of programs that might be found in HLC. To show the contents of the various bytes, we shall use hexadecimal notation. You will recall that hexadecimal notation employs 16 characters to represent all combinations of four bits from 0000 to 1111. The hexadecimal table is repeated in Table 14-1 for convenience.

Table 14-1. Hexadecimal Table

Group of 4 bits	Character
0000	0
0001	1
0010	2
0011	3
0100	4
0101	5
0110	6
0111	7
1000	8
1001	9
1010	A
1011	B
1100	C
1101	D
1110	E
1111	F

To represent the eight bits of a byte, *two* hexadecimal characters are needed. Thus, to represent the bits

0 0 0 0 1 0 0 0

we need the two hexadecimal characters

0 8

To represent the bits

1 0 1 1 1 1 0 0

we need the two hexadecimal characters

B C

Since the instruction format in HLC uses 4 bytes, we need 8 hexadecimal characters to represent the contents of those bytes. If the first instruction of our program contains these 32 bits:

00000001 00000000 00101000 00000000

the hexadecimal characters representing the 32 bits are

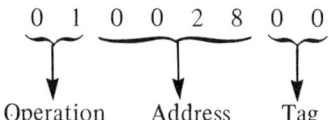

0 1   0 0 2 8   0 0

Operation   Address   Tag

This instruction clears and loads the accumulator with the contents of the 4 bytes beginning at byte position 28_{16}. (The actual bytes are 28_{16}, 29_{16}, $2A_{16}$, and $2B_{16}$.)

INDEX REGISTERS

The operation code 01 found in the Operation Table (Table 14-2) shows that it means "clear and load the accumulator." The address portion of the operation shows *what* is to be loaded in the accumulator. The tag of the instruction, being zero, means that Index Register 0 modifies the address. We shall see later what index registers do.

Instruction Formats

Table 14-2. Operation Table

Group of 8 bits	Hexadecimal code	Operation
00000001	01	Clear and load accumulator
00001000	08	Add to accumulator (integer)
00001001	09	Subtract from accumulator (integer)
00010000	10	Shift accumulator left
00010001	11	Shift accumulator right
00000010	02	Floating add to accumulator
00100001	21	Floating subtract from accumulator
01000000	40	Transfer
01000001	41	Compare accumulator
01000010	42	Transfer on minus
01000011	43	Transfer on zero
01000100	44	Transfer on plus
01010001	51	Store from accumulator
01100000	60	Load Index Register 0
.	.	.
.	.	.
.	.	.

This table shows only a few of the 256 different operations which HLC has been wired to understand. For our purposes these operations will be sufficient to illustrate machine-language programming.

Before we go into the next chapter, it is important that we emphasize that HLC is not a real computer. It was invented simply as a learning tool for this book. There are many makes of computers in existence. Each has its own type of machine language, and these types often differ radically from one another. The student should study the machine-language system given in these chapters simply to understand the concepts. Concepts do not differ greatly from system to system, but the implementation of those concepts does.

SUMMARY

A program is a set of instructions given to a computer to solve some given problem. The process of writing those instructions is called programming.

The most elementary form of computer programming is machine language. To program a computer in machine language, a programmer uses actual zeroes and ones. In instruction formats, he gives the operation (op) as a series of zeroes and ones; then he gives addresses, also in zeroes and ones.

Most computers are known as "stored program computers," since programs to be executed are stored within the memory. You will recall that this concept was first proposed by Dr. John Von Neumann.

In order to execute an instruction, the control "decodes" the instruction, i.e., determines what has to be done. The CPU actually performs the required operation, obtaining any data values required from the memory.

The control has to be told where the first instruction is located. From that point, an automatic sequencer within the control directs the computer from instruction to instruction.

Instructions and data must be kept separated so that the computer does not inadvertently attempt to execute data. Such operations are impossible and will result in error messages' being given.

Many instructions affect an accumulator. Values may be placed into an accumulator. Computations may be done within it. Results or partial results may be stored from the accumulator.

QUESTIONS

1. What is meant by the term *machine-language programming*?
2. What is the memory size of HLC? Is it a fixed-word-length machine or is it a variable-word-length machine?
3. What computer component decodes an instruction?
4. What is meant by the "stored program concept"?
5. What is the function of the automatic sequencer within the control of a computer?
6. What is a transfer instruction?
7. Name some compiler-level languages.
8. What is an accumulator? What can be done with it?
9. What is the maximum address that may be given in the address portion of an HLC instruction format?
10. Tell how many hexadecimal characters are needed to express the contents of an HLC instruction format.
11. What are the names of the three fields in an HLC instruction format?
12. How many bits are needed to define the operation in an HLC instruction format?

15 | Machine-language Programming

ONE-ADDRESS COMPUTERS

Our hypothetical computer, HLC, is a one-address computer. Let us look at its instruction format again (see Fig. 15-1). Observe that there is only one address in this format. The address portion of the

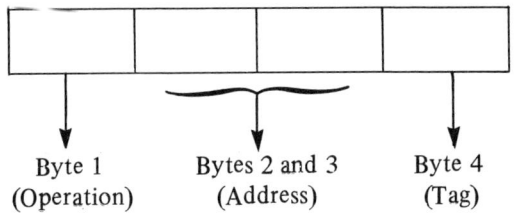

FIGURE 15-1

instruction format requires two bytes (16 bits). Whenever an operation is given, the operation (or "op" for short) usually uses the address given in the instruction in one form or another. Suppose, for example, the instruction is

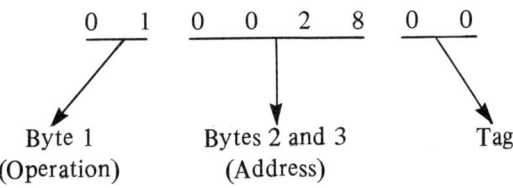

From the table given in the last chapter, we see that the operation 01 orders the computer to clear the contents of the accumulator, then load into it the *contents* of byte locations 28_{16} through $2B_{16}$. These 4 bytes constitute a "word." A word is generally used to store an integer or a floating-point number. Half-words (2 bytes) and double words (8 bytes) are also used to store values.

TAG

In this example, the tag tells what index register modifies this instruction. Since the tag contains 00, Index Register zero is referenced. If Index Register zero contains only zeroes, the instruction we see is not modified. We shall discuss index registers soon.

TWO-ADDRESS COMPUTERS

Computers may contain two addresses or three addresses in instruction formats. A two-address format might have the form shown in Fig. 15-2.

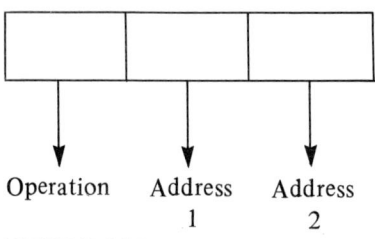

FIGURE 15-2

If the operation is "add," the instruction may be to have the computer add the *contents* found at address 2 to the contents located at address 1. The contents of address 1 change, but the contents of address 2 do not change.

THREE-ADDRESS COMPUTERS

A three-address format might look like that in Fig. 15-3.

If the operation is "add," the instruction may be to have the computer sum the contents of address 1 and address 2, and then

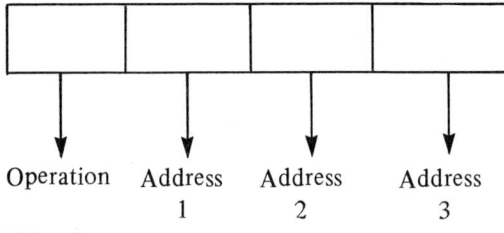

FIGURE 15-3

store the result at address 3. The contents of address 3 change, but the contents of addresses 1 and 2 do not.

Since one-address systems are easy to understand, HLC uses a one-address format. Many of the operations affect the accumulator register. Thus, to add two values and store the result in a memory word, we would give these three instructions:

$$0\ 1\ 0\ 4\ 0\ 0\ 0_{16}$$
$$0\ 8\ 0\ 4\ 0\ 4\ 0_{16}$$
$$5\ 1\ 0\ 5\ 0\ 0\ 0_{16}$$

The first instruction clears the accumulator, then loads into it the contents of bytes 400_{16} through 403_{16}. Assume that the 32 bits found at those four byte locations contain an integer value.

The next instruction adds to the accumulator the contents of bytes 404_{16} through 407_{16}. Assume that these bytes also contain an integer value.

The third instruction stores the result of the computation, the value currently in the accumulator, in the four-byte word beginning at byte location 500_{16}.

INDEX REGISTERS

The tags of these three instructions were 00. Index Register zero was used to modify the instructions. Let us assume that the contents of Index Register zero contained zeroes and therefore did not affect the actions that we have just discussed.

At the conclusion of the execution of these three instructions, we find that the contents of the 4-byte word beginning at byte location 400_{16} has not changed. Neither have the contents of the 4-byte word beginning at byte location 404_{16}. The 4-byte word beginning at byte location 500_{16} contains the sum that was computed in the accumulator. The accumulator still holds that sum after the store instruction has acted upon it. In other words, further calculations may be made using the value still in the accumulator. Should the accumulator need to be cleared, though, another "clear and add" instruction could be issued.

Finally, the action of these three instructions has not affected Index Register zero. It still contains zeroes.

Let us assume that HLC has been built with 16 index registers in the CPU. These registers are numbered Index Register 0_{16} through Index Register F_{16}. Let us assume further that each index register is able to hold an integer value from 0_{16} through $FFFF_{16}$ ($65,536_{10}$).

The contents of an index register are *added* to the address given in an instruction. Consider this example instruction:

$$0 \ 1 \ 0 \ 8 \ 0 \ 0 \ 0 \ 6$$

The instruction is 01 (clear and load the accumulator). The address is 800_{16}. This means that the instruction appears to load the value found at byte locations 800_{16} through 803_{16}. But we must also consider the contents of Index Register 6_{16} indicated in the tag. Suppose that the current contents of Index Register 6_{16} are 200_{16}. This number must be added to the address to give the actual address (the "effective" address) that actually will be used. Since 800_{16} plus 200_{16} gives $A00_{16}$, the actual address used by the instruction is not 800_{16} but $A00_{16}$.

Index registers are used for two basic reasons:

1. To conduct a count without using the accumulator.
2. To modify an existing instruction so that its effective address may be derived from its apparent address.

We shall give examples in the next chapter of how index registers may be used in practical applications for both purposes.

Since there are only 16 index registers in HLC, each of those registers could hold a value for a different purpose. For example, you may wish to assign to Index Register 1_{16} a certain value so that it may modify one type of instruction and you may wish to assign to Index Register 2_{16} another value to modify another type of instruction. The contents of these two registers, as well as those of the other 14 registers, may be independently changed, checked, or cleared by programming operations. If an instruction is not to be modified by an index register, the normal practice is to show Index Register 0_{16} in the instruction tag, and to make sure that the contents of that register are zero.

Now we can analyze HLC's instruction format with a greater depth of understanding. Figure 15-4 shows the format. The first byte contains 8 bits. There are 256 ways that 8 bits can be arranged. These ways vary from 00000000_2 to 11111111_2. Since two hexadecimal characters are needed to express 16 bits, a table of operation codes would have 256 entries and the codes would vary from 00_{16} to FF_{16}.

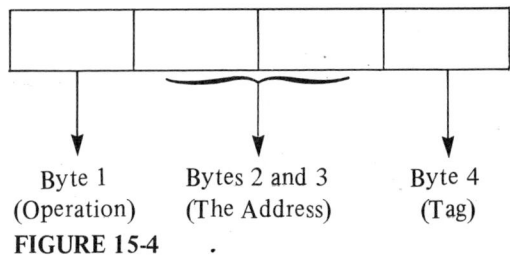

Byte 1   Bytes 2 and 3   Byte 4
(Operation)   (The Address)   (Tag)
FIGURE 15-4

The first few codes would be 00, 01, 02, ..., 09, 0A, 0B, 0C, 0D, 0E, 0F, 10, 11, 12, ..., 19, 1A, 1B, 1C, 1D, 1E, 1F, 20, 21, 22, ..., 29, 2A, etc.

The second and third bytes contain 16 bits. Four hexadecimal characters may be used to express the addresses. These range from 0000_{16} through $FFFF_{16}$. In decimal, the smallest address that can be referenced is 0000_{16} and the largest is $65,535_{10}$. Now you can see why HLC's memory size is 64K bytes. If it had more bytes than 64K bytes, the bytes having addresses larger than $65,535_{10}$ ($FFFF_{16}$) could not be accessed.

The fourth byte contains the tag. The tag is more generous than it needs to be, since there are only 16 index registers. The only values that a tag may have, expressed in two hexadecimal characters, are

         00, 01, 02, 03, 04, 05, 06, 07
         08, 09, 0A, 0B, 0C, 0D, 0E, 0F

These tags always show a zero as the leftmost of the two hexadecimal characters. Built to its fullest potential, HLC could have up to 256 index registers, the first one being 00_{16} and the last, FF_{16}.

SUMMARY

Many computers are of the one-address type. That is, an instruction format contains an operation field (op) and an address field. If an instruction is a two-address system, the instruction format includes an operation field and two address fields. Similarly, if the machine is a three-address type, the instruction format includes an operation field and three address fields.

If the computer is byte-oriented, a series of bytes is used to make up the instruction format as well as the data format. A word often consists of four bytes; a half-word, two bytes; and a double word, eight bytes.

Index registers are used to modify the addresses in instructions. The value of the named index register is added to the address given in the instruction. This way, an instruction may be written in a given way, but when it is executed the address field can be made to vary by changing the contents of the index register.

QUESTIONS

1. Tell the difference between a one-address, two-address, and three-address instruction format. What format does HLC use?
2. What is the function of the tag in an HLC instruction format?
3. What is the function of an index register?
4. How many index registers does HLC use? What is the maximum number of index registers it could use?

16 | Assembly-language Programming

MACHINE-LANGUAGE PROGRAMMING

A program written in machine language can contain hundreds, if not thousands, of instructions. These instructions must be coded in hexadecimal characters where each character represents 4 bits. Then the instructions are punched on cards, 10 instructions per card, and read into a computer via its card reader.

As the instructions are transferred into the memory of the computer, each byte location within memory is loaded from two sequential hexadecimal characters found in the program deck. Suppose, for example, that a program contains 800 instructions. The programmer punches 80 data processing cards, placing 10 instructions on each card. As you will recall, each instruction is designated by 8 hexadecimal characters. There is just room enough on an 80-column card to hold 10 instructions each consisting of 8 hexadecimal characters.

The programmer may direct that the instructions be read into memory beginning at byte location $5{,}000_{16}$. Since 800 instructions require $3{,}200_{10}$ byte locations (4 bytes per instruction), the memory bytes needed to store the program will extend from byte location $5{,}000_{16}$ through byte location $5C7F_{16}$ ($20{,}480_{10}$ through

$23,679_{10}$). The programmer then tells the computer to find the first instruction at location $5,000_{16}$ and to execute the program.

As you can see, machine-language programming requires a programmer to worry about bytes, bits, words, locations, op codes, addresses, and many other details too numerous to mention. When an attempt is made to execute the final program, it probably will not work, and the programmer may have to spend days, weeks, even longer in an attempt to weed out all the problem areas.

ASSEMBLY-LANGUAGE PROGRAMMING

In the early 1950s, it was decided that machine-language programming should give way to a better method of programming. Assembly-language programming was developed. In assembly-language programming, a person no longer had to worry about the hexadecimal code representing machine operations. Instead of recalling that 01 means "clear and add," he could use a mnemonic CLA. Instead of 08 for "add to accumulator," he could use ADA, etc.

Further, he did not have to worry about the binary, octal, or hexadecimal representation of addresses. He could always use decimal numbers.

Let us look at how a program for HLC could be written in assembly-language (see Fig. 16-1).

CODING FORMS

The program has been written on a coding form having the field divisions shown. In the NAME field, various names for values are given. Also the beginning points of subdivisions of the program are given. The name BEGIN shows the one and only subdivision in this example. A name for a value or for a program subdivision may be any name a programmer selects. Let us assume that for HLC, names must always be alphabetic and they may contain a maximum of six characters.

In the OP field, a machine-language operation may be given. Examples of operations that may be given would include:

1	11	21	31	41
NAME	OP	VALUE OR ADDRESS	INDEX	NOTES
X	DEC	1.5		Establish fp 15.6
Y	DEC	1.75		Establish fp 1.75
A	INT	16		Establish integer 16
B	INT	26		Establish integer 26
C	INT	0		Storage for $A - B$
Z	DEC	0		Storage for $X + Y$
BEGIN	CLA	X	0	X to accumulator
	FAD	Y	0	ADD Y
	STA	Z	0	Store in Z
	CLA	A	0	A to accumulator
	SUB	B	0	Subtract B
	STA	C	0	Store in C
	PRINT	C	0	
	PRINT	Z	0	
	HALT	0	0	
	END			

FIGURE 16-1

CLA   clear and load accumulator

STA   store from the accumulator

FAD   add a number in floating-point mode

ADD   add a number in integer mode

FSB   subtract a number in floating-point mode

SUB   subtract a number in integer mode

SHL   shift the accumulator left

SHR   shift the accumulator right

In a table given later in this chapter we shall show several op codes that are used in examples used in the chapter. The table will show the mnemonics for the op codes (CLA, STA, ADD, etc.), the corresponding hexadecimal codes, and the meaning of the operations.

The field labeled "Value or Address" shows what integer or floating-point value is being created with a DEC or INT operation or what is the name of the address being referenced.

The "Index" field shows what index register is used to modify an instruction. *Every* instruction is modified, but, of course, if the contents of the named index register contain zeroes, then the instruction addresses will not be modified.

In the "Notes" field, a programmer tells himself and others what is happening in a particular portion of a program. It is true that an assembly-language program is more clear to a reader than a program written in machine language; nevertheless, the notes help if a person has to come back to a program several months or years after he first wrote it.

This coding form is now keypunched. The information found on each card of this program is punched on a card: one line, one card. On cards, names begin in Column 1; ops begin in Column 11; values or addresses begin in Column 21; index register information begins in Column 31; and notes begin in Column 41.

SOURCE DECK

The deck of resulting cards is known as the "source deck." and the program punched upon the cards is known as the "source program." Since there are 16 instructions in the program, there are 16 cards forming the source deck.

ASSEMBLY

These cards are submitted to a computer with instructions to "assemble" the program. The term "assemble" means to convert the program to machine language. A computer such as HLC can be conditioned to accept assembly-language instructions and convert them to machine language. (The actual conversion is done by a program called an "assembler.")

The process of assembly may or may not be successful. If there are

Assembly-Language Programming   117

clerical errors in the program, such as the misspelling of op codes, the computer will give error messages. If there are no errors, the computer will give an "object" deck containing the same instructions as those in the source deck except that the instructions will be in machine language.

EXECUTION

The object deck may now be submitted to the computer for an execution. The execution itself may or may not be correct. If the programmer's logic was correct when he wrote the program, results will be valid; if his logic was wrong and he told the computer to do things he really did not intend to tell it, then the results will be incorrect. (Computers are fussy. They do only what programmers tell them to do—not what programmers intended to tell them.)

At times a programmer may exercise an option called "load and go." He gives the computer his source deck and tells it to assemble his program (change it to machine language), and then execute it. The two steps are merged into one. If the program assembles correctly, it will execute; if not, the program will give error messages, and make no attempt to execute.

Programmers must make corrections to their source decks if assembly attempts fail. They may then submit their programs to the computer again.

If one were to examine an object deck, he would see how the computer has converted source language to machine language. The machine language is generally identical to or close to the language that the programmer would have generated if he himself had written the program in machine language. Let us consider the example program given above, for instance.

The first four instructions in the program

```
X    DEC    1.5
Y    DEC    1.75
A    INT    16
B    INT    26
C    INT    0
Z    DEC    0
```

cause the creation and storage of the various values shown. DEC ops set up floating-point numbers and INT ops set up integer numbers. The computer uses 24 consecutive byte positions to set up the values indicated. The contents of those bytes, expressed in hexadecimal, are

        41180000   (the floating-point value 1.5)

        411C0000   (the floating-point value 1.75)

        00000010   (the integer value 16)

        0000001A   (the integer value 26)

        00000000   (the integer value 0)

        80000000   (the floating-point value 0)

The computer places these six values beginning at a byte location that the programmer has specified. From that point the values follow in sequence. Suppose the programmer specified that the first value must begin at byte location $2,000_{16}$. The floating-point value 1.5, which the computer will remember has the name X, falls into byte locations $2,000_{16}$ through $2,003_{16}$. The value of Y falls into byte locations $2,004_{16}$ through $2,007_{16}$, etc.

The remainder of the program is changed to machine language. The instruction

        CLA X 0

for example, converts to

        0 1 2 0 0 0 0 0

The 01 is HLC's op code for clear and add, and 2000 represents the byte address of X. Since Index Register zero modifies the instruction, the tag is 00.

The entire example program converted to machine language is shown in Table 16-1.

HLC OPS

Most of the op codes can be found in the table of op codes given in Chapter 14. Observe that some op codes make a distinction as to

Assembly-Language Programming 119

Table 16-1

Name	Contents of Memory	Byte Locations (Hexadecimal)
X	41180000	2000 - 2003
Y	411C0000	2004 - 2007
A	00000010	2008 - 200B
B	0000001A	200C - 200F
C	00000000	2010 - 2013
Z	80000000	2014 - 2017
BEGIN	01200000	2018 - 201B
	02200400	201C - 201F
	51201400	2020 - 2023
	01200800	2024 - 2027
	09200C00	2028 - 202B
	51201000	202C - 202F
	75201000	2030 - 2033
	75201400	2034 - 2037
	00000000	2038 - 203B

whether the work is being done in integer or floating-point mode. There are two "add" op codes: 08 (for integers) and 02 (for floating-point values). There are also two "subtract," two "multiply," and two "divide" op codes.

Note that END does not become converted to a machine-language operation. The END card must be the very last card of every assembly-language program. It signals the computer that the process of assembly is to terminate.

This program must be told where to begin in order to execute properly. Since the byte labeled BEGIN is located at byte position $2,018_{16}$, the computer is told to begin executing the program at that location. Execution continues instruction after instruction until op code 00 is detected.

HLC has the ability to perform 256 different kinds of actions. You have already been introduced to some of them: CLA, STA, ADD, etc. We repeat some of those operations in Table 16-2 and give a few new ones. The example programs on the next pages require that you understand the selected operations shown in Table 16-2.

Table 16-2. Selected HLC Operations

OP	Hexadecimal Code	Function
DEC	NONE	Establish a floating-point number.
INT	NONE	Establish an integer number.
CLA	01	Clear the accumulator and load the value named in the address.
STA	51	Store the value in the accumulator to the memory location identified by the address. The accumulator is not changed.
ADD	08	Add the named integer value to the accumulator.
FAD	02	Add the named floating-point value to the accumulator.
SUB	09	Subtract the named integer value from the accumulator.
FSB	21	Subtract the named floating-point value from the accumulator.
MPY	80	Multiply the named integer value by the contents of accumulator. The result replaces the old value in the accumulator.
LDX4	94	Load Index Register 4 with the value named in the address. The accumulator is not used to accomplish this task.
LDX5	95	Same as for LDX4, except that the Index Register is 5.
ADDX4	A4	Add the integer value named in the address to Index Register 4. The accumulator is not used for this calculation.
ADDX5	A5	Same as for ADDX4, except that the Index Register is 5.
CMPX4	B4	Compare Index Register 4 with the integer value named in the address. A special sign indicator is set to minus, zero, or plus depending upon the result of the compare. To establish the result, the named integer value is subtracted from the current contents of the index register. The accumulator is not used for this calculation.
CMPX5	B5	Same as for CMPX4, except that the Index Register is 5.
TMI	42	The program jumps to the named address if the contents of the sign indicator is minus. Other-

Assembly-Language Programming

Table 16-2. Selected HLC Operations (Continued)

OP	Hexadecimal Code	Function
		wise, the program proceeds to the next instruction.
TZE	43	The program jumps to the named address if the contents of the sign indicator is zero. Otherwise, the program proceeds to the next instruction.
TPL	44	The program jumps to the named address if the contents of the sign indicator is positive. Otherwise, the program proceeds to the next instruction.
TRA	40	The program jumps unconditionally to the named address.
PRINT	75	The named value is printed in a standard format on output paper.
HALT	00	The program stops.
END	NONE	This must be the last instruction of any assembly-language program.

COUNTING USING INDEX REGISTERS

Figures 16-2 and 16-3 are two programs that illustrate how index registers may be employed. Suppose we need to compute 2.5^{10}. Index Register 4 (or any of the other 15 index registers) may be used to count from 1 to 10.

Index Register 4 is given an initial value of 1. Then the value 2.5 is loaded into the accumulator.

ADDX4 ONE adds 1 to Index Register 4. It then has the value 2. The accumulator is multiplied by 2.5, giving 2.5^2. The value in Index Register 4 (2) is compared against 10. The compare makes the calculation $2 - 10$ (not in the accumulator) and finds that the result is negative (-8). The TMI instruction returns the program to AGAIN.

One is added to Index Register 3, making its value 3. The accumulator is multiplied by 2.5, giving 2.5^3. The compare gives -7. The program returns to AGAIN.

This procedure continues until Index Register 4's value becomes 10. The final value, 2.5^{10}, is computed, and the compare instruction gives a zero result. Since the TMI instruction does not return the program to AGAIN, the program continues to the next statement,

NAME	OP	VALUE OR ADDRESS	INDEX	NOTES
ANS	DEC	0		Place to store answer
V	DEC	2.5		The value to be raised to 10th power
ONE	INT	1		Integer 1
TEN	INT	10		Integer 10
BEGIN	LDX4	ONE	0	1 ⟶ Index Register 4
	CLA	V	0	V ⟶ Accumulator
AGAIN	ADDX4	ONE	0	1 added to Register 4
	MPY	V	0	Accumulator multiplied by V
	CMPX4	TEN	0	Compare Register 4 with 10
	TMI	AGAIN	0	Not done. Go to AGAIN.
	STA	ANS	0	Done. Store accumulator in answer.
	PRINT	ANS	0	
	HALT	0	0	
	END			

FIGURE 16-2

where the contents of the accumulator are assigned to ANS and ANS is printed.

In this program, Index Register 4 merely counted. It was not used to modify any instructions. (Index Register zero modified instructions, but its value was automatically initialized with zero when the program began, and it therefore had no effect on the instructions it modified.)

ADDRESS MODIFICATION

This next program uses Index Register 5 to count and to modify instructions. The problem is to write a program that will sum the eight values 1.2, 2.6, 7.7, 8.4, 9.9, 3.6, 4.4, and 1.8.

Index registers always begin with zeroes, so the instruction to load zero into Index Register 5 (at BEGIN) is not really necessary, but it is good programming practice.

The value W is loaded into the accumulator. The instruction is modified by Index Register 5, which contains the value zero. The instruction is, therefore, not modified and the first W value is loaded into the accumulator. The value 4 is then added to Index Register 5. Index Register 5 is checked to determine whether its contents are 32. Since the register contains 4, not 32, the program does not jump to DONE. Instead, it adds W to the accumulator. The fact that the instruction is modified by Index Register 5 means that 4 is added to W's byte address. The actual W accessed is not the first one, but the second.

As the program continues, Index Register 5's contents grow by 4's. Each time a FAD command is executed, the next W is retrieved. Finally, when Index Register 5's value becomes 32, the summing is complete, since all eight values of W have been processed.

The program assigns the contents of the accumulator to SUM and prints it.

NAME	OP	VALUE OR ADDRESS	INDEX	NOTES
SUM	INT	0		Place to store sum
THTWO	INT	32		Establish integer 32
ZERO	INT	0		Establish integer 0
FOUR	INT	4		Establish integer 4
W	DEC	1.2		First W value
	DEC	2.6		2nd W value
	DEC	7.7		3rd W value
	DEC	8.4		4th W value
	DEC	9.9		5th W value
	DEC	3.6		6th W value
	DEC	4.4		7th W value
	DEC	1.8		8th W value
BEGIN	LDX5	ZERO	0	0 ⟶ Index Register 5
	CLA	W	5	W ⟶ Accumulator
AGAIN	ADDX5	FOUR	0	Add 4 to Index Register 5
	CMPX5	THTWO	0	Compare Register with 32
	TZE	DONE	0	Jump to DONE when done
	FAD	W	5	Not done, add another W
	TRA	AGAIN	0	Go back to Add 1 to Register 5
DONE	STA	SUM	0	Store accumulator in SUM
	PRINT	SUM	0	
	HALT	0	0	
	END			

FIGURE 16-3

SUMMARY

Programming in machine-language is tedious, and a programmer has to know a great deal concerning binary bits, operation codes, addresses, etc. With the advent of assembly languages, programming became easier, since much of the tedious work connected with programming was assumed by the computer itself.

Programs written in assembly language are first written on coding forms. Then source decks are punched. Finally, the source programs are assembled. That is, they are changed to machine language by the computer. During the process of assembly, errors may be detected. If so, execution of the program does not take place. The programmer receives an error listing telling him what he did wrong. The programmer may then correct his errors and try again. When assembly succeeds, the programmer obtains an object deck, which contains the machine-language instructions of the program.

Object decks may be used to execute programs; or, in "load and go" operations, programs are first assembled, then immediately executed if there are no errors.

In assembly languages, index registers permit the modification of instructions. Also, index registers may be used simply to have the computer count the number of times that it executes a given series of instructions.

QUESTIONS

1. How does assembly language differ from machine language?
2. Tell how many hexadecimal characters are required to express a machine-language instruction, for the HLC computer.
3. What is meant by the term *assembly*?
4. What is the function of the Name field on an assembly-language coding form?
5. Tell how the op DEC differs from the op INT.
6. What is the function of the Index field on an assembly-language coding form?
7. How many different ops is the HLC computer able to understand?
8. Discuss the advantages of the Notes field on an assembly-language coding form.
9. What is the difference between the terms *source deck* and *object deck*?

10. Are assembly attempts always successful? Explain.
11. What is meant by the term "load and go"?
12. What is meant by the term "execute"?
13. Discuss the difference between ADD and FAD, between SUB and FSB.
14. How are decisions made in machine-language programming?

17 | A Survey of FORTRAN–*Part I*

UNIVERSAL LANGUAGES

It became apparent around 1955 that machine-language and assembly-language programming had its disadvantages. These methods of programming were tedious. They required a programmer to make sure that he gave the most minute of instructions to the computer and in precise sequence. Should he deviate in the slightest from these requirements, the program would either not run properly or give trouble while running.

Another disadvantage was the fact that a program written in machine language or in assembly language would run only on one type of computer. If a new computer were received at a computer site, new languages would have to be learned. These disadvantages became more serious as computers were improved and began replacing older ones.

A further disadvantage was that programs written in machine language or assembly language were cryptic in nature and difficult to understand. A programmer would have difficulty understanding how another programmer had solved a problem, especially if the first programmer had used tricky methods. A programmer who, himself, had written a program might well have difficulty understanding it if he were to come back to it a year or so after it had been written.

FORTRAN

A new method of programming seemed necessary, one that would make programming easier, would be more "universal" and would better act as its own documentation. By "universal" is meant that the language could be used on many computers, not just one or a few. Programmers got together and invented a programming language called FORTRAN. This language was to be a scientific programming language. The name of the language indicates that it was to be used where formulas are to be evaluated: *FOR*mula *TRAN*slator. The IBM Corporation backed the development of this new language, and it flourished.

To use the new language, a programmer had to learn only a few kinds of activities that a computer could perform. For example, computers can read information from punched cards and magnetic tape. The FORTRAN command READ was assigned to this function.

Computers can make calculations. The FORTRAN assignment statement as exemplified by

$$P = (W * R) / Y$$

was developed for this purpose.

Computers can make decisions. The FORTRAN IF statement was assigned for this purpose.

Computers can print lines of output on high-speed printer paper. The FORTRAN PRINT statement was developed for this purpose. The word WRITE may today also be used.

the FORTRAN programmer was required to learn how to use several English words in giving instructions to a computer. Some of the English words were

READ	END
PRINT	GO TO
WRITE	RETURN
DIMENSION	FORMAT
IF	
COMMON	
CALL	
SUBROUTINE	
STOP	

CALCULATIONS

The foregoing list contains about half the list of English words that were made available. Having learned how to use the words in writing computer instructions, the programmer was relieved of many of the tedious details that he previously had to worry about. For example, if the programmer wanted the computer to add two values, then take the square root of the result, he could write the simple instruction

$$D = (A + B) ** .5$$

He would not have to give an instruction to bring the value of A into the accumulator, then an instruction to add B to the accumulator, then an instruction to raise the contents of the accumulator to the .5 power, and finally an instruction to store the result from the accumulator to a memory cell called D.

The more complex the formula that a programmer had to program, the more tedious the details from which he could be relieved.

It must be pointed out that a program written in FORTRAN was almost always not as efficient as a program written in machine language or in assembly language. It might be only 80 or 90 percent as efficient. Though the efficiency penalty seems large, it could be tolerated because the pluses of writing in FORTRAN far exceeded the minuses. If a program had to be highly efficient, a programmer could always go back to machine language or assembly language. Furthermore, selected portions of any program could be written in machine language or assembly language.

CODING FORM

Now for the actual mechanics of writing a program in FORTRAN. A programmer uses a coding form like the one shown in Fig. 17-1. The form is marked off in 80 columns. (It is no coincidence that a standard data processing card also is marked off in 80 columns.)

1	5	6	7	72	73	80

FIGURE 17-1

A Survey of FORTRAN—*Part I*

The form is also divided into four fields (see Table 17-1).

Table 17-1. **FORTRAN Form**

Field	Columns	Use
1	1-5	Statement number
2	6	Continuation
3	7-72	FORTRAN instruction
4	73-80	Identification

STATEMENTS

A programmer writes instructions on the coding sheet in the form of "statements." Statements look like this:

READ 8, X, Y

IF (P − Q) 9, 17, 4

GO TO 23

PRINT 27, W

These four examples are independent statements, and the reader should not interpret them as a portion of an actual program.

The programmer writes statements like these, one per line on the FORTRAN coding form. They begin at column 7 of the coding form and are written so that each character of the statement is given within a single column of the coding form. There is always one column per character and one character per column when one is writing FORTRAN statements. Such characters as open parentheses, minus signs, and commas require a column, as do letters of the alphabet and digits. Statements may not go beyond column 72.

Some statements, not all, require statement numbers. Those numbers are placed within columns 1 through 5.

Columns 73 through 80 may optionally be used by a programmer to give any identification information he wishes to give. That is, he may place his name there, or the name of the program, or sequence numbers of the FORTRAN statements themselves.

If a statement cannot be completed on one line of the coding form, the programmer may continue it on the next line. In doing so, he places any nonblank or nonzero character in column 6 of the next coding line. Column 6 is called the "continuation column."

Statements may be continued upon several coding lines, not just one.

Figure 17-2 shows an example of a complete FORTRAN program written on a FORTRAN coding form:

1	5	6	7	72	73	80
			A = 23.7			
	3		READ 7, X			
	7		FORMAT (F 15.2)			
			IF (X) 20, 130, 20			
	20		Q = A * X			
			PRINT 99, A, X, Q			
	99		FORMAT (1H , 3F 10.2)			
			GO TO 3			
	130		STOP			
			END			

FIGURE 17-2

The programmer has asked the computer to assign the value 23.7 to A. Then he has directed it to obtain another value from a data card and to call that value X. Next the programmer has asked for the value of A to be multiplied by the value of X. The result has been assigned to Q. Finally, the computer has been directed to print the values of A, X, and Q. It has then been directed to obtain another data card.

The program keeps cycling, making computation after computation and giving answers until data cards run out. The last data card in the data deck contains the value zero. When that value is detected, the program stops.

This illustrative program can only hint at the power of FORTRAN, since programs are usually much more complex and contain many more statements.

The FORTRAN program, once coded, is delivered to a keypunch operator who punches one standard 80-column card for every statement in the program. Since there are 10 statements in the program, the keypunch operator punches 10 cards. The operator makes sure that the punched cards reflect the coding forms in every detail. This means that wherever characters are shown on the coding form, the keypunch operator punches those characters in the corresponding columns of the 80-column cards.

SOURCE DECK

The deck of punched cards is called the "source deck." The FORTRAN program punched upon the cards is called the "source program."

INPUT DATA

Now the programmer punches any input data cards that his program might require. These cards are placed behind the source deck (see Fig. 17-3).

JOB CONTROL LANGUAGE (JCL) CARDS

Now "job control language" (JCL) cards are woven among the source and data decks. JCL cards vary from computer to computer. They tell the computer who you are, what kind of a job you want

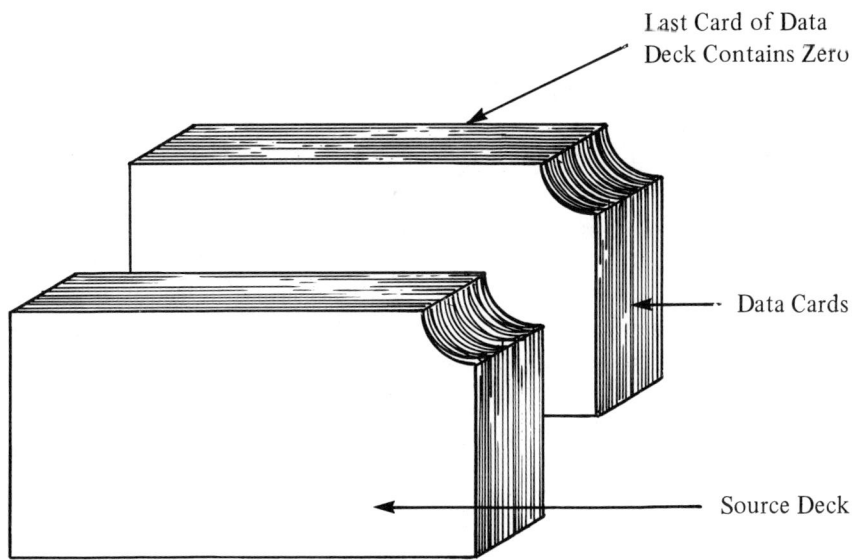

FIGURE 17-3

processed (FORTRAN, COBOL, PL/I, etc.), what your charge number is, and other items of information. JCL cards are distinguished from FORTRAN statements or data cards, since they contain unique characters in column 1. For example, all job control language cards of a certain IBM computer may require an asterisk (*) in column 1, while all job control cards of a certain UNIVAC computer may require a slash (/) in column 1.

Figure 17-4 shows the job setup that a programmer has.

COMPILATION

The setup is delivered to the computer for a process called "compilation." In the compilation process, the computer converts all FORTRAN statements to machine language. then it executes the program. If compilation fails, perhaps because some FORTRAN words were spelled wrong, the program will not execute. The programmer will get a report telling what was wrong with his program. The programmer must replace bad cards with good ones and make an attempt to obtain another compilation. This time the compilation may be successful and the execution of the program will occur. The programmer will obtain the results he asked for.

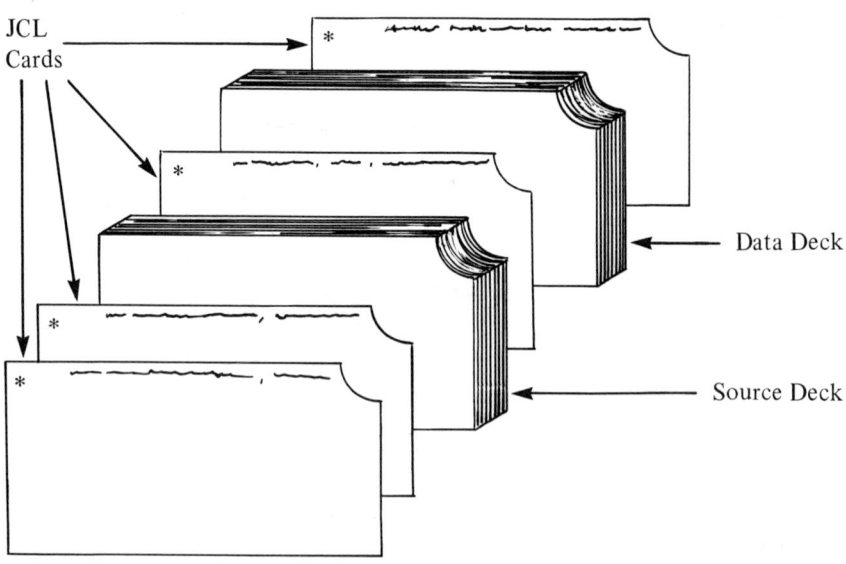

FIGURE 17-4

The compilation process is actually performed by a computer program called a "compiler." This elaborate program is provided by the computer manufacturer at the same time that the computer is delivered.

EXECUTION

At times you may hear the term "load and go." This means that a programmer presents a job to the computer and directs it to compile his job (change it to machine language), and then execute it (run the program). Optionally a programmer may ask for only a compilation.

When a program runs, it may or may not give correct answers. The program may execute but give answers that are obviously wrong. For example, the program may issue million-dollar checks to every employee in the company. Obviously, the program was not written correctly. (Maybe wrong equations were given.)

DEBUGGING

The process of finding out what is wrong with a program is called "debugging." Since a job runs in two stages, (1) compilation and (2) execution, there may be problems with both stages. Errors that are discovered during the time that compilation is in progress are called "compile-time errors"; errors that are discovered while a program is in execution are called "run-time errors." Both types of errors must be discovered and eliminated before a run from a computer may be accepted.

OBJECT DECK

An optional output from a compilation is an "object deck." This deck of punched cards contains a program in machine language. If a program is to be executed many times, the object deck should be used rather than the source deck. The executions are less expensive, since repeated compilations are avoided.

SUMMARY

While assembly-language programming is less difficult and tedious than machine-language programming, it still is too difficult to be really effective. The need for a better programming language led to the development of FORTRAN in the mid-1950s.

FORTRAN was developed for three reasons:

1. To provide an easier method of programming a computer.
2. To enable easier conversion of departments or companies from one computer to another.
3. To help make the listing of a program easier to understand.

English words are used in FORTRAN to tell a computer what to do. The entire vocabulary of the FORTRAN language incorporates little more than thirty words. With the proper use of these words, highly complex programs may be written.

In FORTRAN, one can direct the computer to obtain input data (READ), process it, then write out answers (WRITE and/or PRINT).

In actual practice, a person writes a program on a coding form; punched cards forming a source deck are then obtained. Then compilation takes place. If successful, compilation is followed by execution.

FORTRAN programs are written in the form of statements, some of which are numbered with statement numbers. If necessary, certain longer statements may be continued.

Input to a FORTRAN program may be given in the form of punched data processing cards. (Magnetic tape may also provide input.) Intermingled with source or object decks and data cards are Job Control Language (JCL) cards. JCL cards give the computer information it needs to know in order to execute the given program.

In "load and go" situations, a program can be submitted for the joint activities of compile and execute. If there are no compilation errors, the program is executed. If there are programming errors, the user is told what they are and he is permitted to make the appropriate change.

QUESTIONS

1. What are the reasons that FORTRAN was developed? What type of problems is FORTRAN ideally suited for?
2. What is a universal language?

3. What kind of statement does FORTRAN use to cause input data to be read?
4. What kind of statement does FORTRAN use when decisions have to be made?
5. About how many English words does the FORTRAN language employ?
6. What is meant by the term *compilation*?
7. What is meant by the term *execution*?
8. What is a FORTRAN statement? What is a statement number?
9. What is a source deck? How does it differ from an object deck?
10. What are JCL cards?
11. What are some of the problems that may arise when an attempt is made to compile a program?
12. What is meant by the term "load and go"?
13. Discuss the differences between compile-time and run-time errors.
14. What is meant by the term "debugging"?

18 | A Survey of FORTRAN–*Part II*

INTEGER NUMBERS

FORTRAN makes a distinction between two types of numbers. They are the "integers" and "reals." Integer values are the kind that we discussed in Chapter 9. In recent IBM equipment, integer values may be expressed using 16 bits (a half-word) or using 32 bits (a full word). A half-word employs two 8-bit bytes, and a full word employs four 8-bit bytes. The maximum value that may be expressed in 16 bits is $\pm 2^{15} - 1$ ($\pm 32{,}767$), and the maximum value that may be expressed in 32 bits is $\pm 2^{31} - 1$ ($2{,}147{,}483{,}647$).

REAL NUMBERS

The real numbers are the ones that we discussed in Chapter 10 under the topic of floating-point. A floating-point number may be as large as $\pm 10^{76}$. Though the number is immense, only the first seven significant (nonzero) digits are known accurately. In FORTRAN, there is the ability to store real numbers in "double precision." This means that numbers are stored in floating-point format in 8 bytes (64 bits). The characteristic employs one byte as it does in single precision, but the mantissa employs 7 bytes. Since 8 bytes are double 4 bytes, a double precision value in FORTRAN is said to occupy two computer words.

The exact number of bits assigned to real and integer values in non-IBM computers depends upon the design of those other computers. Though details may vary, basic principles are the same.

Real numbers are numbers that show decimal points and integer values are those that do not. These numbers are real:

```
4.5
 .2945
-4.35
24.
```

These numbers are integers:

```
10325
 -36
 24
```

A real number is assigned to a computer word consisting of four bytes by employing a statement like

ALPHA = 9.567

and an integer number is assigned to a computer half-word or full word by employing a statement like

ITEM = 645

In the above two statements, the names ALPHA and ITEM are called variable names. The computer is instructed to store the given values in 4-byte (sometimes 2- or 8-byte) computer words and name the words ALPHA and ITEM.

VARIABLE NAMES

FORTRAN variable names may consist of up to six characters composed of letters of the alphabet and digits. The first character of a name must always be a letter of the alphabet.

Variable names are also divided into two types: real and integer. Real names always store real values. Those names begin with letters of the alphabet A through H and/or O through Z. The dollar sign ($) may also be used as a real alphabetic "letter."

These variable names are real:

BETA
EPSILN
A12345
X

Integer variable names begin with the letters I through N. These names are integers:

IPSWCH
J12345
K
NABC

ASSIGNMENT STATEMENT

In FORTRAN the assignment statement may have simple forms, such as

W = 4.5
N = 25

or more complex forms such as

P = (A+B)**3−X/Y
L34 = N+5

The calculations given at the right of the equals sign are to be performed, and the results are to be assigned to the variables shown to the left of the equal sign.

A statement such as

K = K + 1

is legal. The integer value 1 is added to the current value of K and the result *replaces* K. The old value of K disappears.

Assignment statements in FORTRAN must be made in proper sequence. The statements

   A = 5.6
   B = A + 1.2

give different results from

   B = A + 1.2
   A = 5.6

The value 0. will be used as A's value when the first statement is computed. At the conclusion of the statement's execution B's value will be 1.2. In the earlier example, B's value will be 6.8.

PRINT AND FORMAT STATEMENTS

The PRINT statement is used in FORTRAN to print the current values of the named variables. Consider, for example:

   PRINT 85, X,Y
   85 FORMAT (1H ,2F10.2)

The values *last assigned* to X and Y will be printed. The purpose of the FORMAT referenced in the PRINT statement (85 is the FORMAT) is to show *where* on the output paper the values of X and Y are to be printed. In this example, X and Y each use 10-character positions (120 or 132 are available on most printers), and the answers are rounded to two decimal places.

FORMATs are difficult for new programmers to work with. In general, for output, FORMATs tell where values are to be printed on output paper. For input, FORMATs tell where on a punched card values are to be found. Example:

   READ 60,A,B,C
   60 FORMAT (3F20.1)

The program reads a data card and assigns the values found thereon to variable names A, B, and C. The FORMAT (60) tells the computer where to obtain the numbers from a punched card. In this example, the three values will be found within the leftmost three fields of an 80-column punched card. As you will recall, 80 columns (sometimes 90 or 96) are available on a punched card for the purpose of providing input data.

IF STATEMENT

The IF statement is used for having a program make a decision. Example:

IF (P – X) 4,9,7

The computer evaluates $P - X$. If it finds that the result is negative, the program jumps (branches) to statement 4, where it resumes execution of statements; if the result is exactly equal to zero, the program jumps to 9; if the result is positive and greater than zero, the program jumps to statement 7.

The IF statement always gives three statement numbers. The leftmost number always tells where to go if the program finds a negative value within parentheses; the middle number always tells where to go if the program finds a value exactly equal to zero; the rightmost statement tells the program where to go if the value within parentheses is greater than zero.

All FORTRAN systems provide the IF statement form shown above. Many FORTRAN systems also provide an IF form like this one:

IF (P.EQ.Q) GO TO 75

This is called the "logical" IF as opposed to the "arithmetic" IF described earlier.

If P is equal to Q, the program jumps to statement 75. If P is not greater than Q, the program advances to the next statement in sequence.

STOP AND END STATEMENTS

STOP terminates the execution of a program. STOP must be distinguished from END. The END statement is always the very last statement of every source program. Its purpose is to signal the end of the compilation phase of a computer run. STOP goes into action only when compilation has been completed and execution has begun. It terminates the execution of a program.

It might be well to point out at this point that compilation is a relatively expensive process. If a program is to be run more than one time—say, once a week—the programmer may request that during the compilation process an "object" deck be provided by the computer. An object deck is a deck of punched cards that contains the same instructions as are found in the source deck. The difference lies in the fact that the object deck contains machine-language instructions. When an object deck is used in computer runs at times other than the first time, the object deck is given in place of the source deck. The compilation process is thus avoided and the cost of the run therefore is less.

READ STATEMENT

Let us examine a program that reads a series of manufacturing costs, totals them, and prints the sum of those costs (see Fig. 18-1).

1	5	6	7	72	73	80
			SUM = 0.			
	4		READ (25, END - 45)X			
	25		FORMAT (F15.1)			
			SUM = SUM + X			
			GO TO 4			
	45		PRINT 50, SUM			
	50		FORMAT (1H , 30X,F10.1)			
			STOP			
			END			

FIGURE 18-1

The variable SUM is initialized to hold the value zero. Then a data card is read. The value on the card is assigned to the variable name X. X is then added to SUM, and the program is then directed to return to the READ statement. Additional values of X are then read and added to SUM. When the data cards are exhausted, the program jumps to statement 45, where the value of SUM is printed. The execution of the program then terminates.

We repeat that this chapter and the last were designed not to teach the FORTRAN language but merely to give an idea of its flavor. There are many excellent texts that teach all of FORTRAN, using hundreds of pages to do so. The interested reader is advised to select one and peruse it thoroughly if he wishes a deeper knowledge of FORTRAN than has been given here.

FORTRAN V

We might also point out that since 1955, FORTRAN has been improved several times. With each improvement, FORTRAN's name was changed slightly. Simple FORTRAN became FORTRAN I, then FORTRAN II, then FORTRAN III, and finally FORTRAN IV. FORTRAN IV is the latest FORTRAN in general use.

FORTRAN has always been "upwards compatible." This means that a computer that has been conditioned to understand FORTRAN IV will correctly run programs written in all previous FORTRAN versions. Of course, the reverse is not necessarily true. A computer conditioned to understand FORTRAN II will not necessarily be able satisfactorily to run a program written in FORTRAN IV.

These days most new computers being built understand FORTRAN IV. Further, many computers permit extensions to this FORTRAN, but the extensions are not universally recognized. If and when a FORTRAN V is defined and announced, the chances are good that many of the extensions mentioned will be incorporated in the improved FORTRAN.

SUMMARY

In FORTRAN, there are two types of numeric values, real and integer. Similarly, there are two types of variable names, real and integer. In general, real numbers are assigned to real names, and integer values are assigned to integer names. However, exceptions are permitted to this rule.

Some important kinds of FORTRAN statements are READ, PRINT (or WRITE), IF, GO TO, and assignment statements. (Assignment statements are those that use equals signs.)

READ statements are used to obtain input values, PRINT statements to print answers, IF statements to make decisions, GO TO statements to cause unconditional transfers, and assignment statements to cause calculations.

FORTRAN has always been upwards compatible. Programs written in FORTRAN II will run on machines that understand FORTRAN IV; the reverse is not true. In the wings is the pending release of FORTRAN V. When made available, FORTRAN V will undoubtedly be found to be a significantly improved language over FORTRAN IV.

QUESTIONS

1. What are the two types of numbers and variable names used in FORTRAN?
2. What is a double-precision number?
3. What is the maximum number of characters that may be used in defining a variable name? What must be the beginning character?
4. What is an assignment statement?
5. What is the function of FORMATs in input/output FORTRAN statements?
6. What FORTRAN statement is used for making decisions? What are the two kinds available?
7. What is the difference between STOP and END statements?
8. What is meant by the term "upwards compatible"?
9. Discuss the development of FORTRAN. What is the designation of the language in current use?
10. Under what circumstances would a FORTRAN object deck be used?

19 | COBOL Concepts

COBOL OBJECTIVES

Another programming language which had its beginning around 1955 is COBOL. The acronym COBOL comes from the words *Co*mmon *B*usiness *O*riented *L*anguage. As the name indicates, COBOL was intended to be a universal language enabling programmers to prepare business programs for computer solution.

The objectives of COBOL were to be fourfold:

1. To alleviate conversion problems. Jobs that had been programmed for a computer would not have to be reprogrammed if an old computer was updated.

2. To provide a language that would be available on most computers. Once learned, a person would not have to learn a new language if an old computer were updated.

3. To provide a language that programmers would find easier to use for business purposes than FORTRAN, which was then being popularized, or any of the multitude of assembly languages that were available on the various computers in existence.

4. To provide a language that would help serve as its own documentation. A person should be able to look over COBOL instructions in a program and get a good idea of what the program did.

BUSINESS FILES

COBOL was oriented around business files. The business world is a world of files. Up-to-date information is maintained concerning personnel records, customer records, inventory records, and many others. It is important that these files, which sometimes hold millions of items of information, be kept up to date so that meaningful reports may be obtained from them.

COBOL is a language that enables a programmer to:

1. Describe files.
2. Sort files.
3. Update files.
4. Obtain reports from files.
5. Make calculations, using various numeric values found in files.

These and several other functions may easily be performed with the use of COBOL.

COBOL CODING FORM

A COBOL program is written upon a coding form in much the same way that a FORTRAN program is written upon a coding form. Figure 19-1 shows a form containing only a small portion of a COBOL program. The coding form is divided into five areas. Within columns 1 through 6, sequence numbers are placed. These numbers have minimum utility value and optionally may be omitted in many systems. When cards are eventually punched from lines on the coding forms, the sequence numbers may act as a safety measure in case the card deck is dropped and the cards are scrambled. The codes may be sorted, a mechanical sorter being used, to their original positions.

Column 7 is used for continuations. If a COBOL word is begun on a coding line and that word cannot be completed before column 72 is reached, the word may be continued on the next coding line, provided that a hyphen (-) is placed in column 7 of that next coding line.

Column 8 begins the "name field." Certain COBOL names must begin at column 8. The name field extends from column 8 through

```
401480  TAX-CALC.
401490      MULTIPLY GROSS-PAY BY
401500      DED-PERCENTAGE GIVING S-NET.
401510  DED-CALC.
401520      IF NUMBER-OF-DEPENDENTS =
401530      ZERO GO TO COMP-DED-O.
401540      IF NUMBER-OF-DEPENDENTS = 1
401550      GO TO COMP-DED-1.
                    .
                    .
                    .
406030  COMPUTE-CHECK.
406040      SUBTRACT TOT-DEDUCTIONS FROM
406050      GROSS-PAY GIVING NET-PAY.
406060      GO TO WRITE-CHECK.
```

FIGURE 19-1

column 72. Names may, therefore, begin at column 8 and extend well beyond column 12, where the next field begins.

Column 12 begins the "text field." This field extends from column 12 through column 72. Much of the material on a coding form begins at column 12.

Column 73 begins the "identification field." The programmer may place anything he pleases there: his name, the program's name, sequence numbers, etc. Whatever is placed within columns 73 through 80 is never transformed to a computer instruction. Instead the field is used for whatever identification purposes the programmer might wish to employ. Many programmers leave the field blank.

Once a coding form, or set of coding forms, has been filled in, they are delivered to a keypunch operator who punches cards from the forms. One card is punched for every line on the coding form. As with FORTRAN programming, the keypunch operator is very careful to match what is written on a coding form with what is punched on cards.

SOURCE AND OBJECT DECKS

Punched cards form a deck called the "source" deck. The program recorded on the cards is called the "source" program.

Source cards are submitted to the computer for the process called compilation. Compilation in COBOL means exactly what it means in

FORTRAN programming. the COBOL source program is converted to machine language, and usually an "object" deck is produced. The object deck contains the same instructions as in the source deck, except that those instructions are in machine language.

The object deck is submitted to the computer, and the program executes. Input data to a COBOL program are usually provided either from magnetic tapes or from magnetic disk. Punched data processing cards may also be used.

There is the problem of debugging in COBOL as there is in FORTRAN. A COBOL program (or any program, for that matter—seldom runs correctly the first time that an execution attempt is made. Bugs (errors, omissions, misunderstandings, etc.) must be worked out before the program may be permanently assigned to the job it must perform.

DIVISIONS

COBOL programs always have four divisions of coding. The divisions are called

      IDENTIFICATION DIVISION
      ENVIRONMENT DIVISION
      DATA DIVISION
      PROCEDURE DIVISION

The coding associated with these divisions must always appear in the order that the above names are given (see Fig. 19-2).

The IDENTIFICATION and ENVIRONMENT divisions are generally short, requiring only about 10 to 20 lines of coding; the DATA and PROCEDURE divisions are generally much longer, requiring up to several hundred lines of coding.

The IDENTIFICATION division is used mostly for documentation. It tells what the name of the program and programmer are, what the date is, and a few other items of information.

The ENVIRONMENT division tells what computer is to be used in solving the problem, what input/output devices are to be used, what special conventions are to be followed, and several other items.

The DATA division is the division in which a programmer spends about half of his programming effort. In this division, he describes in great detail the organization of the files that his program is to deal with. He gives general characteristics of the files, such as file name,

1	6	7	8	12	72	73	80
				IDENTIFICATION DIVISION.			
				ENVIRONMENT DIVISION.			
				DATA DIVISION.			
				PROCEDURE DIVISION.			

FIGURE 19-2

recording mode, block size, and others. Then he describes in detail the records that the files use. He tells how many fields there are on a record, what the field names are, what the field sizes are, what kind of information (numeric or alphanumeric) the fields contain, and others. For example, Fig. 19-3 is a portion of a COBOL program, showing the beginning of the DATA division. The file being described is PERSONNEL-MASTER.

The coding shows that the file has records that provide data such as social security number, last name, middle initial, etc. On each record, the items of information are recorded in the same order in which they are shown in the description.

The sizes of the various data items are also shown. Social Security Number is described as consisting of nine numeric digits; Last Name is described as consisting of 18 alphanumeric characters; Middle Initial is described as consisting of a single alphabetic character. In the PICTUREs that follow the field data names, the leading 9's refer to numeric data; X's refer to alphanumeric data and A's refer to alphabetic data. The numbers within parentheses give sizes. Thus 9(9) means 9 numeric characters; X(18) means 18 alphanumeric characters, and A or A(1) means one alphabetic character.

```
DATA DIVISION.
FD  PERSONNEL-MASTER RECORDING MODE IS
        BINARY HIGH DENSITY LABEL
        RECORDS ARE STANDARD BLOCK CONTAINS
        60 RECORDS DATA RECORD IS PERSONNEL-RECORD.
01  PERSONNEL-RECORD.
    05  SOC-SEC-NUMB       PICTURE 9(9)..
    05  LAST-NAME          PICTURE X(18)..
    05  MID-INITIAL        PICTURE A.
    05  FIRST-NAME         PICTURE A(8)...
    05  PAY-RATE           PICTURE 99V99..
    05  JOB-CODE           PICTURE X.
    05  YTD-EARNINGS       PICTURE 9(5)V99..
    05  YTD-FED-TAXES      PICTURE 9(5)V99..
```

FIGURE 19-3

A PICTURE often shows where an assumed decimal point is located. In YTD-EARNINGS, for example, the PICTURE is 9(5)V9(2). The size of the information is shown to be 7 numeric characters. There is to be an assumed decimal point pointed off two places from the right. If the information in seven consecutive bytes of memory is

| 0 | 3 | 6 | 9 | 4 | 8 | 5 |

the earnings to date are assumed to be $3694.85. The characters do not give dollar signs or decimal points, but these can be inserted in COBOL by the use of COBOL's editing feature.

A numeric item without a decimal point might look like this

| 0 | 6 | 0 | 1 | 8 | 1 | 3 | 8 | 9 |

and be described with the PICTURE 9(9). (This means nine digits with no assumed decimal point.)

An alphabetic item like this

| S | M | I | T | H | | | | | | | | | |

would be described with the PICTURE(14). (Blanks are considered alphabetic characters.)

An alphanumeric item (combination of alphabetics, digits and other symbols) might look like this:

| W | 2 | Z | 0 | V |

and be described with the PICTURE X(5). Alphanumeric characters may include special data processing symbols. For example,

| $ | * | * | * | 1 | 4 | 4 | | 8 | 9 |

would be described with the PICTURE X(10).

The PROCEDURE division instructs the computer how to process the data that are described in the DATA division. In this division, we may see such instructions as these disjointed examples:

ADD THIS-WEEKS-PAY TO YTD-EARNINGS.
OPEN INPUT PERSONNEL-MASTER.
IF SOCIAL-SECURITY-NUMBER IN
    PERSONNEL-MASTER EQUALS
    SOCIAL-SECURITY-NUMBER IN
    TRANSACTION-FILE GO TO PROCESS-PAY-CHECK.
WRITE OUTPUT-REC.

COBOL VOCABULARY

COBOL provides a vocabulary that programmers may use. That vocabulary contains about 300 words. The programmer is free to invent words, however, should he need them. A requirement is that when a programmer invents a word, he must describe it fully in the DATA division or in the PROCEDURE division.

In the above example statements, such words as ADD, TO, OPEN, INPUT, IF, IN, EQUALS and others, are words found in the COBOL vocabulary. Words such as THIS-WEEKS-PAY, YTD-EARNINGS, and others, are words that a programmer invents. When inventing a word, a programmer may employ up to thirty characters, some of them being letters of the alphabet, some digits, and some hyphens.

COBOL programs tend to be rather lengthy. Figure 19-4, however, shows a relatively short COBOL program, which merges two files.

The reader should not try to understand everything that is happening in the program, since this chapter could not begin to describe all COBOL features thoroughly. The interested student is advised to select any of the excellent COBOL texts available on the market for further study.

SUMMARY

COBOL is a universal language available for solving business problems. The language is highly business-oriented, permitting such operations as describing files, opening and reading them, writing records, closing files, and others. COBOL also permits calculations to be performed.

The language uses about 300 words in a vocabulary. Programmers

```
00001    100010 IDENTIFICATION DIVISION.
00002    100020 PROGRAM-ID. aPAYDAYa.
00003    100C30 AUTHOR.
00004    100040 ENVIRONMENT DIVISION.
00005    100050 CONFIGURATION SECTION.
00006    100060 SOURCE-COMPUTER. IBM-360.
00007    100070 OBJECT-COMPILTER. IBM-360.
00008    100080 INPUT-OUTPUT SECTION.
00009    100C90 FILE-CONTROL. SELECT PAY-FILE ASSIGN TO SYSCC9-UR-2540P-S.
00010    1001C0 DATA DIVISION.
00011    100110 FILE SECTION.
00012    100120 FD  PAY-FILE  LABEL RECORDS ARE OMITTED   DATA RECORD IS
00013    100130    PAY-CARD.
00014    100140 01 PAY-CARD.
00015    100150     C2 EMPLOYEE-NUMBER PICTURE X%4a.
00016    100160     C2 HOURS-WORKED    PICTURE 99V99.
00017    100170     02 PAY-RATE        PICTURE 99V99.
00018    100180     C2 FILLER          PICTURE X%68n.
00019    100190 WORKING-STORAGE SECTION.
00020    100200 01 HDG1.
00021    100210     C2 FILLER    PICTURE X%59a VALUE SPACES.
00022    100220     C2 FILLER    PICTURE X%14a VALUE aPAYROLL REPORTa.
00023    200C1C     C2 FILLER    PICTURE X%59a VALUE SPACES.
00024    200C20 01 HDG2.
00025    200030     C2 FILLER    PICTURE X%5a VALUE SPACES.
00026    200C40     C2 FILLER    PICTURE X%8a VALUE aEMP. NO.a.
00027    200050     C2 FILLER    PICTURE X%10a VALUE SPACES.
00028    200C60     02 FILLER    PICTURE X%11a VALUE aHRS. WORKEDa.
00029    200C70     02 FILLER    PICTURE X%10a VALUE SPACES.
00030    200C80     C2 FILLER    PICTURE X%8a VALUE aPAY RATEa.
00031    200C90     02 FILLER    PICTURE X%35a VALUE SPACES.
00032    2001C0     C2 FILLER    PICTURE X%9a VALUE aGROSS PAYa.
00033    200210 01 DETAIL-1.
00034    200220     C2 FILLER    PICTURE X%5a VALUE SPACES.
00035    200230     C2 EMP-NO    PICTURE X%8a.
00036    200234     C2 FILLER    PICTURE X%13a VALUE SPACES.
00037    200250     02 HRS-WK    PICTURE 99.99.
00038    200260     C2 FILLER    PICTURE X%15a VALUE SPACES.
00039    200270     02 PAYRTE    PICTURE 99.99.
00040    200280     C2 FILLER    PICTURE X%37a VALUE SPACES.
00041    200290     C2 GRS-PAY   PICTURE $$$,$$$.99.
00042    200310
00043    300010 PROCEDURE DIVISION.
00044    300C20 OPEN-PROC.
00045    300C30     OPEN INPUT PAY-FILE.
00046    300C40     DISPLAY HDG1.
00047    300050     DISPLAY HDG2.
00048    300060 READ-PROC.
00049    300070     READ PAY-FILE, AT END GO TO EOJ.
00050    300080 DISPLAY-PROC.
00051    300090     MOVE EMPLOYEE-NUMBER TO EMP-NO.
00052    3001C0     MOVE HOURS-WORKED TO HRS-WK.
00053    300110     MOVE PAY-RATE TO PAYRTE.
```

FIGURE 19-4

may invent their own words, but those words must be completely defined.

Programs written in COBOL must be organized in four divisions—IDENTIFICATION, ENVIRONMENT, DATA, and PROCEDURE. The two divisions requiring the most effort are the DATA and PROCEDURE divisions. In these divisions, programmers describe data items in records, then instruct the computer what to do with the data items described.

COBOL is widely used in industry, since it permits the easy programming of complex problems and acts as its own documentation. Once it is learned, a programmer does not have to learn another language should the department in which he works replace an old computer with a newer one. Conversion problems are alleviated for management as well as programmers, since programs written in COBOL generally do not have to be rewritten when a new computer is installed.

QUESTIONS

1. What are the *four* objectives that the COBOL language was designed to meet?
2. What are some of the actions that COBOL may perform in connection with files?
3. Name the *five* fields on a COBOL coding form and tell what they are used for.
4. Discuss the difference between COBOL source and object decks. How do they differ from FORTRAN source and object decks?
5. What is meant by the term "compilation"? How does COBOL compilation differ from FORTRAN compilation?
6. Name the *four* COBOL divisions and tell what each is used for.
7. What kind of information does COBOL's PICTURE give?
8. In PICTUREs what do 9's represent? X's? A's?
9. What is meant by the term "editing"?
10. What is the COBOL vocabulary? Approximately how many words does it contain?
11. What is a programmer's responsibility when he invents a name for a data item?
12. From what media may the input data to a COBOL program come?

20 | The BASIC Language

Over the years since their inventions, the FORTRAN and COBOL languages were improved. With each improvement the languages became more complex and difficult to learn. Programming computers became the domain of professional programmers.

In the meantime other languages also became popular. The IBM-developed language PL/I was developed in the early 1960s and earned a number of loyal fans. The language spread and is today used on computers other than those built by IBM.

PL/I, which looks a little like FORTRAN and a little like COBOL, was designed to be the one universal language for solving both scientific and business problems. This objective the language meets admirably, but it is even more difficult to learn than either FORTRAN or COBOL.

The language ALGOL, especially suited for scientific work, is popular in Europe and in many universities in the United States. It is not used much in industry. ALGOL's adherents claim that it is a much more powerful language than FORTRAN and that all it needs is a chance to prove itself. ALGOL, too, is moderately difficult to learn.

BASIC'S DEVELOPMENT

With programming languages evolving far beyond the reach of technicians and business people, a vacuum developed. There was a need for an easy-to-learn, easy-to-use programming language. In the mid-1960s, the language came along, BASIC (*B*eginner's *A*ll-purpose *S*ymbolic *I*nstruction *C*ode).

The BASIC programming language was developed by Professors Kemeny and Kurtz at Dartmouth College. Having the appearance of a simplified FORTRAN, the language became an overnight success. A student could learn to write programs in the language after only a few minutes' instruction. With two or three weeks of experience, persons who had never programmed before could be writing really remarkable programs to solve highly complex problems.

TIMESHARING MODE

At first the language could be used in only an interactive mode. That is, a person would seat himself at a teletypelike terminal, call up the computer on the phone, then begin "conversing" with the computer via typed messages. The user would type something; the computer would type a reply. The user would type something else, and the computer would reply. This procedure could continue for hours on end (and often did) until the user had obtained the answers he wanted. Users employed a mode called *timesharing,* since they shared a computer's processing time.

Today BASIC is used not only in a timesharing mode. It is also available at some installations in a form that enables one to punch BASIC programs on cards.

When we discuss timesharing in an upcoming chapter, we shall give further details as how one uses a computer in a conversational mode. In this chapter, we shall describe the language and give some illustrative problems.

When a person enters a BASIC program he types it, using the keyboard of a typewriterlike terminal. Then he tells the computer to "run" his job. The computer compiles his program and, if no errors are found, executes it.

BASIC'S VOCABULARY

The BASIC programming language has a vocabulary just as the FORTRAN and COBOL languages do. That vocabulary includes only a few words. The most commonly used ones are LET, IF, GO TO,

PRINT, READ, DATA, FOR, NEXT, DIM, GOSUB, RETURN, STOP, END, and a very few more. By writing instructions that begin with those words, highly complex problems may be solved. The complexity of programs that may be solved rivals the complexity of programs that FORTRAN and COBOL can handle. In some ways BASIC is more powerful than the other languages.

Here is a complete program that illustrates what BASIC looks like:

```
10  DATA 2.6, 18, 44, 94, 7.8, 99.99
20  LET S = 0
30  LET C = 0
40  READ V
50  IF V = 99.99 THEN 90
60  LET S = S+V
70  LET C = C+1
80  GO TO 40
90  PRINT S, S/C
100 END
```

SEVEN BASIC STATEMENT TYPES

This program uses seven types of statements—DATA, LET, READ, IF, GO TO, PRINT, and END. Following is a thumbnail explanation of what each statement type does.

DATA

This statement provides input values that a program is to use. If one DATA statement is not sufficient to provide all the values, additional DATA statements may be given.

LET

This statement is called the "assignment" statement. Whatever value is shown to the right of the equal sign is assigned to the variable named at the lefthand side of the equal sign. Examples:

```
20  LET S=0
```

The value zero is stored in a memory word called S.

    25 LET T=(A+B)*C

The calculation (A+B)*C is made, and the result of the calculation is assigned to the memory word T. It is assumed that values were established earlier in the program for A, B, and C.

    70 LET C=C+1

The value 1 is added to C, and the result is assigned back to C. The value of C is, therefore, updated as a result of this statement's execution.

READ

One or more values are obtained from the DATA statement. Those values are assigned to the variable/s named in the READ statement. Examples:

    100 READ P

A value is obtained from the DATA statement. That value is the next one not yet used in the DATA statement. The value is assigned to P.

    110 READ A,B,C

Three values are obtained from the DATA statement. Those values are the next ones not yet read from the DATA statement. The three values are assigned to A, B, and C.

Suppose we have these four statements near the beginning of a program:

    20 DATA 2.6, 8.3, 9.9, 7.2, 98, 6.7, 99.99
    30 READ X
    40 READ P,Q,R
    50 READ M,N

Values are assigned as follows:

>2.6 is assigned to X
>
>8.3 is assigned to P; 9.9 to Q; 7.2 to R
>
>98 is assigned to M; 6.7 is assigned to N

The value 99.99 waits for another READ statement.

If

The IF statement causes decisions to be made. An example is this:

>300 IF J < K THEN 600

The program checks to determine whether J is less than K. If it is, the program jumps to line 600, if it is not, the program "falls through" to the next sequential statement of the program. If that next statement is at line 310, the program goes there.

An IF statement may check six kinds of relationships between values. Those relationships are

>=   (equal)
>
>\>   (greater than)
>
><   (less than)
>
><=   (less than or equal)
>
>>=   (greater than or equal)
>
><>   (not equal)

Values being tested may be in the form of variable names, actual numeric values, or expressions. The following IF statements are all correct.

>700 IF A=B THEN 1200
>
>710 IF A < 6 THEN 1300
>
>720 IF 16 > X THEN 1400

The BASIC Language

```
730 IF (C-D)*E <> B THEN 1500
740 IF W >= (A+B)/C THEN 1600
750 IF A-Y <= R+S THEN 1700
```

GO TO

The GO TO statement causes an unconditional jump from one part of a program to another. Example:

```
GO TO 2000
```

PRINT

The PRINT command tells the program to print one or more values that are being used or computed in the program. These statements are valid.

```
1200 PRINT M
1300 PRINT U, X
```

The computer will print the value *last* assigned to M. Then the computer will print the values last assigned to U and X. Spaces are automatically provided by the program to go between printed data values.

The PRINT statement may be used to have the program print headings or messages. Here is a statement that causes a heading to be printed:

```
650 PRINT "COST REPORT YEAR TO DATE"
```

The program prints the heading given within quotes.

An example of a message:

```
690 PRINT "ERROR IN TRANS CODE"; C
```

The program prints the words shown within quotes and also gives the actual value held by the variable C. When the statement is executed, you may see a printed line like this:

ERROR IN TRANS CODE 3

The PRINT statement may also be used as a dual-purpose statement. A calculation can be requested and caused to be printed at the same time. For example;

780 PRINT (W−X)*(A+C)

The program will compute (W − X) times (A + C) and print the result.

When calculations are made, either in a LET or a PRINT statement, the symbols +, −, *, /, and ↑ may be used. The symbol + means add; − means subtract; *, multiply; /, divide; and ↑, raise to a power. These statements may be written:

800 LET W = A−B/C
805 LET P = M ↑ 3.5+N ↑ (−2)
810 LET Q = (P+R)/(S−T*V)
815 LET B = (R+C)/(3.5/(D − E))
820 PRINT (A−B)/C

The statement at line 800 computes A − B/C and assigns the result to W. The statement at line 805 computes $M^{3.5}+N^{-2}$ and assigns the result to P. The statement at line 810 computes (P+R)/(S−TV) and assigns the result to Q. The statement at line 815 computes

(R+C)/(3.5/D−E)

and assigns the result to B. Finally, the statement at line 820 computes

(A−B)/C

and prints it. The result is not assigned to any variable.

Observe that parentheses may be used in an expression in order to make clear what the program is to compute. Contrast the statement at line 800 with the statement at line 820.

BASIC offers several built-in functions to facilitate the calculation of sines, cosines, square roots, logs, and other values. For example, to obtain the square root of M + N, a statement could be written

    F = SQR (M+N)

STOP

The STOP statement terminates the execution of a program.

END

The END statement must be the very last statement of a BASIC program. Some BASIC systems implemented on some computers do not require an END statement at the end of a program. In those systems its use is optional.

In this chapter, we shall not discuss FOR, NEXT, DIM, GOSUB, RETURN. Again, interested readers are referred to the texts available that fully describe the BASIC programming language.

BASIC statements are always executed in the order that they appear in a program. The order of statements is determined by their line numbers. Every statement must have a line number. Numbers must be given in increasing sequence. The gap between numbers may be anything the programmer desires, and that gap does not have to be a constant one. The smallest line number that may be used is 1; the largest, on most systems, is 99999.

Now for some example programs. Suppose that it is necessary to obtain the sum of a series of numbers in a DATA statement and compute their average. The program below almost explains itself.

    10 DATA 2.6, 18, 44, 94, 7.8, 99.99
    20 LET S=0
    30 LET C=0
    40 READ V
    50 IF V = 99.99 THEN 90
    60 LET X=S+V
    70 LET C=C+1

```
80  GO TO 40
90  PRINT S, S/C
100 END
```

The variable S is to hold the sum of the values found in the DATA statement. In that statement, 99.99 is not to be summed. It is a "sentinel" value that signals the end of the data values.

The variable C counts the values that are added to S.

In execution, the program first initializes S and C by assigning zeroes to those variables. Then it reads a value and assigns it to V. That value is 2.6. Since the value is not 99.99, the program adds 2.6 to S and 1 to C. The resulting values of S and C are 2.6 and 1, respectively. The program then returns to line 40 to obtain another data value. That value is 18. That value is assigned to V, thus replacing the old value of V. Since V is not equal to 99.99, the program adds V to S and 1 to C. The new values of S and V are 20.6 and 2, respectively.

The program repeats the procedure until the sentinel value is found. At that time the program does not add 99.99 to S and does not add 1 to S. Instead, it jumps to statement 90, where the last value is assigned to S is printed. The calculation S/C is also made and the result is printed. The program then terminates.

In this next program the objective is to find the largest value in a series of values found in the DATA statement. That value is printed.

```
100 DATA 9,4,6,14,7,2,-6,-2,99.99
110 READ L
120 READ X
130 IF X = 99.99 THEN 170
140 IF X <= L THEN 120
150 LET L=X
160 GO TO 120
170 PRINT L
180 END
```

This program obtains the first value in the DATA statement and assigns it to L (for largest). Then it reads additional values until it finds the sentinel value 99.99. Whenever the value read, X, is less than or equal to the value currently stored in L, the program goes to get another X value. Whenever X is larger than L, that value replaces L, thus updating it. When the sentinel value is found, it is not compared with L. Instead, the program jumps to the statement at line 170, where L is printed. This is the largest value.

The sentinel value in both above examples has been 99.99. The programmer may select any sentinel value he desires, so long as he knows for sure that the sentinel value will not be confused with an actual value in the DATA statement.

These examples have shown that while statements in a BASIC program are normally executed in the same order that they appear, a deviation from that order, when necessary, may be caused by a GO TO, or IF statement.

In BASIC no distinction is made between integer and floating-point values. When modes are mixed, as in the statement

280 LET F = 2.6+L/3

the computer will automatically change integer values to floating-point, then make the required computations.

SUMMARY

As the major compiler languages, COBOL, FORTRAN, and PL/I, became more complex, the need arose for a simple language that persons could employ to program their own problems. At Dartmouth College in the mid-1960s, Professors Kemeny and Kurtz developed BASIC for use in a timesharing, interactive mode. The language quickly became popular.

The BASIC language reminds one of a simplified FORTRAN. Statements that accomplish a great deal are written in brief form. In compensation for this brevity, the language imposes a few restrictions insofar as input and output are concerned.

The language permits calculations to be performed (LET), values to be input (READ), results to be printed (PRINT). In addition, the program can be directed to make conditional (IF) or unconditional (GO TO) transfers. With a knowledge of only these functions, a person can begin writing actual computer programs after only a few minutes' study.

QUESTIONS

1. Why was the BASIC language developed?
2. What are some of the principal words used in the BASIC programming language and what do they accomplish?
3. How does one give the computer data values in BASIC?
4. When BASIC is used, how is the computer instructed to make decisions?
5. Discuss the difference between conditional and unconditional transfers.
6. What does the BASIC statement

    LET C = C + 1

    accomplish?
7. Why would one use parentheses in a BASIC LET statement?
8. In a DATA statement, what is a "sentinel" value?

21 | Flowcharting

FLOWCHART CONCEPTS

When programs to be written are simple, the programmer can hold in his head the required instructions that he must give to the computer. However, if the program is a complex one, he must first draw a flowchart. A flowchart is a "road map" that the programmer uses in developing the instructions he must give to the computer. The flowchart shows the steps he wants a computer to take and the order of the steps.

Figure 21-1 shows an example of a flowchart. This is the flowchart of the program that computes the sum and average of a series of numbers found in a DATA statement.

Figure 21-2 shows another flowchart. This is the flowchart of the program which finds the largest value in a series of values found in a DATA statement.

When faced with a complex problem to be solved, a programmer spends a good deal of time in developing the flowchart. A flowchart does not spring full-blown out of the air. The programmer writes a portion of it, then determines whether what he has put down is valid; sometimes he crosses out what he has done and replaces it with something else, or he may add to it. Eventually, after some effort, the programmer has a flowchart that he thinks can be used to solve the problem. He writes the program and submits it to the computer.

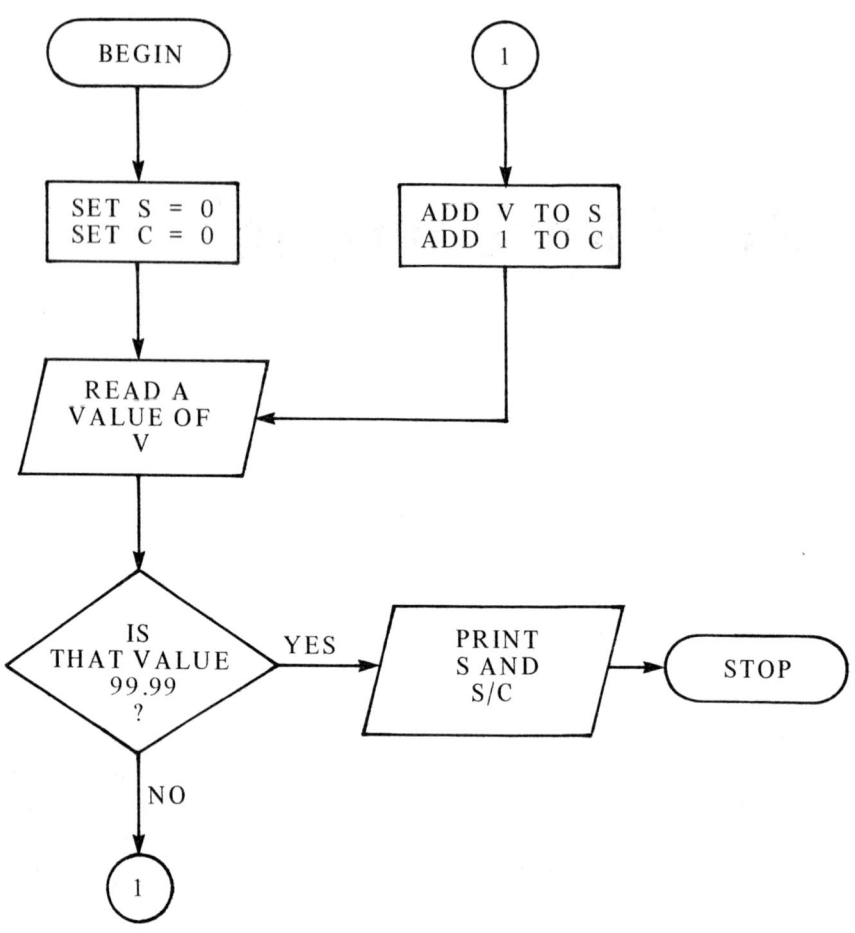

FIGURE 21-1

FLOWCHART AND PROGRAM EXAMPLES

Let us try some problems. Suppose that we must write a BASIC program to compute the sum of all integers from 1 through 100. The flowchart is shown in Fig. 21-3.

The arrows show what the order of the statements must be as the program advances from the BEGIN symbol.

A flowchart is semi-independent from the language that will be used in the program. The flowchart in Fig. 21-3 could be used with languages COBOL, PL/I, FORTRAN, ALGOL, and other languages

FLOWCHART SYMBOLS

This is an input or output symbol and is used for READ and PRINT statements.

This is an assignment symbol and is used where values or the results of calculations are assigned to variables.

This is a decision diamond and is used in a program where a decision is to be made. Two labeled arrows must exit from a decision diamond.

This is the terminal symbol and is used to indicate where a program begins and where it terminates.

This is a connection symbol. It is used to shorten the lines which would otherwise crisscross over a flowchart.

besides BASIC. The flowchart can be more meaningfully written, though, if the programmer knows ahead of time what programming language is to be used.

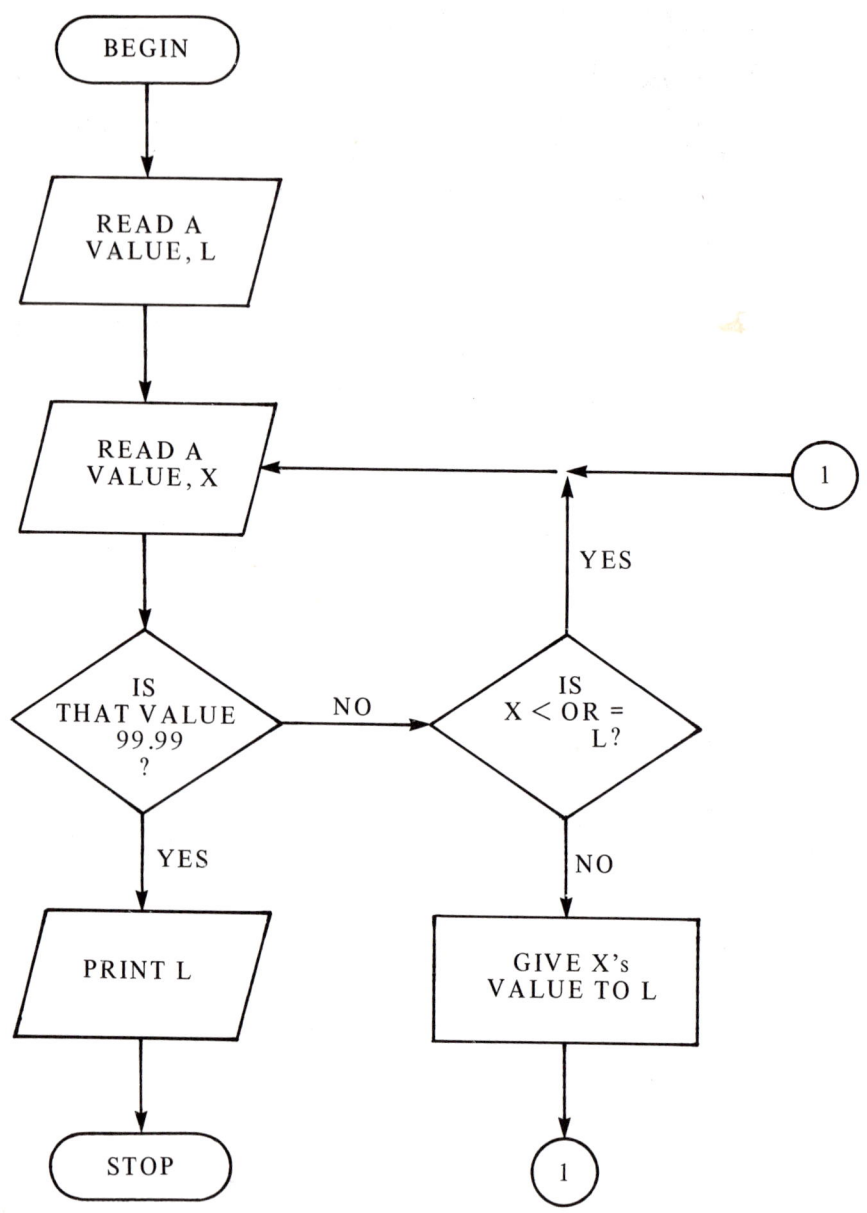

FIGURE 21-2

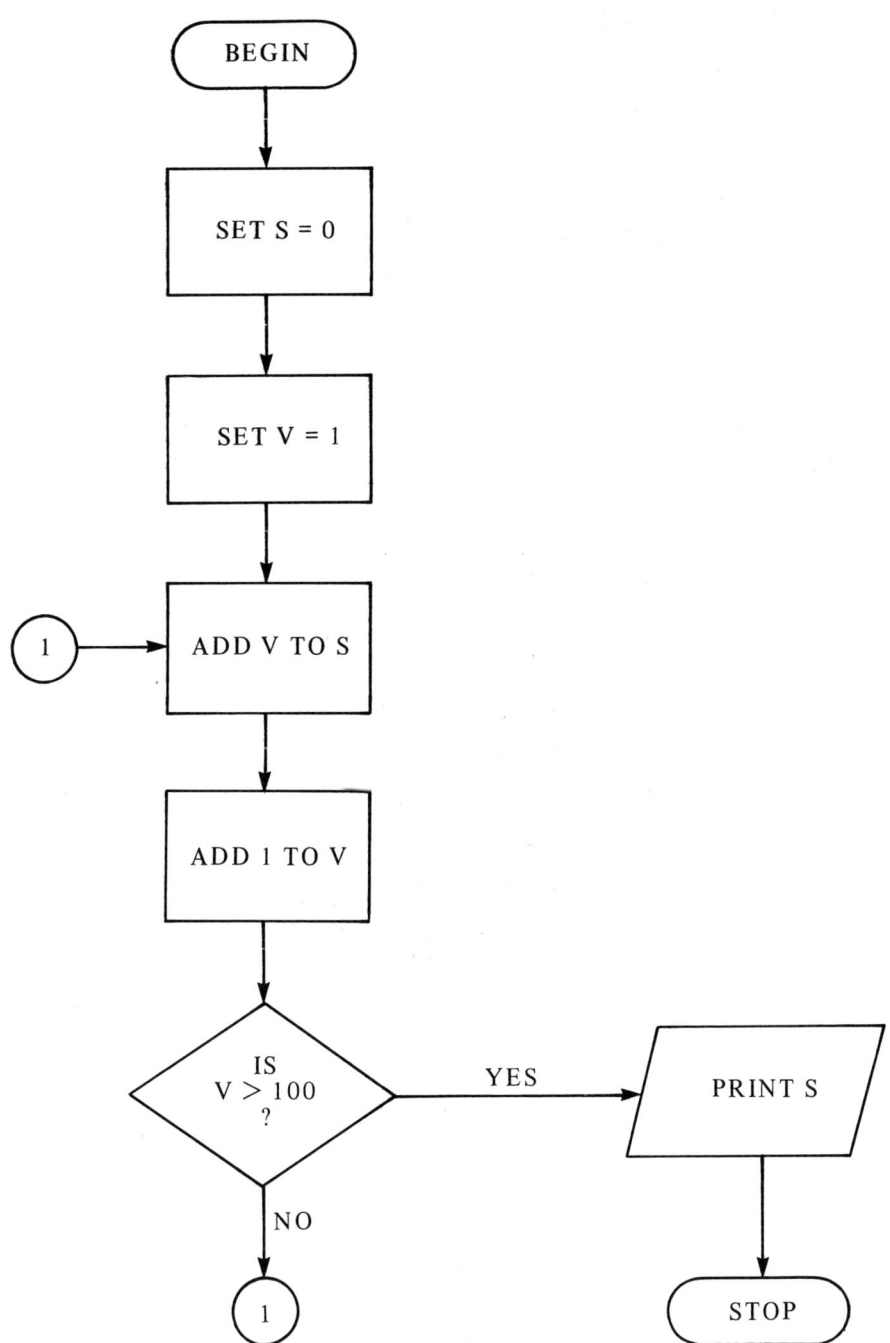

FIGURE 21-3

In this example, the resulting BASIC program is

```
100 LET S=0
110 LET V=1
120 LET X=S+V
130 LET V=V+1
140 IF V > 100 THEN 160
150 GO TO 120
160 PRINT S
170 END
```

The words given in flowchart symbols may be given in ordinary English; there is nothing formal about what may be written therein. For example, all the instructions in Fig. 21-4 mean the same thing.

```
┌─────────────────┐
│                 │
│    SET S = 0    │
│                 │
└─────────────────┘

┌─────────────────┐
│    GIVE S AN    │
│  INITIAL VALUE  │
│     OF ZERO     │
└─────────────────┘

┌─────────────────┐
│   ASSIGN ZERO   │
│      TO S       │
│                 │
└─────────────────┘
```

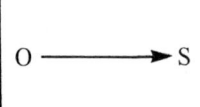

```
┌─────────────────┐
│                 │
│    LET S = 0    │
│                 │
└─────────────────┘
```

FIGURE 21-4

Flowcharting

Similarly, the words associated with the symbols in Fig. 21-5 all mean the same thing.

Figure 21-6 shows a flowchart for a somewhat more complex problem. The program to be written from this flowchart solves for the two roots of the equation

$$ax^2 + bx + c = 0$$

The BASIC program is this:

```
10 DATA 4,6,2,9,-3,4,2,9,1,0,0,0
20 READ A,B,C
30 IF A=0 THEN 110
40 IF B ↑ 2 - 4*A*C < 0 THEN 90
50 LET R1 = (-B+SQR(B↑2-4*A*C))/(2*A)
60 LET R2 = (-B-SQR(B↑2-4*A*C*))/(2*A)
70 PRINT R1,R2,A,B,C
80 GO TO 20
90 PRINT "IMPOSSIBLE CASE"; A,B,C
100 GO TO 20
110 END
```

A more efficient way to write the program, and one which still follows the flowchart is this one:

```
10 DATA 4,6,2,9,-3,4,2,9,1,0,0,0
20 READ A,B,C
30 IF A=0 THEN 110
40 LET D = B↑2-4*A*C
50 IF D < 0 THEN 90
60 LET Q=2*A
65 LET R1 = (-B+SQR(D))/Q
67 LET R2 = (-B-SQR(D))/Q
70 PRINT R1,R2,A,B,C
80 GO TO 20
90 PRINT "IMPOSSIBLE CASE";A,B,C
100 GO TO 20
110 END
```

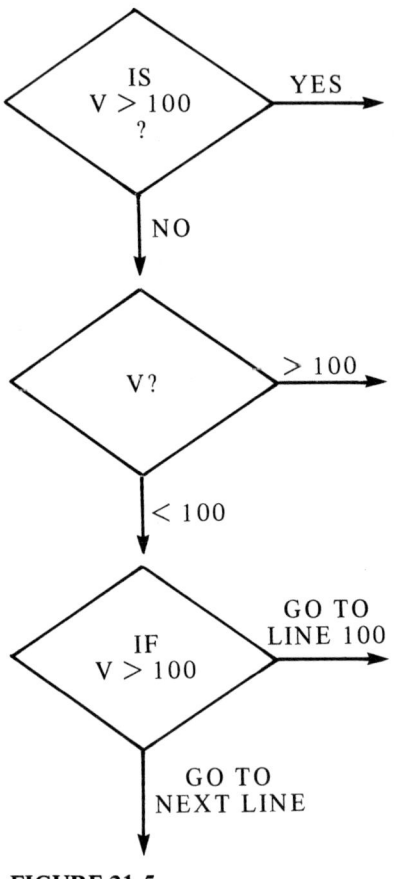

FIGURE 21-5

SUMMARY

A flowchart is a "road map" that a programmer prepares before he codes the solution to a problem. In developing the flowchart, most of the programming effort is expended. If the flowchart is well conceived, the program should be relatively easy to write and should exhibit relatively fewer bugs when placed in execution.

While flowcharts can be prepared in highly informal ways, certain symbols have been accepted for common usage. The parallelogram is used for input/output operations; the rectangle for assignments; the diamond for decisions; the oval for begin and stop operations; and

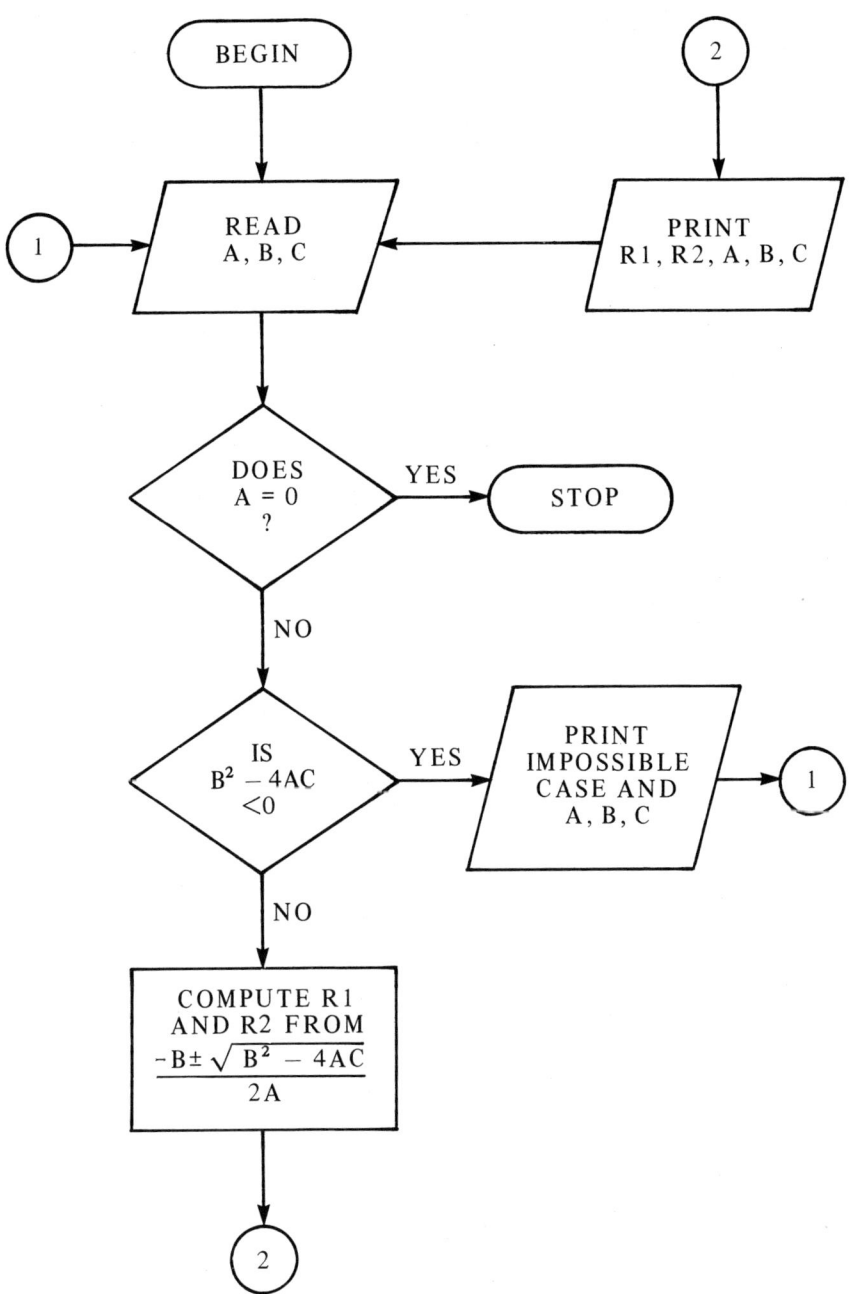

FIGURE 21-6

the small circle for connectors. In addition to symbols, arrows connect one symbol with another. These arrows indicate the order in which program statements are to be executed.

QUESTIONS

1. What is a flowchart and what is its purpose?
2. What are the symbols used in flowcharts and what are their uses?
3. What is the function of arrows in flowcharts?
4. How does a programmer select the words to be used within flowchart symbols?

22 | Batch Mode

COMPUTER USAGE MODES

A modern computer system may be used in three ways: batch mode, remote batch mode, and conversational timesharing mode. In this chapter, we shall discuss the batch mode. In the next two chapters we shall cover the remote batch and conversational timesharing modes.

BATCH MODE PROGRAMMING STEPS

In batch mode, a programmer follows the steps outlined below:

Step 1. Programming

The programmer flowcharts the solution to a problem, and then he codes the program, usually in FORTRAN, COBOL or PL/I, and submits his coding forms to a keypunch operator. The operator delivers a deck of punched cards. These cards form a "source deck."

At a later time that source deck may give rise to an "object" deck. If an object deck already exists, the programmer uses it for the next step instead of the source deck.

Step 2.   JCL Cards

The programmer provides cards punched in the job control language of the computer he is using. These job control language cards (JCL cards) tell who the programmer is, what the charge number is, what the programming language is, and other items of information. In connection with providing JCL cards, the programmer must tell the computer where to obtain input data. If the input data are on magnetic tape, one or more of the JCL cards must tell what the reel serial numbers of the input tapes are. If the input data are on magnetic disk, the disk must be identified. If the input data are on punched cards, the cards must be placed behind the source or object deck, as the case may be.

Step 3.   Submitting

The programmer prepares his job for the computer. The job may consist of source deck, data cards, and JCL cards, or it may consist of object deck, data cards, and JCL cards. Possibly, the job may more simply consist of a source or object deck and JCL cards.

The programmer must now briefly fill out a form called a submittal form. This form tells the computer center personnel who the programmer is, what his charge number is, where the programmer is located, whether any magnetic tapes or disk packs are needed for the job, and a few other items of information.

It is true that the programmer has given some of this information on JCL cards, but JCL cards are used more for communicating with a computer system than with computer center personnel. Both computer and computer center personnel must be given certain facts.

Having filled out the submittal form, the programmer delivers his job to the "control desk" at the computer center. The folks at the control deck receive the job, log it in, and give the programmer an idea of when results will be ready.

If the computer center is a large one serving hundreds of persons, there may be a courier service that serves the users. Couriers visit pickup points at regular times and either pick up jobs that have to be processed or deliver results that were processed earlier.

Step 4.   Debugging

A programmer will receive results from his job either a few hours after he submitted it or the following day. (Sometimes jobs are not run for several days, but these kinds of instances are rare.) The programmer may check at the control desk to determine whether a job is ready, or he may phone. Possibly, the center provides a closed television circuit which flashes on screens located at various points the identification numbers of those jobs that have been completed. If the center has a courier service, the programmer checks to see what the courier delivers from time to time.

The programmer must examine the computer output to determine whether it appears correct. Checking this output may take only a few moments, or it may require several days of close scrutiny. If the programmer discovers errors, he must correct them, then submit his corrected job to the center.

COMPUTER CENTER PROCEDURES

The personnel at the center have their own procedures. When they receive a program from a user, they must log it in, and then prepare it for the computer. The various steps that computer personnel go through are the following.

Step 1. Logging In

Logging in a job may simply mean assigning the job an identifying number and entering that number in a log book. The book contains the job's identifying number, the name of the person who submitted it, and the time that the job was received.

Step 2. Job Preparation

In getting the job ready for the computer the center personnel may have to retrieve reels of magnetic tapes from the "tape library." A tape library is a room located at the computer center where user reels of tape are stored. These tapes are stored under ideal conditions of temperature, humidity, and security. Certainly a user may hold a reel of tape at his own desk, but there is really no necessity for his doing so, since having the computer center do this offers so many advantages.

In addition to a tape library, there may be a "disk pack library" where user disk packs are stored available for use.

In preparing a job for running, the computer personnel may have to convert program cards to magnetic tape. To do this they use a device called a card-to-tape converter. (A small computer may be used for card-to-tape conversion.)

Where computers work directly with card programs, card-to-tape conversion is not necessary. Computers having the ability to perform multiprogramming do not mind working with card programs. We shall discuss the full meaning of multiprogramming later. In general, the point is that a multiprogramming computer can perform several tasks of input and output at the same time that it computes. It may easily read in a deck of cards containing a program while, at the same time, it is computing in connection with another program.

Step 3. Executing

Once all loose ends have come together, a program may be run. That is, the program has been delivered to the computer console area in either card or tape form, the input data have been identified and are ready to be read, and all the special instructions have been recognized. The job is then ready to be run.

The job, if on cards, is placed into the card reader or, if on tape, is mounted on a tape handler. The computer takes over and executes the job in a period of time ranging from one-hundredth of an hour to several hours. Output is given by the computer's printing lines on an "on-line" high-speed printer or by recording results on reels of magnetic tape or on the surfaces of disk units.

Step 4. Processing Output

Some of the information that is recorded on tape or disk may never be recorded on paper (hard copy), since it can later be used in tape or disk form. Some of the information that is intended for human eyes, though, will have to be converted by using tape-to-printer or disk-to-printer devices.

There are off-line devices that convert output on tape or disk to output on hard copy. Processing output off-line is often desirable to processing it on-line, since off-line processing does not use computer time and is therefore less expensive. Even multiprogramming computers employ extensive off-line output processing, since attempting to do it all on-line would require so many high-speed printers that a computer center could not find places to put them.

Output that has been processed must be returned to the original users who submitted the jobs. In doing so, output reports have to be matched with original program decks. Users want their original decks as well as reports generated by the computer.

Often output from jobs is inserted in plastic bags so that it may be kept clean as it wends its way back to the user. (Couriers have been known to inadvertently drop program decks and reports in puddles or in mud.)

When jobs have been processed, the time that the job was completed is recorded in the log. Many computer centers pride themselves on their ability to provide good service. They keep records on "turnaround" time. Turnaround time is the time it requires for a center to process a job. It covers the interval of time since a job is logged in to the time it is logged out. Turnaround times of two hours are not unusual at efficient computer centers.

SUMMARY

Modern computer systems may be used in three modes—batch, remote batch, and timesharing.

In the batch mode, programmers must deliver programs to the computer center. In order to do this, they must first code programs, have them punched on cards, supply the JCL cards, then provide the input data. Then, the programs are either given to a courier for delivery to the computer center, or programmers may deliver them personally.

Programs, once processed, are returned to programmers. If errors in compilation have been found, programmers must correct them, then resubmit to the center. If output has been obtained, programmers must check over the results to determine whether the results are reasonable. If so, the job is done; if not, "bugs" must be found and the programs corrected.

At the computer center, the center's personnel log in programs, then begin processing them through the system. After jobs have been processed, they are returned to programmers. A computer center attempts to keep its turnaround time down to a minimum. Turnaround time of two hours is considered very good.

QUESTIONS

1. What are the *three* modes by which modern computer systems may be used?
2. What is the meaning of "batch" when one is discussing this mode of employing a computer system?

3. In batch modes, what functions fall under the classification of Programming?
4. What are JCL cards and what are they used for?
5. In batch mode, what functions fall under the classification of Submitting?
6. What is meant by the term "debugging"?
7. Discuss the responsibilities of the personnel who work at the computer center.
8. What do computer center personnel do in connection with logging in programmer jobs?
9. What do computer center personnel do in connection with job preparation?
10. What is a tape library and what is its function?
11. What do computer center personnel do in connection with executing programmer jobs?
12. What do computer center personnel do in connection with processing output?
13. What is meant by the term "turnaround time"?
14. Give some reasons why you believe turnaround time should be kept as short as possible.

23 | Remote Batch

REMOTE BATCH MODE

Operating in the remote batch mode, a programmer may use a distant computer by entering his programs at a local terminal. The distance between terminal and computer is usually only a few miles, but the distance could be thousands of miles. Communication between terminal and computer is established over ordinary telephone lines.

Suppose that there is a large-scale computer located at some central site. Figure 23-1 shows how the computer may be accessed remotely. Positions A, B, C, and D show where remote terminals may be located. Those terminals are usually small computers. The small computers are true computers in every sense of the word. They may read cards or tape, process data, write output. As terminals to large computers, they serve a very simple function, that of reading cards, transmitting the data thereon to the large computer, and of printing results obtained from the large computer.

There are only four users shown in Fig. 23-1. There could be dozens. There is little danger of overloading the large computer. It is so fast and efficient that even while serving many remote users, it could also be providing batch and conversational timesharing service for many other users.

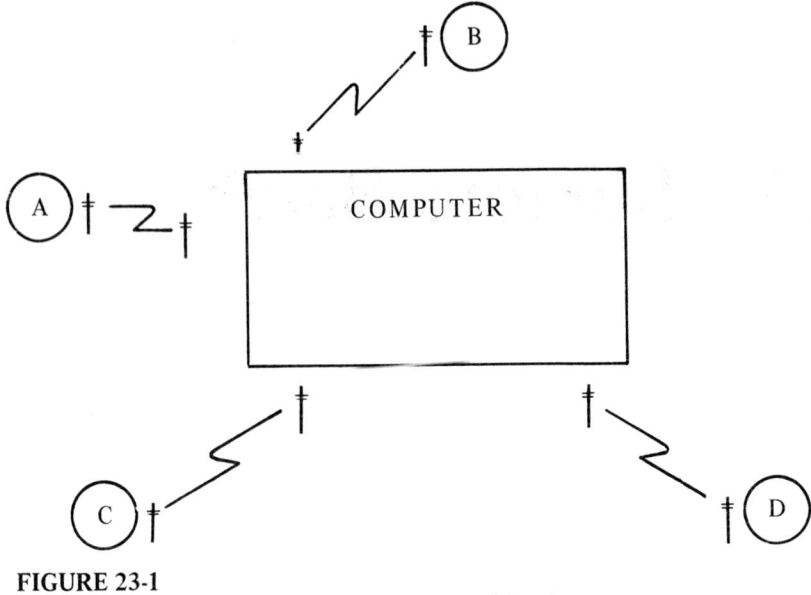

FIGURE 23-1

Why would a user, say user A, want to use a large remote computer when he could do his data processing using the local small computer? The answer is one of economics. Historically, it has been true that the larger and faster a computer is, the less expensive is any given application. User A may use the large computer for only an hour or so each day. He pays only for the time he uses. His cost for using the large computer, is, therefore, very low. True, the user must own or lease his smaller machine. This computer costs him a certain amount regardless of whether he uses it or not. Still, it is the final cost that counts. A user may well find that leasing a small computer and paying for time actually used on a larger computer is two to five times less expensive than doing his processing on local equipment.

A small remote computer may be thought of as a simple card reader attached to a distant large computer over a long telephone line, and as a simple on-line printer also attached to the large computer in the same way.

The advantage of cost is apparent, but there is also another advantage in using the remote batch mode: Turnaround time is greatly improved. There are no humans needed to process a job that a user submits in remote batch mode. The job goes directly to the large computer. The larger computer logs the job in and schedules it. Then it executes the program at its earliest opportunity. Results are automatically routed back to the remote user. These actions all take place within an hour or so, and it is unlikely that any operator, administrator, or clerk at the computer center has been aware of the activity. The computer itself bills for the service. At the end of the month, users get computer-prepared bills that often are even automatically paid. If the computer center serves several large departments of a large company, for example, the computer takes certain bookeeping actions that transfer funds from the account of one department to the account of another. These actions are preplanned, and perfectly legal, and they save a great deal of time. Computer-prepared reports, of course, keep interested persons informed of what actions have been taken.

TERMINALS

In addition to small computers, users may also use typewriter-like terminals to communicate with a remote computer. Let us consider how users E, F, G, and H in Fig. 23-2 may operate. These users sit at terminals and converse with a computer over telephone lines. Instead of speaking, though, users type messages to the computer in a specially developed language. The computer responds by typing messages, which appear on the paper flowing from the user's terminals.

User E may wish to enter a complete FORTRAN program. Though the process is slow, the user types the complete program, then tells the computer to run the job in the batch mode. The computer executes the program at its earliest convenience, which may be an hour later, then provides output either upon the user's terminal or upon its own on-line high-speed printer.

OBTAINING OUTPUT

If the user requests it, the computer will give all the output or selected portions of it on the paper attached to the user's terminal. The computer types at a rate of up to 1200 characters per second. While this speed sounds impressive, it is really slow compared to the speed at which an on-line printer is able to print. Therefore, after the

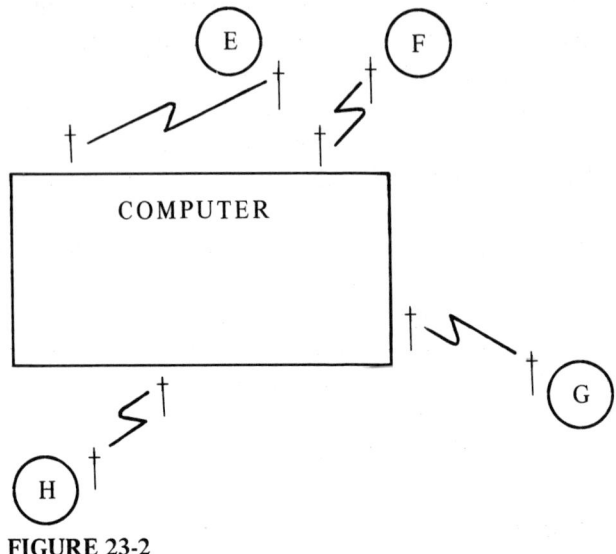

FIGURE 23-2

user has glanced at the terminal output and decided that it looks OK, he may direct the computer to give him complete output printed on the on-line high-speed printer. That output may be delivered to the user either over the control counter (that is, by normal batch methods) or via a local small computer, should the user have one at his disposal.

Figure 23-3 shows how batch and remote batch programming methods complement each other.

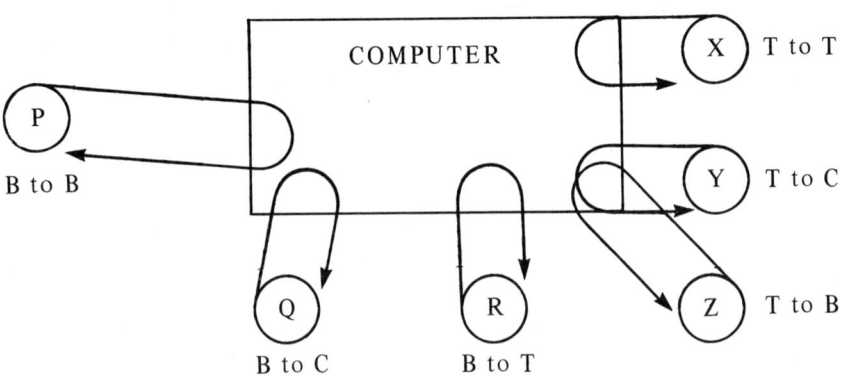

FIGURE 23-3

User P submits a program in batch mode and obtains output in normal batch mode (B to B).

User Q submits a program in batch mode and obtains output via his local small computer (B to C).

User R submits a program in batch mode and obtains output via his typewriter-like terminal (B to T).

User X submits a program via a typewriter-like terminal and receives output via the same terminal (T to T).

User Y submits a program via a typewriter-like terminal and receives output via his local small computer (T to C).

User Z submits a program via a typewriter-like terminal and receives output in normal batch mode (T to B).

Not illustrated are three other optional modes: C to C, C to B, and C to T.

> C means small local computer.
>
> B means normal batch mode.
>
> T means typewriter-like terminal.

Programs may be saved at the computer center, usually on magnetic disk. This means that a programmer may submit a program in card form over the control counter (batch mode) and direct that its insturctions be stored on disk. Another programmer may submit a program in card form, using his local small computer. He too may request that the instructions punched upon the cards be stored on disk at the computer center. Finally, a programmer may laboriously type a program and then ask the central computer to store it on disk.

Stored programs all have names. Whenever a programmer wishes to access a program, he may use any of the three modes of entry (batch, small computer, typewriter-like terminal) and ask for his program by name.

Having obtained it, he may change the program or simply run it without changes. He may also request that the program not be saved if he no longer has use for it.

There is no danger that the programs of one user will be confused with the programs of another user. Programs are segregated first by user ID, then by program name. Thus if the ID of user A is 346X21 and the ID of user E is 956W76, both users may store a program called QUADROOT, EXTFORM, or INTRTN.

Special control languages are provided for programmers who wish to operate a computer in the remote batch mode. We shall not go into the details of those languages here, since to do so would require several chapters. Suffice it to say that the languages are flexible and easy to use. Furthermore, many users may be doing work at the same time. The users mentioned above could all be doing something at the same time. The computer's speed and flexibility gives each user the illusion that he is the only person using the large remote computer. Actually, as many as 200 persons may be doing some type of remote work while, in its "spare time," the computer may be processing pure batch jobs that are being submitted to it by computer operators.

COSTS

Then, of course, there is the inevitable bill. Each user is periodically charged for the remote batch work that he has asked the computer to do. Batch and remote batch applications cost approximately the same on a job-by-job basis.

SUMMARY

A large computer located at some central site may be accessed via telephone lines. A user may place a program in the card reader of a small computer located near his place of business, and then transmit the data punched on those cards to the central computer over ordinary telephone lines. Output from the computer is returned over the same lines and printed on the small computer's printer.

The advantages of remote access are twofold. First, it enables persons who are located far from a large computer to use that computer and thereby save on computing costs. Second, it provides better turnaround time. No humans are directly involved as middlemen in remote access operations; users submit their programs directly to the central computer.

Operating under the remote access mode, users may instruct the central computer to run or change and run programs that were earlier stored at the central site on magnetic disk. Users sit at a terminal that looks like a typewriter and begin to converse with the central computer while connected by phone lines. The user may type a complete program in FORTRAN, COBOL, or some other language if he wants to. More commonly though, the user instructs the computer on what to do with a program that the computer already has.

Operating from the terminal, a user may instruct the central computer to return results via terminal, remote computer, or via the central site's courier service.

QUESTIONS

1. What is meant by the term "remote batch"?
2. How many users may a large-scale computer service in remote batch mode at one time?
3. What are *two* benefits obtained from operating in the remote batch mode?
4. What are *two* types of devices that may be used when one is accessing a distant central computer?
5. Approximately how long does a remote user have to wait before he obtains output from a remote batch submission?
6. What are some of the ways in which a user may receive results from a remote batch application?
7. How does a programmer operating from a typewriter-like terminal identify a particular program that he wants the computer to work with? How are one user's programs distinguished from those of another programmer?
8. What are the relative costs between batch and remote batch jobs?

24 | Conversational Timesharing

CONVERSATIONAL TIMESHARING MODE

In addition to the batch and remote batch modes of using a computer, there is available the timesharing mode. In this mode, a user sits at a terminal that looks a great deal like an overgrown typewriter. He picks up a nearby phone (any phone will do) and dials a distant computer. Then, as soon as he hears a high-pitched tone coming from the receiver, he places the receiver in a special receptable (an "acoustic coupler") on his terminal and snaps it into place. The user is now connected with the distant computer.

Figure 24-1 shows how several users (as many as 200) may be connected to a computer via phone lines all at the same time. Users M, N, O, and P are connected to the computer. These persons may use the computer at the same time. Since the computer is fast and efficient, it serves all these persons in such a way that each person has the illusion that he is the only one using the system. The user is operating in a mode called conversational timesharing.

So far, the situation appears identical to the mode that we described in the last chapter—that of remote batch. There is this important difference: in remote batch a user may have to wait an hour before he obtains results from a job he inaugurates; in

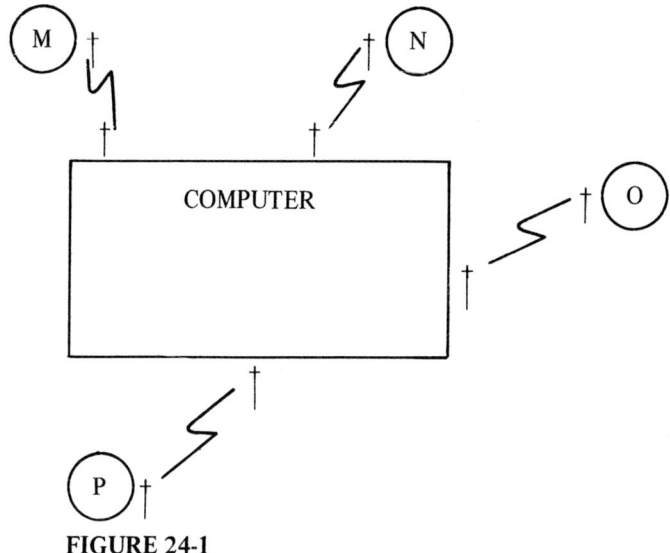

FIGURE 24-1

conversational timesharing, a user begins to obtain answers only a few seconds after he tells the computer to execute his job.

The computer gives results so promptly that a user may examine his output and decide what he wants to do next. He may decide to make some changes in his program and request another execution. Again the computer will respond in seconds.

If a user makes a typographical error when typing his statements, the computer will find those errors and inform the user about them. The user may then correct his mistakes and keep right on going.

Timesharing is practical, but it is expensive. It costs roughly ten times as much to obtain timesharing results as it does to obtain batch or remote batch results. This mode of using a computer should be employed only when it is important that the user obtain instantaneous answers to his problems.

TIMESHARING LANGUAGES

In a previous chapter, we described the BASIC programming language. This is one of the three very popular languages that are used when a person operates in the conversational timesharing mode.

The BASIC language is easy to learn and easy to use, but its main vehicle of use has been in conversational timesharing. A few computer centers do offer BASIC as a batch language, but these sites are few in number.

FORTRAN, which may be used in batch and remote batch modes, is also available in conversational timesharing mode. ALGOL, too, is available upon some timesharing systems. This language, which has a strong similarity to FORTRAN, is not very popular in this country for industrial computer processing. It has, nevertheless, a strong following in Europe and in several universities.

To show why conversational timesharing is described as such, let us look over the shoulder of user M as he uses a remote computer in conversational mode. In the examples that follow, the underlined text is what the user has entered. The computer begins by identifying itself and asking for the user's ID.

```
T/S SERVICE    JAN 16, 1975    16:40
USER-ID?    A36P74
```

The computer asked for user M's ID. The user gave it (A36P74) and it was accepted by the system. In order to avail homself of the services of a computer center, a user must first apply to receive the service. When accepted, he is given a User ID. This ID informs the system that person M is authorized to use the timesharing system.

After the user has identified himself, and the system has checked out the ID to make sure that it is correct, the system requests SYSTEM? and the user replies BASIC:

```
SYSTEM?   BASIC
```

The system has asked whether the user wishes to employ the BASIC, FORTRAN, ALGOL or any other of the other programming languages that may be available. This user has replied BASIC, but he could, as an example, also have replied FORTRAN, a language available on the majority of timesharing systems.

Next the computer sets aside a working area for the user. You may think of the working area as looking like Fig. 24-2. You can see that the working area has information recorded on it. This information was placed there by the last user and is of no value to the current user. The system must either erase what is in that working area or

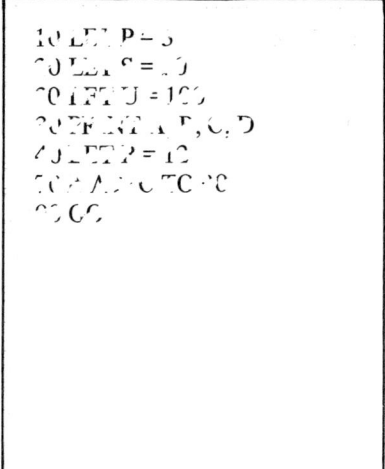

Working Area

FIGURE 24-2

replace it with something that the user actually can use. Therefore, the system next asks:

NEW OR OLD?

The system wants to know whether the working space should be erased (cleared) or whether the system should replace it. If the user replies NEW BAKER,

NEW OR OLD?   NEW BAKER

the system clears the working space so that it appears as shown in Fig. 24-3. The user has identified the new program that he is going to create (BAKER).

If the user replies OLD:

NEW OR OLD?   OLD TEST-4

the system replaces what is in the working space with the user's program called TEST-4. The working space now looks like Fig. 24-4.

TEST-4 was a program that the user prepared at some earlier time and requested the system to save for him. TEST-4 was saved on

```
┌─────────────────────────┐
│ BAKER                   │
│                         │
│                         │
│                         │
│                         │
│                         │
│                         │
│                         │
│                         │
└─────────────────────────┘
```

Working Space

FIGURE 24-3

Working Area

FIGURE 24-4

magnetic disk in a portion reserved especially for him. Conceptually, though not actually, the disk looks like Fig. 24-5.

In seeking for program TEST-4 the system first goes to A36P74's disk portion, since that code was the ID given when the user signed on. Then it finds program TEST-4 and *makes a copy* of it. The copy

Conversational Timesharing 193

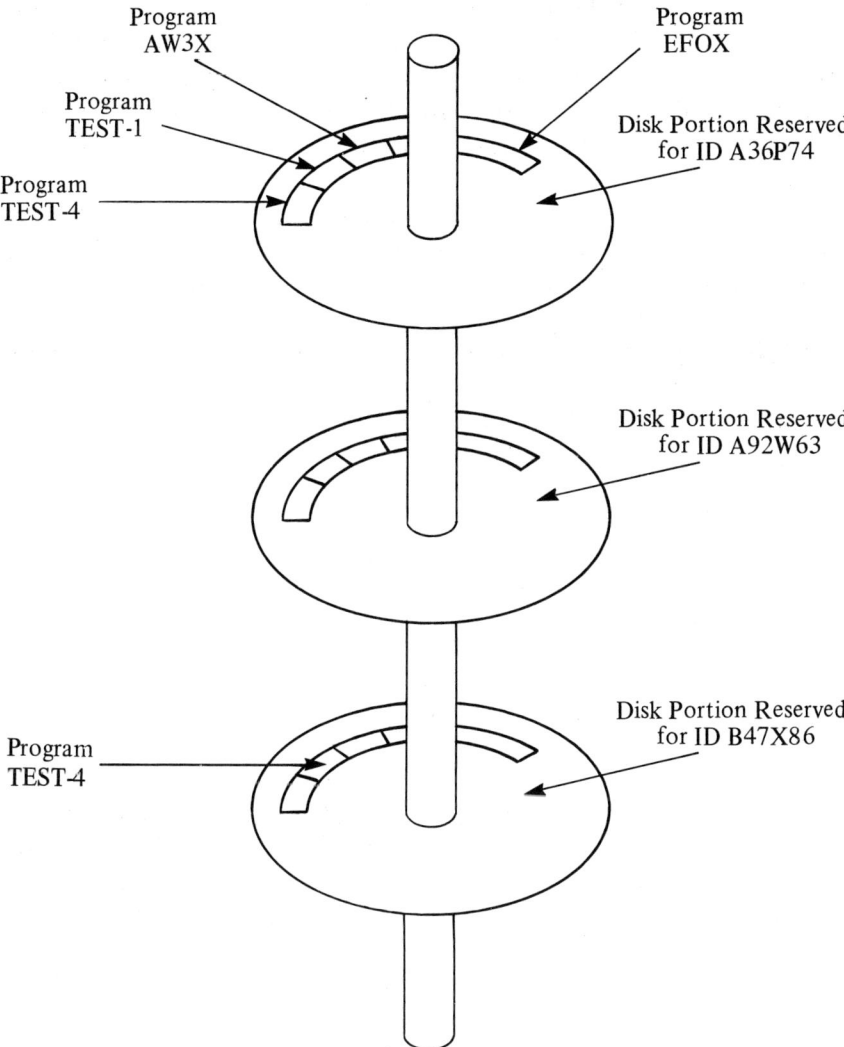

FIGURE 24-5

is brought to the user's working space. The original copy of TEST-4 remains saved on a disk in unchanged form.

Note that the program TEST-4 under ID B47X86 was ignored throughout this procedure.

Once TEST-4 is in the working space, the user may list it (using a LIST command), execute it (using a RUN command), or change it (using various techniques). When the user no longer wants TEST-4 in his working space, he may erase it from working space by typing NEW or OLD. (We shall see examples soon.) Erasing a program from working space does not affect the stored copy of that program. To remove TEST-4 from its permanent storage area on disk, the user will have to type UNSAVE at the proper time. We shall show you how soon.

After the user has responded to the question NEW or OLD? the system types READY. The user is now on his own. Let us follow the conversation between user and computer from this point.

```
NEW OR OLD? NEW BAKER
READY
10 PRINT "THIS IS JUST A TEST"
20 LET P=4.9
30 PRINT P ↑ 3
40 END
RUN
THIS IS JUST A TEST
117.649
READY
BYE
```

From our discussion of the BASIC programming language, you can see that the user typed four statements. Then he asked the computer to run the program. Since there were no errors in the program, the computer gave its output a few seconds after the RUN command was issued.

The user then disconnected himself from the system by typing

BYE

Program BAKER *was not saved* on the user's portion of disk. To save a program, a user must give the SAVE command. Let us see how this user saves a program the next time he comes to the system.

We shall pick up the conversation from the point where the system asks NEW OR OLD?

```
NEW OR OLD? NEW EFOX
READY
```

Conversational Timesharing

```
10 LET F=1.4
20 LET G=F+F
30 PRINT F AND G
40 PRINT "END OF JOB"
50 END
RUN
LINE 30 INCORRECT PUNCTUATION
LINE 40 ERROR IN QUOTED LITERAL
READY
30 PRINT F, G
40 PRINT "END OF JOB"
RUN
1.4    2.8
END OF JOB
READY
SAVE
READY
BYE
```

The user entered lines 30 and 40 incorrectly. In response to RUN, the system detected the incorrect statements and typed messages telling, as best it could, what was wrong with the statements.

The timesharing system should not be expected to repair incorrect statements, but merely to report them. Some errors are so serious that the system could not possibly know what the user had intended. For example, if a user types

```
80 LET W = 6.78.2 + (P+Q/
```

it is impossible for another human, let alone a computer, to know what the original user had in mind when he typed this statement.

To correct statements, a user merely retypes them. This user retyped lines 30 and 40. The new statements replaced the old ones. When the user typed RUN a second time, the system gave the desired output.

SYSTEM COMMANDS

To save the program, the user types SAVE. The system types READY, indicating that it has done so. After the user has saved a program, his disk area looks like Fig. 24-6.

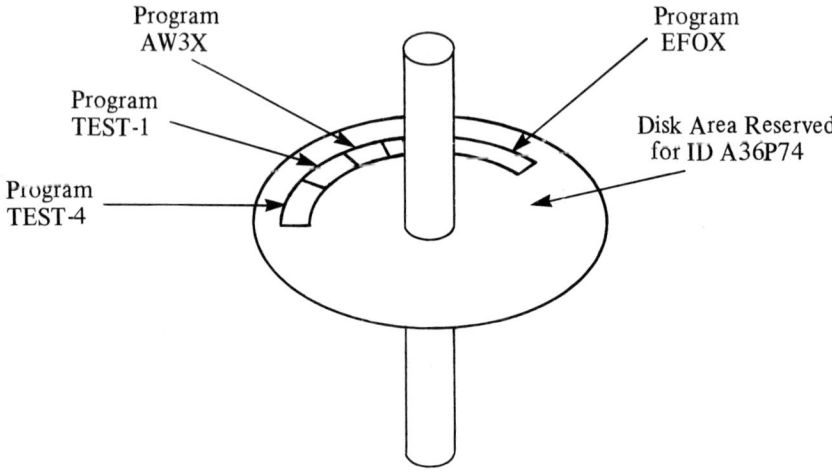

FIGURE 24-6

The working space was not affected by the SAVE command. After the SAVE command had been executed, the user's working space looked like Fig. 24-7. Observe that working space reflects the changes that were made to lines 30 and 40. If the user wishes, he may continue working with EFOX, changing it, running it, etc.

Suppose that instead of typing BYE, the user had continued in this way (we shall pick up the conversation from the SAVE command):

```
SAVE
READY
LIST
10 LET P=1.4
20 LET G=F+F
30 PRINT F, G
40 PRINT "END OF JOB"
50 END
```

```
         EFOX

    10 LET F = 1.4
    20 LET G = F + F
    30 PRINT F, G
    40 PRINT "END OF JOB"
    50 END
```

Working Space

FIGURE 24-7

READY
20 LET G=F*F
RUN
1.4   1.96
END OF JOB
READY
REPLACE
READY
BYE
OFF AT 18:04

The user typed LIST, requesting the computer to provide a printout of working space. The computer did this. Then the user must have realized that line 20 should be

20 LET G = F*F

rather than

20 LET G=F+F

The user made the change and requested an execution. Then, to replace the incorrect copy of EFOX in permanent disk storage, the user typed

    REPLACE

The program currently in working space replaced the stored copy of EFOX. If the user had typed BYE without giving the replace command, the incorrect copy of EFOX would have remained on disk.

The command SAVE differs from REPLACE in this way: When a person wants to save a new program, giving it a name that the user is not currently using as the name for a stored program, he uses the command SAVE; when a person wants to replace an already saved program with either a changed version of that program or an entirely different program, he uses the command REPLACE.

Any program may be replaced as often as the user wishes to replace it.

Let us again look over the shoulder of user M as he enters a new program and finds that he must make corrections as he does so.

```
NEW OR OLD?  NEW K-ITEM
READY
10  LEX ← T D = 1.1
20  LET E=1.2
30  LET F = D+A ←← *E+1.3
30 PRIN DELETED
40 PRINT D, E, F
20  LET E=2.1
50  END
LIST
10  LET D = 1.1
20  LET E=2.1
30  LET F=D*E+1.3
40  PRINT D,E,F
50  END
READY
SAVE
READY
```

$\underline{\text{RUP} \leftarrow \text{N}}$
3.61
READY
$\underline{\text{UNSAVE TEST-1}}$
READY
$\underline{\text{BYE}}$
OFF AT 13:42

This time user M had a difficult time in typing his statements correctly. In line 10 he typed LEX when he intended to type LET. Giving the backwards arrow immediately after typing the incorrect character permitted him to correct that character.

In other words, when the user typed

10 LEX ← T D=1.1

the actual information received by the computer was

10 LET D = 1.1

Similarly, in line 30, the user typed two backwards arrows to correct the last two characters typed. When the user typed

30 LET F=D+E ← ← *E+1.3

the actual statement received by the computer was

30 LET F=D*E+1.3

To replace line 20, which the user realized was typed incorrectly, the user retyped the statement. The *last* line 20 that the user typed replaced the earlier one.

You will observe that the user inadvertently began retyping line 30, which was correct and did not need to be replaced. As soon as the user realized that he was inadvertently working with line 30, he simultaneously depressed the two keys CRTL and X. These keys are located on the terminal's keyboard. The system typed DELETED, and the system did not change line 30 in any way.

To see what his program looked like after having made all these changes, the user typed LIST. The listing showed that the program appeared ready to run. User M saved the program, then ran it. A program may be listed, saved, and/or executed in any order.

Observe that the user had difficulty typing the word RUN. When he typed

        RUP ← N

the system replaced P with N, and the command was correctly interpreted as RUN.

Before signing off, this user typed

        UNSAVE TEST-1

The program TEST-1 was removed from permanent disk storage. Disk storage then looked like Fig. 24-8. The UNSAVE command did not affect the user's working space. Program K-ITEM located there remained unchanged.

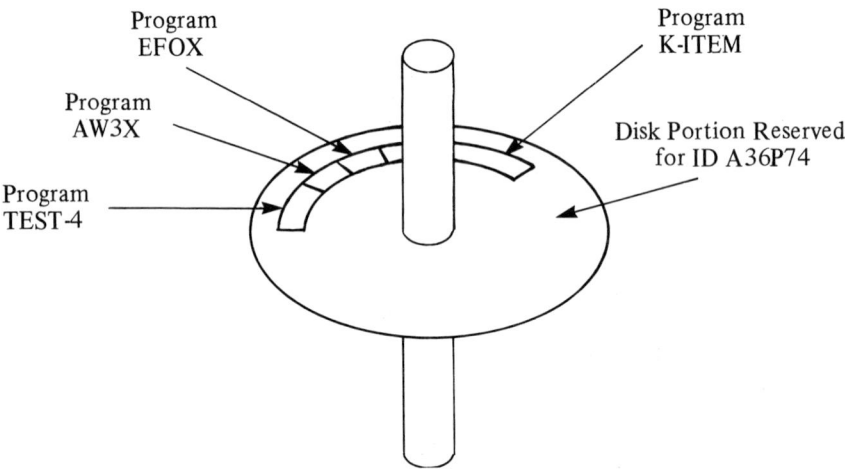

FIGURE 24-8

If, instead of typing BYE, the user had wanted to retrieve EFOX and do some more work with it, he could have typed

        OLD EFOX

instead of BYE. Let us see what could have been done:

UNSAVE TEST-1
READY
OLD EFOX
READY
LIST
10 LET F = 1.4
20 LET G = F*F
30 PRINT F,G
40 PRINT "END OF JOB"
50 END
READY
25 PRINT "THE VALUES OF F AND G FOLLOW"
RUN
THE VALUES OF F AND G FOLLOW
1.4   1.96
READY
REPLACE
READY
NEW TOM
READY
10 DATA 9.4,7.6,3.6
20 READ X
30 PRINT X
40 GO TO 10
50 END
RUN
 9.4
 7.6
 3.6
OUT OF DATA IN 20
READY
BYE
OFF AT 13:50

The user retrieved EFOX by typing

OLD EFOX

Then he listed it so that he could refresh his memory as to what E-FOX contained.

The user caused line 25 to be *inserted* between the already existing lines 20 and 30. He next ran the program with the results shown.

In permanent storage the user replaced the old version of EFOX with the new one.

Next, the user wanted to begin work on a program called TOM. He typed

NEW TOM

The working space assigned to user M was cleared, and the user was permitted to begin entering a new program. As you can see, the user entered and executed the new program but did not save it. He did not lose it, though. TOM is still saved in the permanent storage area for later retrieval.

If a person is a poor typist, he should not type in a program while he is actually connected to the distant computer. Instead, he should punch his program on paper tape off-line ahead of time; then, when connected, employ the paper tape reader attached to most terminals. Some installations decree that all computer programs must be entered via paper tape regardless of whether the user is a poor typist or a good one. Reading paper tape is always faster than on-line typing.

In this chapter we have explored conversational timesharing, but not to the depth that a professional programmer would have to go in order to use the system effectively. We have given the major principles, including the most-used system commands, OLD, NEW, RUN, SAVE, UNSAVE, LIST, BYE, but there is a great deal more to be learned.

As we have said before, the interested student may obtain a textbook dealing with conversational timesharing and do some independent work.

SUMMARY

In the batch mode, user programs are actually delivered to a computer; in remote batch, they are sent via telephone lines. In either case, the user may have to wait some considerable time before he obtains output. If the necessity for obtaining fast results is urgent, a third mode of computer usage may be employed, conversational timesharing.

In the timesharing mode, a person accesses a distant computer and tells it what he wants it to do. The computer gives results in seconds rather than in minutes or hours.

Timesharing gets its name from the fact that many persons may access the computer at the same time. Each person shares the time that the computer is able to devote to users. Since the computer is fast and gives intermittent attention to each person, users have the illusion that they are the sole users of a central computer.

A programming language especially suited to timesharing is BASIC. The language is easy to learn and easy to use. It has built-in features that permit easy conversational communications between users and the computer. Other programming languages, FORTRAN, ALGOL, APL, and others, can also be used in the timesharing mode.

Timesharing is expensive, about ten times as expensive as batch or remote batch for the same task. Timesharing should be used only when the results justify the expense.

QUESTIONS

1. What is meant by the term "conversational timesharing"?
2. How long does a person generally have to wait for output after he has asked the computer to run his job?
3. How many users can a large-scale central computer accommodate in timesharing mode at any one time?
4. What type of terminal device is most often associated with timesharing?
5. What is the name of the programming language developed especially for timesharing?
6. Discuss the differences in cost between batch (or remote batch) and timesharing service.
7. Give *two* benefits of conversational timesharing.
8. What does an individual have to do in order to become a user of a timesharing service?
9. What is the function of a working area when one is operating in timesharing mode? Contrast this area to a permanent storage area.
10. What hardware device is associated with stored programs in the permanent storage area?

11. What is the difference between the SAVE and REPLACE commands?
12. What are *two* ways that a user may make corrections while operating in the timesharing mode?
13. Why is the use of paper tape advantageous while one is operating in timesharing mode?
14. What is the meaning of the term "system command"? Give some examples.

25 | Software

SOFTWARE

The term software means "programs." When a computer is purchased, a customer obviously receives "hardware." He receives cabinets containing electronic components, card readers, printers, tape handlers, etc. These items are manufactured items that people have no trouble seeing.

But computers do not run on hardware alone. They require standard programs that have been written by programmers who work for the computer manufacturer. These programs take the form of "assemblers," "compilers," "operating systems," and others.

ASSEMBLER

You will recall that when we discussed assembly-language programming we mentioned the fact that programs written in assembly language are converted to machine language. It is not hardware that does the converting; it is software. In other words, computers are not wired to convert assembly-language programs to computer language.

Rather, an actual program called an assembler performs this task. The assembler was programmed by programmers working for the computer manufacturer.

The assembler is delivered to the customer at the same time that the computer is delivered. The assembler is probably recorded upon a large deck of punched cards or upon a reel of magnetic tape. Every time that an assembly is required, the assembler program is read into the memory of the computer. The assembler then accepts assembly-language cards found in the programmer's source deck. There cards are "decoded" one at a time. That is, the assembler determines what machine-language instructions have to be generated for the assembly-language instructions that are provided in the source deck.

Figure 25-1 gives the process in pictorial form.

The assembler has been written so that it also detects typographical errors. If even one typographical error is found, the assembly process is unsuccessful. The punching of object cards is discontinued, and all the programmer receives is a listing containing error messages. The programmer may then correct his source deck and try for another assembly.

What is the purpose for assembly? Simply to provide a deck that may be used if the same program is to be run again in the future. Assembly is expensive and should be done only once. Once an object deck exists, the memory of the computer is cleared and machine-language instructions punched upon the deck are read into the memory. The actual problem solution begins from that point. Figure 25-2 is a diagram illustrating the process.

It is also possible to "load and go." At the same time that the assembler generates the object deck, it also places the machine-language instructions on magnetic tape or disk. Immediately after the assembly has been completed, the computer retrieves the machine-language program and runs the program to obtain the required answers. For all subsequent runs, the object deck is used.

COMPILER

Another item of software is the "compiler." A compiler converts compiler-language programs (not assembly-language programs) to machine language. As you will recall, compiler-language programs are written in the FORTRAN, COBOL, PL/I, ALGOL, BASIC languages, and others.

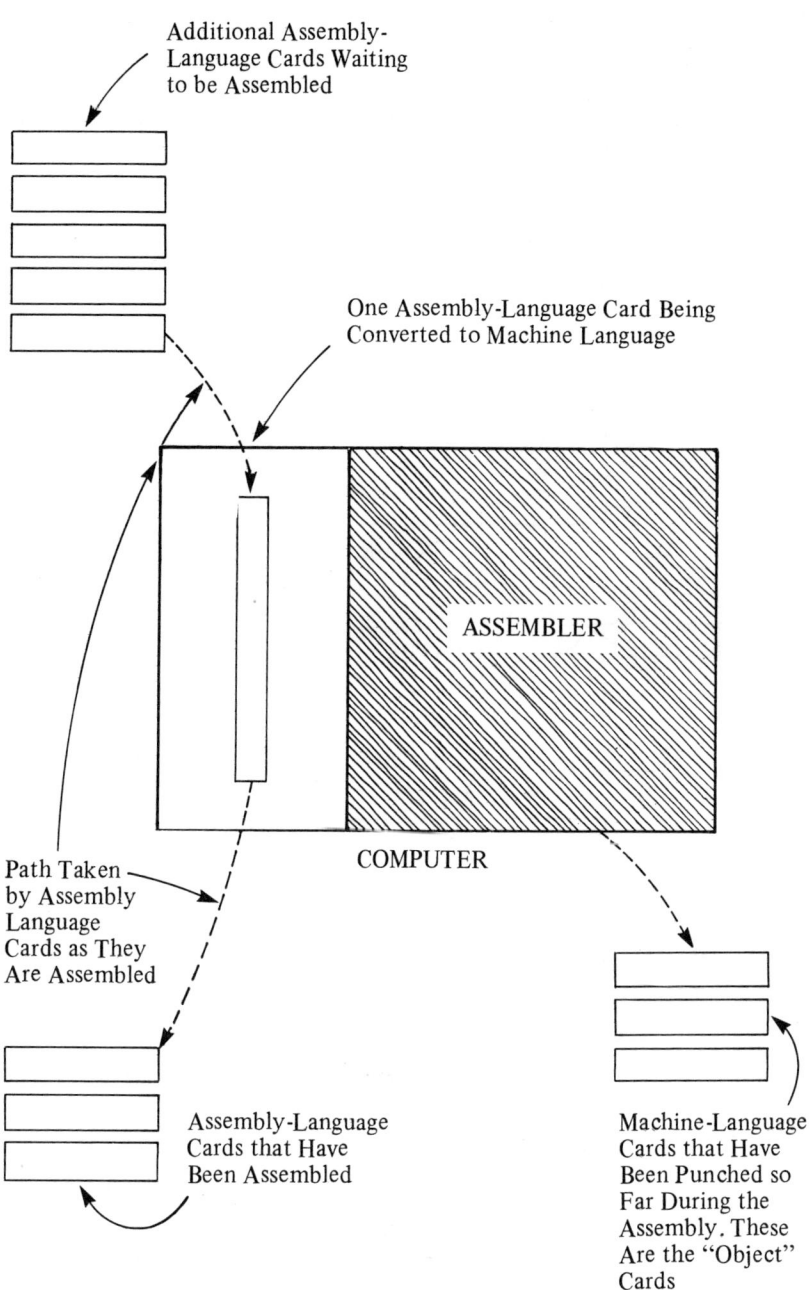

FIGURE 25-1

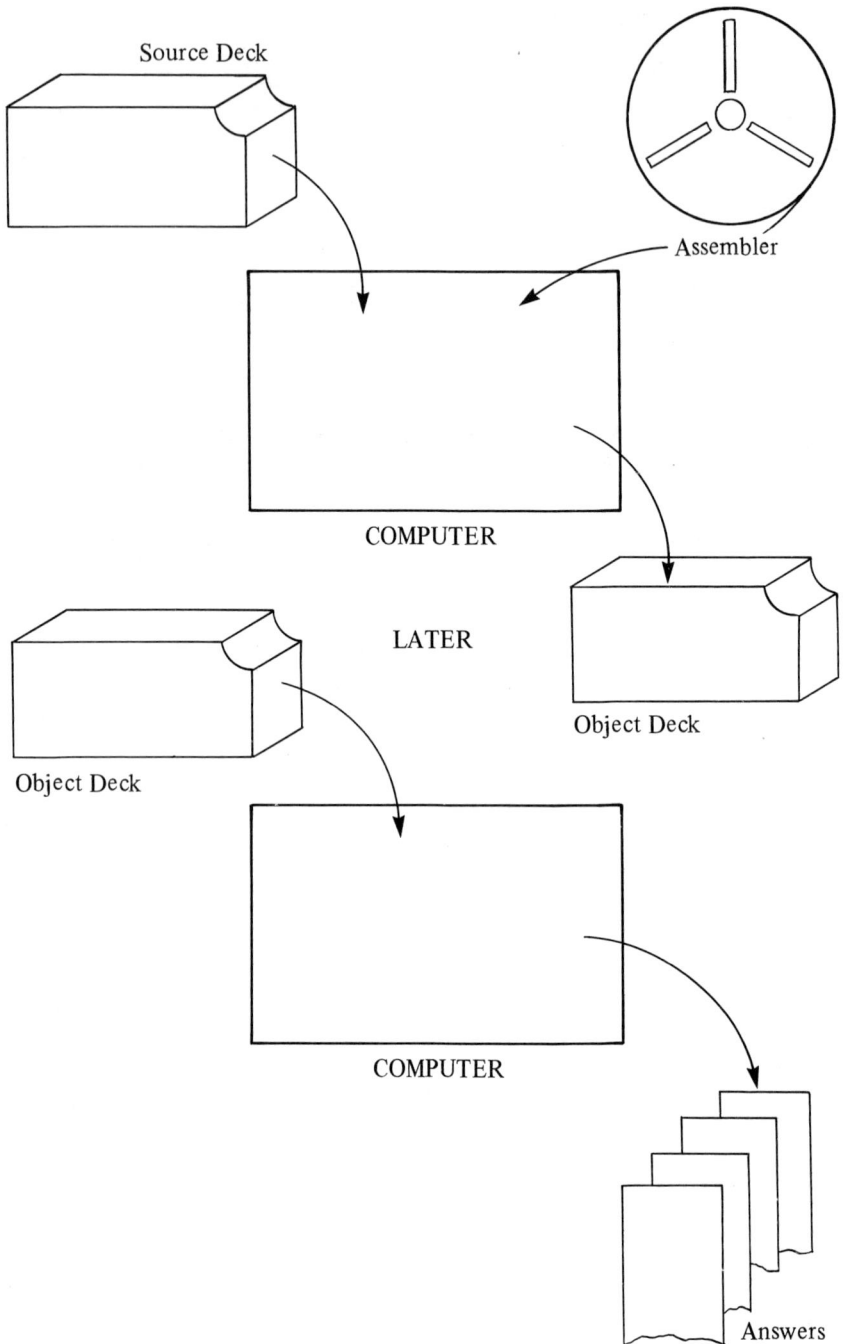

FIGURE 25-2

Other than the fact that assemblers convert assembler-language programs to machine language and compilers convert compiler-language programs to machine language, the principles and procedures are identical. In the illustration given above, wherever you see the word assembly or assembler, substitute the words compilation or compiler.

OPERATING SYSTEM

Another important item of software is the operating system. An operating system is a program that resides in the computer's memory all the time. It controls how the computer is to operate in batch, remote batch, and conversational timesharing modes. Figure 25-3 shows how an operating system controls several programs that may all be in the computer's memory at one time.

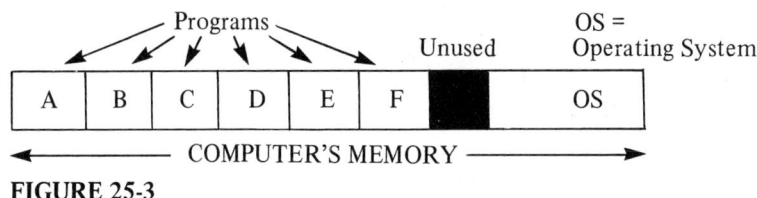

FIGURE 25-3

MULTIPROGRAMMING

At this particular moment there are six programs in the memory besides OS. OS, a very sophisticated program written by personnel at the computer manufacturer's plant, allows each program to execute in certain prescribed ways.

First, OS inquires whether program A would like to use the CPU (central processing unit) to actually do some computing. Let us suppose that program A responds "yes." OS allows program A to use the CPU but only for one millisecond (1/1000 second). At the end of that time program A is interrupted. OS intends to return to program A later to pick up from where it left off.

OS then goes to program B and inquires whether it wishes to compute. Let us say that the answer is "no," that it would rather read information from magnetic tape. OS allows program B to begin reading tape; then OS asks program C what it would like to do.

Program C may want to use the CPU, so OS connects program C to the CPU and permits it to compute for one millisecond. Then it interrupts program C. In the meantime, program B reads magnetic tape.

In like manner, the computer asks programs D, E, and F if they want to use the CPU. Whenever the programs reply "yes," they are connected for one millisecond. Whenever they reply "no,"—that they would rather pursue some input or output tasks—OS permits them to initiate those types of functions. It is possible, therefore, for a computer to be doing several tasks of input and output (I/O) while a single program is actually using the CPU.

If the CPU is kept busy, the computer becomes more efficient. The larger percentage of time that the CPU operates, based upon total time available, the more efficient the computer becomes, and the less each individual user pays for his job.

OS does other things. It removes programs from memory when the programs have ended; it brings in new programs that are waiting to be run; it permits remote batch users to enter the system from distant points; it permits conversational timesharing programs to merge with batch and remote batch programs and provide instant answers to distant users.

These tasks and others OS performs with great effectiveness.

There are many more examples of software that we could give at this point, but space does not allow. It is important to remember that a computer without software is very little more than a maze of wire and metal. You can touch it, speak to it, even kick it, but it will not do a thing. Infuse into it breath in the form of software programs, and the machine comes to life and begins doing wonderful things.

SUMMARY

Computers by themselves cannot accomplish anything. Instructions must be given to them, and then the instructions must be executed. When a computer (hardware) is delivered to a user, the use also receives major programs (software) that the computer understands. These programs may be received in the form of punched cards or magnetic tape.

Software usually involves program packages which accomplish a task or series of tasks that many users require. For example, one such program package is the COBOL compiler. The compiler converts COBOL statements employing English words to a series of zeroes and ones, the machine's language. Another program package is the operating supervisor (OS). The operating supervisor is a program that controls how all other programs are to run. OS makes multiprogramming possible, for example. During multiprogramming, a computer operates upon several programs all at the same time. While any one program is actually using the central processing unit (CPU), other programs may be doing some form of input and/or output (I/O).

QUESTIONS

1. Distinguish between the terms "hardware" and "software."
2. What is an assembler? A compiler?
3. Discuss what an operating system is and what it can do.
4. Why is it that that an assembler or compiler does not attempt to correct errors that it detects in user programs?
5. Tell what multiprogramming is and why it is advantageous.
6. What is the meaning of the term "I/O"?
7. What is the meaning of the term "load and go"?
8. Discuss why computer manufacturers should supply software packages along with purchased computer hardware.

26 | Applications

It has not been our intention in this text to make you experts in data processing. No one that we know of who started with no knowledge of computers became an expert by just studying a single book. It is doubtful whether the study of a whole shelf full of books could accomplish this feat.

Our objective has been to explore with you the world of data processing. We have discussed the reasons why data processing is necessary, what the levels of data processing are, what EAM equipment is, what computers are, and many other topics. We have been able merely to expose you to these topics so that you would have an idea of what is meant by such terms as keypunching, memory, programming, compilation, debugging, software, and others.

It is inevitable that a student will wonder how extensively computers are being used in this world, how they affect him now, what effect they will have in the future, etc.

In this chapter and the next we shall consider these questions. Then we shall try to project what we know in order to predict what the future may bring.

Broadly speaking, computer usage falls into two categories: scientific programming and business programming. About two-thirds of all data processing being done today is business processing; about one-third is scientific. Naturally, there are areas where the business and scientific worlds overlap. A particular application may be a combination of both types.

SCIENTIFIC APPLICATIONS

In the scientific world, computers are used to help design industrial machinery such as steam turbines, diesel engines, and even other computers. In the aircraft industry, computers are used to help design wings, fuselages, and propulsion equipment. In the military, computers assist in the development of new weapons. The strength of computers in design application is the capacity to do a great deal of computing in a very short time without getting bored or tired. As an example, an engineer may need this equation to help design the shape of a rotor in a Wankel engine:

$$Pf = [\sqrt{x+\theta} - \log(B)/e^{2.4m}] \sin(\theta)$$

The engineer knows that the best design is obtained when Pf is greatest as x varies from -5.3 to $+6.7$; as B varies from 2 to 8; as θ varies from 0.3 to 0.4; and as m varies from 8.5 to 10.6. The engineer may use his slide rule to obtain values of Pf, plugging in various values of x, θ, B, and m. He may get some fairly good results when he applies this technique, but he may not be convinced until he has tried many additional values. The engineer may, therefore, request a computer to give him all possible values of Pf as x varies with the range of -5.3 to 6.7 in steps of 0.1; as B varies from 2 to 8 in steps of 0.5; as θ varies from 0.3 to 0.4 in steps of 0.001; and as m varies from 8.5 to 10.6 in steps of 0.01.

The engineer is asking for over 15 million Pf calculations to be made. A fast computer can give the results in just a couple of minutes. If the engineer is experienced in BASIC or FORTRAN programming, he can write the required program in ten minutes or less. The result is a very accurate result obtained in less time than it would have taken to visit a mathematician and obtain his advice.

Sometimes a computer will be requested to give a result by a "trial and error" method. For example, an engineer may need to hook up a hundred or so components of an electronic device. The objective may be to hook up the components while keeping the hookup wire used to a minimum. It may be impractical to try every possible arrangement of the components to determine which combination gives the shortest amount of wire to be used. A computer can be instructed to try several hundred or several thousand arrangements and keep track of which arrangement uses the least amount of wire. That arrangement will be the one actually used in the assembly.

It is true that the arrangement finally chosen may not be the very best solution to the problem, but it will be an acceptable solution based upon the number of combinations that were actually tried. A human might have tried several dozen arrangements; a computer can economically try at least a thousand times as many.

When considering scientific applications, we can not ignore space travel. As a space ship is launched to visit the moon or distant planets, computers on board the spacecraft and on Earth are in constant control of what is happening. If the spacecraft should veer from its course ever so slightly, a computer will detect the deviation and cause corrective actions to be taken. Many of the computers involved are "on-line." This means that the computers have only one job to do, and they work on nothing else except that job. Typically, an on-line computer is idle most of the time, but when it is needed, it is right there.

ON-LINE APPLICATIONS

The importance of some applications justifies the expense of on-line computers. For example, a power station generating electricity for a community of two million persons needs to be right on top of power requirements at any given moment. When requirements increase or decrease, the on-line computer senses the change in requirements and alters the power output of the power-generation equipment within seconds.

On-line equipment is used also to help control the processes in a steel mill or in a chemical plant. Sensors tell the computer how the process is going. If it is going well, the on-line computer does nothing; if something beings to go wrong (a temperature becomes too hot, for example), the on-line computer takes action to make conditions go back to normal. That action may be to close a relay or to open a switch.

BUSINESS APPLICATIONS

The world of business data processing is an entirely different world. In the business environment, people are concerned with inventories, payrolls, reports, forecasts, accounts receivable, etc.

Much of the data that are used in the business world are in the form of files, and much of the work that is done concerns these files. There are programs that sort files, merge them, and update them.

FILE MAINTENANCE

Many business problems are concerned with the maintenance of files. By maintenance is meant that files are periodically brought up to date. There are two ways to update files—serial and random. In serial processing the entire file is examined, record by record. Those records that are to be changed are changed; records that are to be eliminated are deleted; records that are to be added to the file are added. Typically, in serial processing, an old file is used in creating a new one. The following paragraphs show in detail how this is done.

Let us consider a typical business situation. Assume that the Acme Card Company records data concerning its employees on a file called PERSONNEL MASTER FILE. The file consists of records. Each record contains complete details concerning a person—name, address, social security number, job description, pay rate, number of exemptions, year-to-date earnings, year-to-date federal taxes paid, etc.

Files to be processed serially are often recorded on tape. Tapes are used because a great deal of data can be recorded in a relatively small amount of space. Usually, 800 characters of data can be stored per inch. In some installations, 1,600 and even 3,200 characters of information are stored per inch.

Files that contain complete details concerning employees, customers, parts, etc., are called "master files."

Let us assume that the personnel master file that the Acme Card Company maintains has 1954 records of uniform size. There is one record for every employee, and each record contains 3,000 characters of data.

Figure 26-1 shows what the file looks like.

This file is organized by social security number. Those numbers

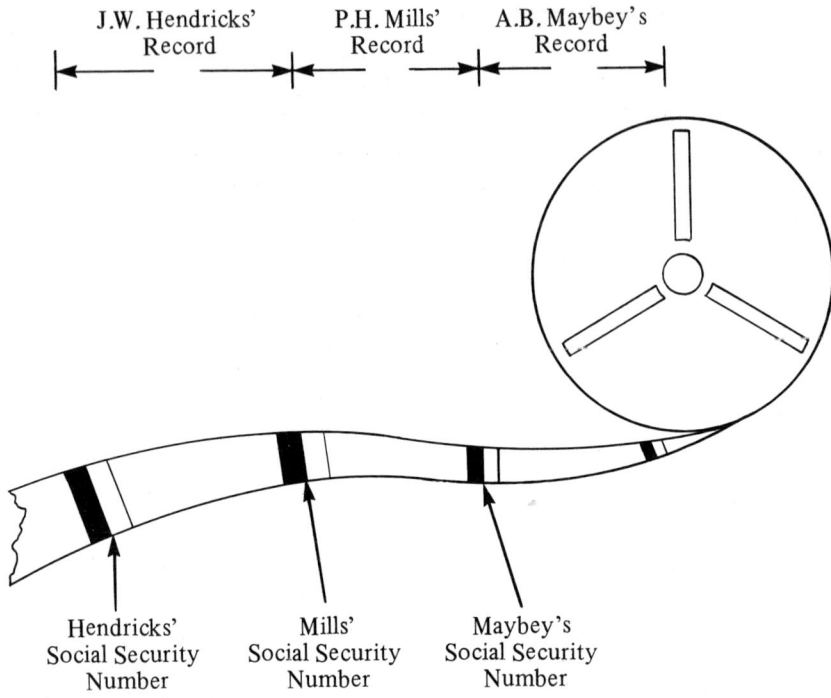

FIGURE 26-1

are in increasing sequence. A. B. Mabey's number is greater than P. H. Mills' number, which, in turn, is greater than J. W. Hendricks' number, etc.

Each record is the same size (3,000). This format was achieved by assigning fixed-length fields to every data item of every record. For example, 9 characters were allowed for social security number, 20 characters were allowed for last name, 1 character for middle initial, 12 characters for first name, 7 characters for year-to-date earnings, etc. If one record does not require the full number of character positions for an item, either zeroes or blanks fill unused positions. As an example, if year-to-date earnings were $12,406.35, then the corresponding field on the record would contain the characters 1240635. (The location of the decimal point is assumed to lie between the 6 and the 3.) If the earnings were $306.00, the record would contain 0030600.

A master file is up to date for only a short time after it has been updated. Within a minute or an hour a person may have his status changed. He may get a raise, or he may change the number of exemptions, or he may resign, etc. Other persons may be hired. These occurrences are termed "transactions" and will have to be reflected in the master file the next time that it is updated.

Transactions that occur are "batched." That is, they are collected for a period of time, say, a day or a week. The period of time during which transactions are collected is called the "batching period."

Transactions are generally recorded on pieces of paper called "source documents." The data on source documents are then punched on cards and the data on those cards are recorded on magnetic tape. Figure 26-2 shows the process.

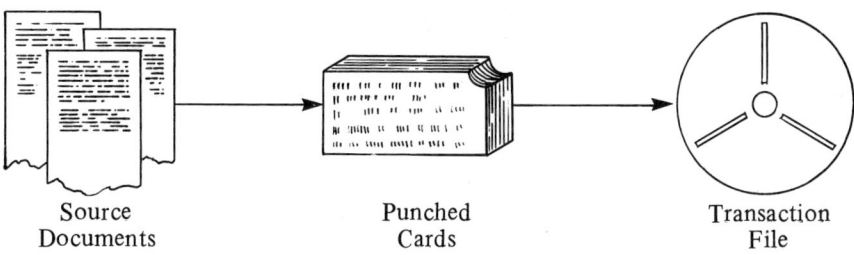

    Source   Punched   Transaction
Documents   Cards   File

FIGURE 26-2

The transaction file has been created and may now be used to update the master file.

To process a transaction file, it must be sequenced in the same order that the master file is sequenced. A "sort" procedure is, therefore, necessary. The sort may take place before the cards have been converted to tape (if a mechanical card sorter is used) or after the transaction tape has been created (if a computer sort program is used). For purposes of this example, let us assume that the transaction file is sorted after the tape has been created.

Figure 26-3 shows how the actual file update takes place.

There are four reels of tape used in the process:

> The old master file
>
> The new updated master file
>
> The unsorted transaction file
>
> The sorted transaction file

The first action is to sort the transaction file. After that process has occurred, transaction records will be sequenced in the same way

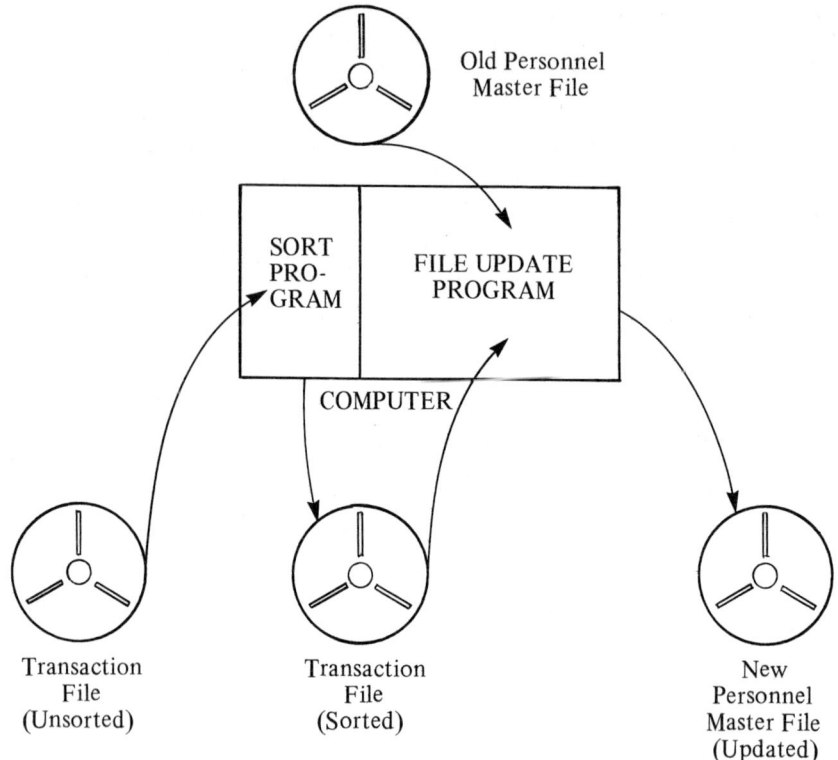

FIGURE 26-3

that the master file is sequenced—that is, in increasing sequence by social security numbers.

The next actions are to read some master records into memory (a block of them) and to read some transaction records into memory (a block of them). Attempts are made to match social security numbers in both groups of records. Where numbers match, the transactions that must be processed are those that make changes or those that delete full records. Where social security numbers do not match, complete records are to be accepted from the transaction file into the new master file, or complete records that need no action are to be copied on to the new master file from the old master file.

The update program never has to look very far in either file to determine what it has to do. The reason for this is that both files are stored on the same key. Consider the situation in Fig. 26-4, for example. Since records having social security numbers 123456789

Applications

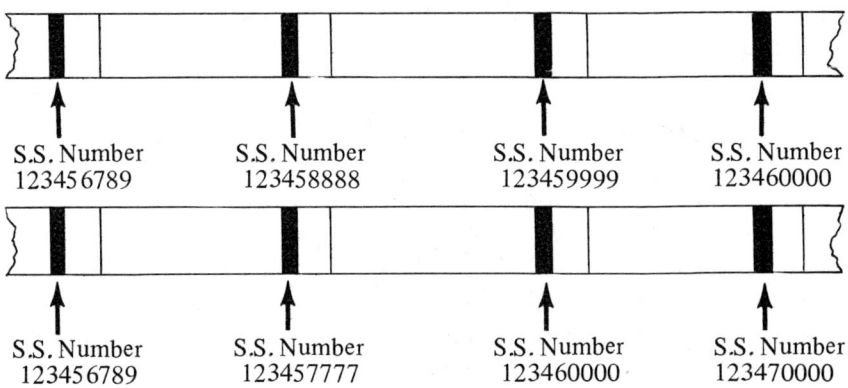

FIGURE 26-4

are found on both files, the transaction must be one that changes the master record or deletes it from the file. (A code in the transaction record tells what condition applies.) That master record is processed. It is then copied on to the new master file in updated form.

Since social security number 123457777 is smaller than 123458888, the transaction record must be for a new person. The data on the transaction record are copied on to the new master file.

Since there is no matching transaction record for master record 123458888, there must have been no transaction applying to that master record. The master record is, therefore, copied on to the new master file. By a similar process of deduction, it can be seen that master record 123459999 had no transaction. Records identified with 123460000 must concern a change or a deletion, etc.

When all records in both master and transaction files have been processed, the file update program terminates. The new master file will contain the information required for paying employees, for processing inquiries, and for making reports during the next interval of time, the "batching period." The new file will itself be updated at the end of the next batching period.

At the same time that files are updated, other outputs may be obtained. Outputs may include paychecks, new employees reports, promotion reports, etc.

You may hear the terms "father file" and "son file" in connection with file update situations. The father file is the old master file. The son file is the new master file. Son files become father files the next time that the file update program is run.

220   Applications

Grandfather files are files that are kept as backup in case something goes wrong and the entire update job has to be done all over again.

SEQUENTIAL AND RANDOM FILE MAINTENANCE

The sequential method of updating files is a good method to use when the number of records in a file is large and the proportion of those records that must be processed is also large. For example, if a file contains 1954 records and over 1900 records must be processed at every file-update time, then it makes sense to use serial processing.

When the number of records in a file is large, say 5,000, but only a small proportion of those records must be processed at file-update time, say 150, then another method of file maintenance should be used. An alternate method is called "random processing."

Files that are to be processed randomly are usually placed on magnetic disk. Each record of the file may or may not be placed next to its logical companion. Also, there may be a good many blank areas on the disk surfaces. Consider the example in Fig. 26-5. The rectangles represent complete records. Observe that the records appear to be placed at random locations on the disk surfaces. However, each record is placed at a certain location based upon rules that the programmer established.

If the records are organized around social security numbers, then a formula has been applied to those numbers. The output from the formula has given the disk location where the record is to reside.

Similarly, if records are organized around part numbers, then the formula is applied against those part numbers.

Let us consider an actual case. Assume that we have a disk unit that enables us to store a maximum of one million (1,000,000) records. Each place on the unit where a complete record may be stored is identified by an "address." That is, the first record storage area is Address 0, the next is Address 1; the next, Address 2, etc. The last record storage area is the one at Address 999,999. Figure 26-6 shows the disk unit.

Let us also assume we have a file that contains 600,000 personnel records. The social security numbers of the persons involved run from 000-00-0000 through 999-99-9999. Let us make these assumptions, even though we suspect that some social security numbers will probably never be assigned to actual persons.

Applications

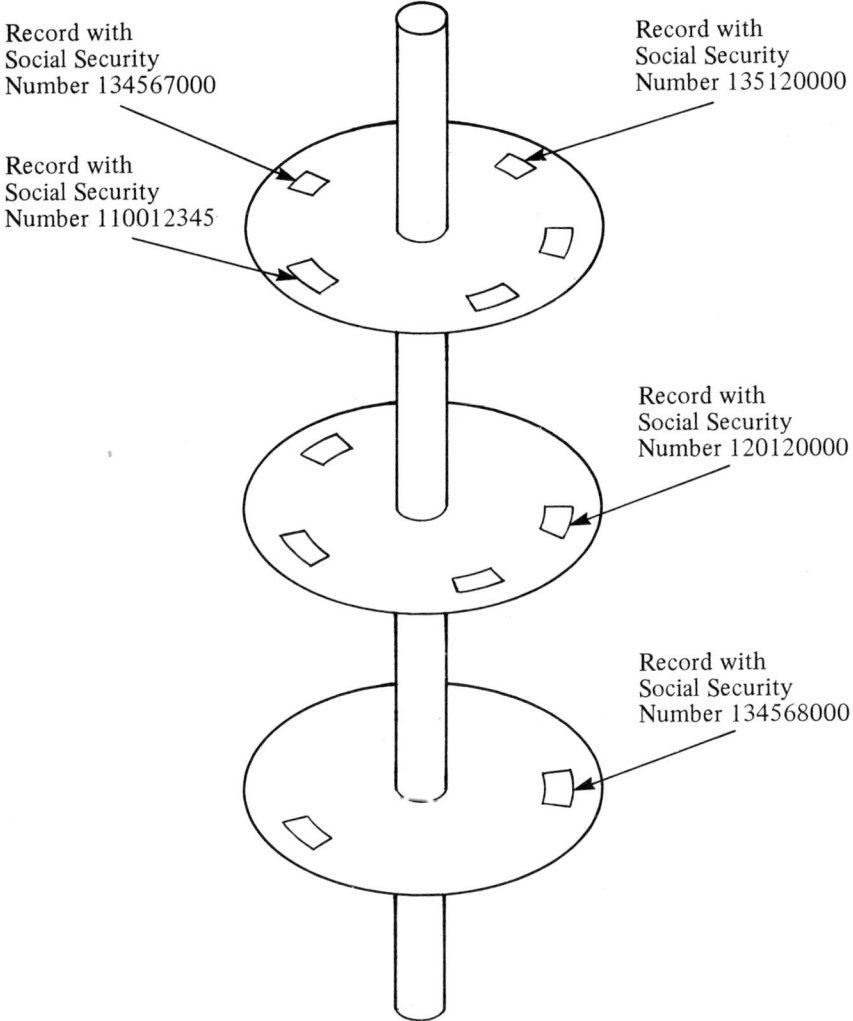

FIGURE 26-5

Can we remove the hyphens and use the social security numbers directly to give us disk addresses? No, because a social security number has nine digits while the addresses referencing record areas on a disk contain only six digits. We could possibly truncate social security numbers. That is, we could drop the leftmost three digits, thus, social security number 060181389 would give disk address 181389. This simple formula establishes the disk address where the record having social security number 060181389 is to reside. To

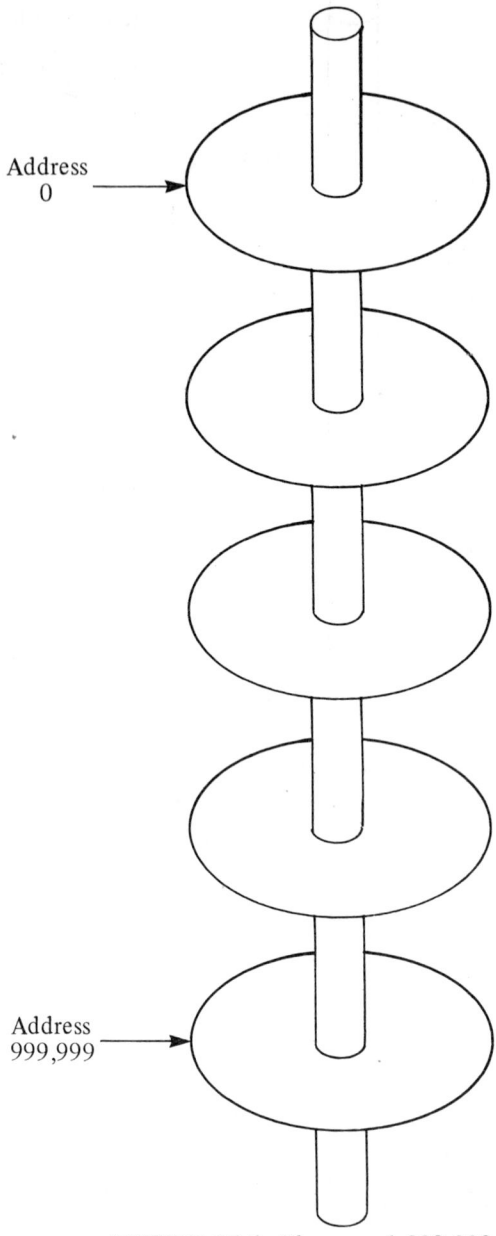

FIGURE 26-6 There are 1,000,000 places on this unit where a complete record may be stored. All places are of equal length. The addresses of the 1,000,000 record storage areas run from 0 through 999,999.

improve the formula, we could add the three leftmost digits to the six rightmost. Thus social security number 060181389 would give disk address 181499. Thus;

```
 181398
    060
 181449
```

If summation causes a number to grow beyond six digits (Example: 123999994), the "overflow digit" at the left is ignored. The address for this example would, therefore, be 117.

```
  999994
     123
 1000117
 ↑
```
The overflow digit

No matter how excellent the formula that is used to store records upon disk, "synonyms" will occur. A synonym is an address that wants to serve two or more records. A synonym could be generated by the two social security numbers 060181389 and 020181429. Each record wants address 181449 as its home. When synonyms occur, the usual method is to allow the first record that claims an address to have it, and then to place any other record that claims it in an "overflow" portion of the disk (see Fig. 26-7).

When it comes time to retrieve a record, the formula (whatever it was) will be applied first. Then if the required record is not located at the address that the formula gives, the overflow area will be searched serially—record by record—until the desired one is found. It is important, therefore, to keep the overflow area of the disk as short as possible. If too many synonyms are possible, then the formula being used is probably faulty and should be changed.

To update files in random mode, a person typically sits at a terminal and calls up the computer. When connected, he tells the computer that he wants to run his program that updates random files. The computer obtains the program and puts it into execution. The program next asks what record the user wishes to retrieve. The user gives the social security number of the record he wants to update. The computer then applies the formula that was originally used to store the record. It finds the record and brings it to a

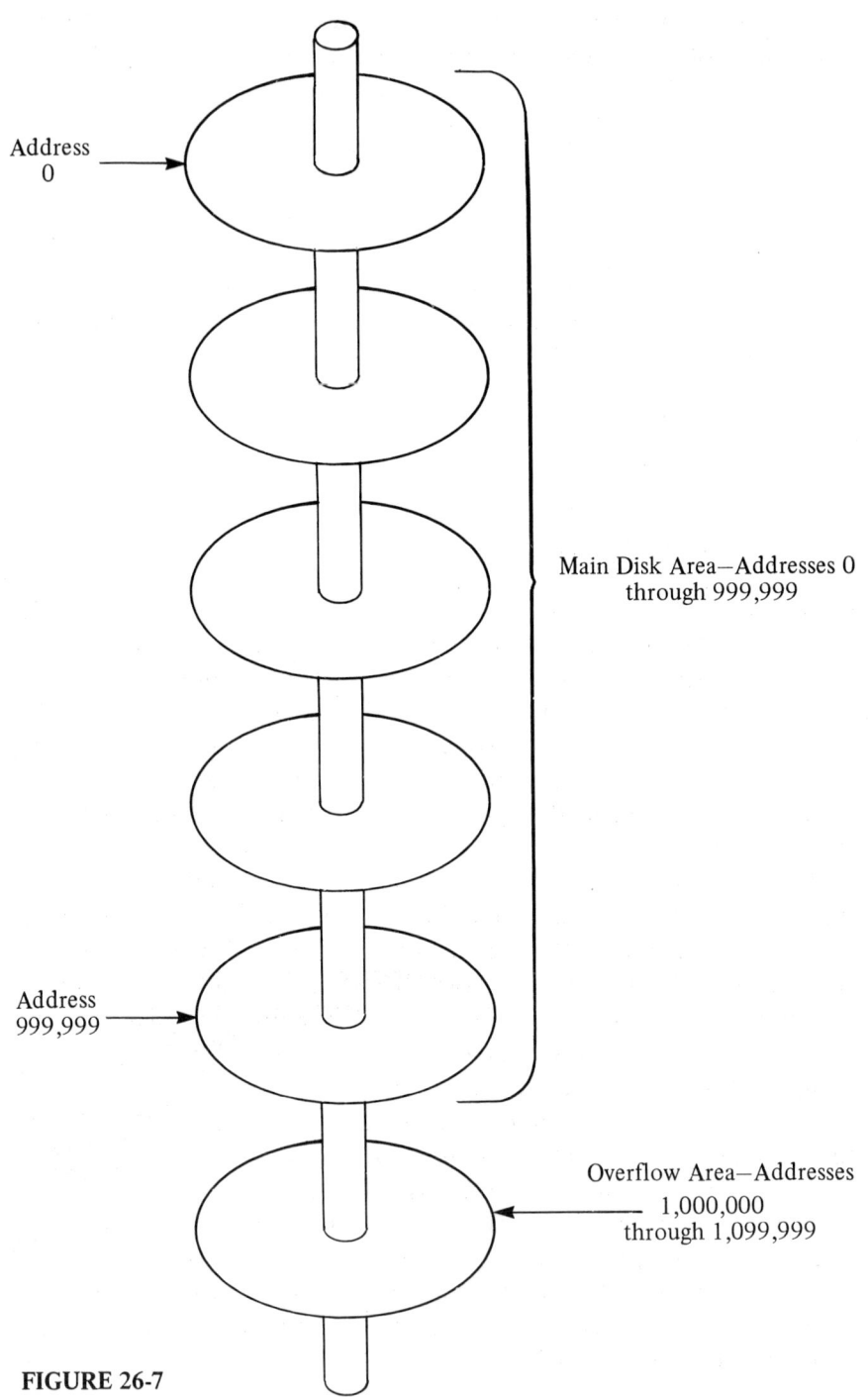

FIGURE 26-7

working space where the user may ask questions about it. He may ask, for example, what the pay rate is or what the year-to-date earnings are. In addition to asking questions, the user may change the record, and then store it back at its home address in updated form.

Keep in mind that random processing is far more expensive per record than serial processing. It should only be used where frequent updating is needed and where the number of transactions is not great when compared to the number of records in the file.

An airline uses random processing effectively, as an example. Picture a customer walking up to the airline counter and asking whether a certain flight is available to him. The customer would be greatly disturbed if he were told to come back at the end of the week when reservation files were updated and he would get his answer. The customer wants an answer "right now."

To serve a customer efficiently, a person at the airline ticket counter, using a terminal connected by phone lines to a distant computer, types a question. The question concerning reservations is answered within seconds.

SUMMARY

Computers may be used for both scientific and business applications. In scientific applications, computers utilize their great ability to perform calculations at very fast speeds, and to perform those calculations accurately. In business applications, computers utilize their ability to move information rapidly, to change it from one form to another (edit).

Typically, a scientific problem uses the general flowchart shown in Fig. 26-8, while a business problem uses the general flowchart in Fig.

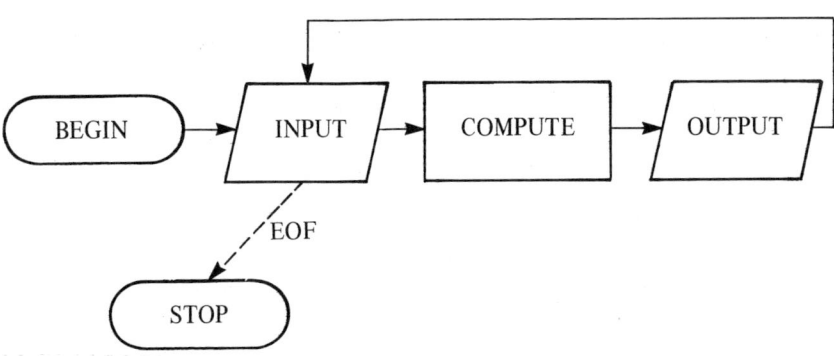

FIGURE 26-8

26-9. The sizes of the symbols illustrate the relative importance of the tasks. EOF means End of File.

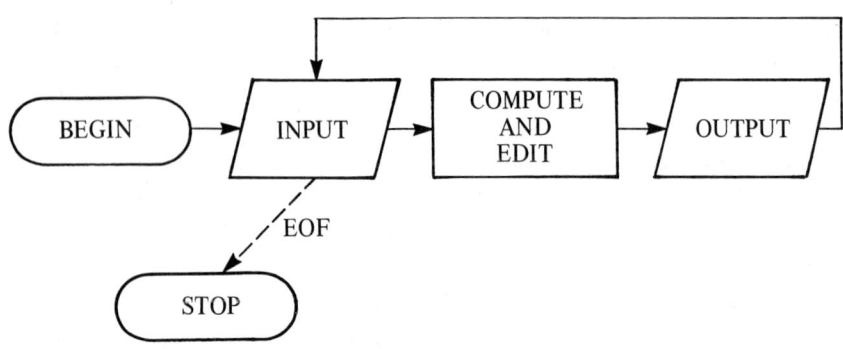

FIGURE 26-9

While scientific programming involves the performing of a great many calculations, business programming often deals with files. One task frequently accomplished in the business data processing world is the updating of files. About two-thirds of all computer usage is devoted to business data processing, and about half that amount involves, either directly or indirectly, the updating of files.

Files may be updated either serially or randomly. Serial updating is feasible if the number of master records is large and if the number of transactions affecting those records is also relatively large. Random processing is feasible if the number of master records is large and if the number of transaction records is relatively small.

QUESTIONS

1. What is the proportion of scientific computer usage versus business computer usage?
2. How does a computer utilize its strengths in performing scientific calculations?
3. Contrast input/output requirements for a scientific job with the input/output requirements for a business job. Contrast also the computing requirements for both kinds of jobs.
4. What is meant by the "trial and error" method of solving a scientific problem?
5. What is meant by the term "on-line"? Give some examples of on-line applications.

6. Give some examples of business applications.
7. What proportion of business applications has some connection, either directly or indirectly, with updating files?
8. What is a master file? Transaction file? Record?
9. What is meant by the term "sort"?
10. Why is it important that files be sorted?
11. Give the meanings of the terms "father file," "son file," and "grandfather file" and discuss their usages.
12. What is the difference between serial and random processing? When should each mode be used?
13. What is meant by the term "batching period"? How long may a batching period be?
14. What are some outputs that may be obtained from a file update application?
15. What is an overflow area? Why should it be kept as small as possible?

27 | System Design

PROCEDURES

The procedures that a company or department uses to achieve certain required objectives constitute a system. A system may, therefore, be simple or complex, manual or automatic.

A small farm machinery manufacturing company may, for example, have an integrated system that controls its operations. Included in the system are the functions of purchasing, engineering, manufacturing, shipping, sales, accounting, and others. The system provides inputs to the various components and obtains outputs from them. When the sales component sells a large machine, for example, the proper documents are prepared which inform engineering, purchasing, manufacturing, and shipping that the sale has been made. The receipt of this information enables the components to take whatever actions are required for the proper functioning of the component. Engineering is alerted that parts and subassemblies have to be designed; purchasing is made aware of components that must be ordered; manufacturing learns which components have to be built; shipping is advised to plan ahead for the eventual shipment of the machine.

In a smooth, well-functioning system, management is able to make timely, informed, effective decisions. But it is a fact of life that not all systems work properly. Some may be too elaborate for what is intended to be accomplished; others may be inadequate. Some systems are well designed but do not work properly for lack of acceptance and cooperation.

SYSTEM STUDY

The system designer is responsible for analyzing and implementing new systems or for replacing old ones. While no two systems are exactly alike and no two require the same design procedures, there are several considerations that apply to all systems. The first and perhaps most important is the system study.

In making the study, the designer must investigate in detail the procedures involved, the equipment used, the duties, the responsibilities, the talents, and the motivations of the employees. The designer must enter the study with an open mind and a willingness to accept conclusions that may be contrary to prevailing opinions.

It is imperative that the designer obtain the confidence of the people with whom he meets while making the study. He should exercise the utmost of tact in making his investigations, striving to dispel fear and anxiety. The designer should make clear that it is not his intention to eliminate jobs but to improve the working environment for all concerned.

Having concluded his study, the system designer's next task is to construct a theoretical model of the new or revised system. In constructing the model, he must give consideration to what constitutes efficient communication between components, what data processing devices are needed for the system, and what should be the interactions between people and equipment. During this phase of system design, the designer will have to develop a flow diagram that illustrates the various interrelationships involved.

The model must be tested on a small scale. If it is a new system, the flow of data and the operation of the new procedures should be closely studied. Deficiencies that become apparent may then be corrected. If the new system replaces an older one, the two systems should operate in parallel until it is clear that the new one operates properly.

COSTS

Of primary importance throughout the development of a system are the costs involved. The result of any new implementation should be a net savings. The savings can come about in a variety of ways. For example, the same amount of benefits may be made available as currently enjoyed, but at lower cost; or a reduced amount of benefits can be made available with a commensurate savings. Finally, benefits may be increased while costs are kept level. A major coup, of course, would be to increase benefits while, at the same time, reducing costs.

In analyzing costs, a distinction should be made between one-time outlays and recurring expenses. It may be justified, for instance, to incur a one-time large amount as investment in new equipment if the recurring costs can thereby be reduced.

The new procedures, once developed and tested, may then be proposed to higher management and, if accepted, be implemented. The new system should be kept under critical observation to ensure that the benefits anticipated are, indeed, being obtained.

DESIGNING THE SYSTEM

The design of new systems or the modifications of older ones is not a trivial task. The best personnel available should be assigned to the project. The greater the thoroughness with which the system is studied and the greater the care with which it is implemented, the better the prospects that it will be a successful endeavor.

THE FEASIBILITY STUDY

Before an application can be considered a candidate for computer application, a feasibility study must be made. In the course of this study, the proposed application will be examined from various angles. Some of the considerations involved in the study are

> What are the objectives to be met by the proposed applications?
> What is the nature of the system being replaced?
> What should be done in the replacement system?
> Who are the people participating in the new system?
> What are the costs and benefits involved?

System Design

Objectives

A clear statement must be made regarding what the objectives of the new system are to be. The main question concerns what is to be accomplished by computerizing. Any assumptions concerning the proposed system and its limitations must be defined at this point.

The Current System

A thorough description must be given of the existing system. The objectives and actions taken in this system are documented. Also documented are the types of persons administering the system. What do they do? Why do they do it? How? When? These questions must be answered in the description of the existing system.

Some of the specific questions that must be asked and answered are these:

1. Why does the system exist? What are its objectives?
2. Where and under what circumstances is the work being done?
3. What are the inputs to the system? Are they reasonable, accurate, timely? What are the outputs?
4. Does the system work well? Does it accomplish its objectives? Will the system continue to perform in the future as it is currently performing?
5. At what points in the operation of the system may controls be applied? May feedback be obtained from those points?
6. What are the problems associated with the system? (If there are no problems, then the system logically should not be changed.)
7. How urgent is the necessity to revise or replace the system?

These and many other questions will occur to and be answered by the system designer. Throughout his study, he should keep constantly in mind that it is not so important what is being done as what should be done.

The New System

Several challenges must be met in the design of the new system. What is to be done? How? Who are the people to do it? When? These are some of the considerations that must be examined.

What Is To Be Done?

1. Decisions must be made concerning what outputs are needed from the new system. Thought should also be given to the system's inputs.
2. The details of data to be maintained in the master file must be defined. How is it to be sorted?
3. It must be decided when and under what circumstances the master file is to be updated.
4. The response time to be offered by the system must be established.

How Is It To Be Done?

1. An analysis of how the work will be accomplished must be obtained.
2. Are reports to be issued? To whom will they be directed?
3. A determination must be made concerning conversion problems from the old system to the new.
4. The kind of equipment to be used must be tentatively defined. If a computer is involved, its type and size should be known.

Who Will Do It?

1. A thorough understanding should be obtained of the people who will operate the new system. The levels of knowledge and experience should be understood.
2. The types of persons needed to implement the system should be known.
3. The supervisory personnel needed should be sketched out at least in rough form.

When Is It To Be Done?

1. A schedule of the time needed to develop, implement, and test the new system should be established.
2. Checkpoints along the way to project completion should be defined.

System Relationships

The relationship of the new system to others already in existence should be understood. Possibly the new system can be incorporated with one that already exists. Or perhaps the system being designed can be enlarged to include the functions of other existing, related systems.

The inputs and outputs connected with the new system should be examined to determine whether they can be used in conjunction with the operation or development of other systems. (Sometimes a little extra effort in analysis or study can reap unexpected dividends from related sources.)

Costs

The costs of the new system could be thoroughly recognized.

1. The feasibility study itself should be considered a fixed cost in the development of the new system.
2. A determination should be made to differentiate the fixed versus variable costs involved in the new system. What are the types of costs for study, programming, implementing, and testing of the system?

CONCLUSIONS AND RECOMMENDATIONS

The system designer is responsible for documenting conclusions reached from the system study. He should also make recommendations for action to be taken. Often, the most valuable recommendation is not to go ahead with the implementation of the proposed new system.

During a system feasibility study, the designer's greatest assets are an open mind and a willingness to be convinced. What should be done should ever be uppermost in his mind rather than what is being done.

SUMMARY

A system is a set of interwoven procedures that a department or company employs to achieve some desired objectives.

One of the important outputs from a system is information. When up-to-date information is available, management is able to make effective decisions. Being able to make good decisions is an advantage that organizations strive for, for it enables them to compete successfully in the business world.

In developing a system, a system designer must marshall all the factors at his disposal and form the most effective combination of those factors as possible. No two systems are alike. The designer must, therefore, make sure that he understands the problem, the assets at his disposal, and the feasibility of combining them in some efficient manner.

A feasibility study is of prime importance in developing a system. The designer has to determine the objectives of the system, to understand the operation of the current system, and to plan the new system with respect to what is to be done, how it is to be done, who will do the work, and when will the work be done. In addition, the designer must investigate and understand the interrelationship of the various parts of the system. He must plan the efficient interweaving of those parts. Finally, the designer must plan the system to minimize its cost commensurate with the benefits obtained.

Having completed the system study, the designer must make recommendations to management and obtain their approval to proceed.

QUESTIONS

1. What is a system?
2. What are some of the important outputs to be obtained from a well functioning system?
3. What is the system study?
4. Explain what the function is of a theoretical model for a system.
5. What is a flow diagram? Why is it important?
6. Why are costs important when one is planning a system?
7. Why should the current system be well understood when one is planning another to replace it?
8. Discuss some of the broad bodies of information that must be obtained in a system study.
9. What is a system designer's responsibility after a study has been completed?
10. Once a new system has been approved, what steps are required in its implementation?

28 | The Future

Computers have been used to process data since only about 1945. In less than thirty years, they have become a major factor in our economy. They have been used to design the most complex of machines. (Space travel would have been impossible without computers.) They have been used to establish the most complex of automated business information system. In these systems, the important functions of a business are computerized and related to each other. When an order is received, for example, all persons responsible for knowing about the order are told. In addition, purchases for needed material are automatically triggered. Shop scheduling for the manufacture of the ordered items is automatically initiated. As the order is processed, status reports are periodically issued. When the ordered items are shipped, a bill is automatically issued.

Computers have been used in the world of finance. Without them, banks and other financial institutions would have great difficulty in keeping up with the billions of transactions that occur every day.

Computers are used in schools. At many high schools and colleges, conversational timesharing is made available to students so that they may do their homework more easily.

Computers are also used for fun. Using a distant computer, persons may play tic tac toe, blackjack, baseball, football, checkers, and other games in a conversational mode. The user gives his play, and the computer gives its response. Invariably, the computer wins—not because it cheats, but because it knows what the best alternatives are in any given situation and always plays the odds.

Needless to say, the government is the largest user of computers in this country. Its uses range all the way from reporting upon the census to auditing tax returns. The use of computers is growing in government faster than it is in industry.

But what about the future? If computers have made such a large impact on our present daily lives, what can we expect from them in the future?

Let us consider finance.

FINANCE

In future years, paper money and metal coins will all but disappear. People will be paid by check, and these checks will be deposited directly into checking accounts. Any amount that you owe the federal government in taxes will disappear out of your account before you have a chance even to see it.

In making purchases, you will use a single credit card. Inserting the card into a slot at a business establishment will remove funds from your account and deposit them into the account of the business. Of course, your credit will be checked. If your balance shows that you can not afford the item you want to purchase, you will not be permitted to do so.

EDUCATION

Computers will become "smarter" in the future. You will be able to speak to them, via teletype-like terminals, in a language that is far less structured than the ones we use today. For example, you may engage in the following conversation with a computer. The underlined remarks are yours:

>HI
>HI
>HOW ARE YOU TODAY?
>FINE. AND YOU?

FINE. ARE YOU BUSY TODAY?

YES. THERE ARE 403 USERS ON LINE RIGHT NOW.

CAN YOU HELP ME WITH A PROBLEM?

CERTAINLY. PLEASE STATE IT.

I HAVE TO FIND OUT WHETHER IT'S BETTER TO INVEST $1000 AT 6% COMPOUNDED QUARTERLY OR $900 COMPOUNDED MONTHLY.

DO YOU WANT TO KNOW WHICH ALTERNATIVE GIVES YOU A HIGHER YIELD?

YES

WHAT IS THE PERCENTAGE RATE OF THE SECOND ALTERNATIVE?

DIDN'T I TELL YOU? IT'S 6½%.

THE FIRST ALTERNATIVE IS BETTER. DO YOU WANT THE EXACT FIGURES?

NO THANKS. YOU TOLD ME WHAT I WANT TO KNOW.

DO YOU HAVE ANY OTHER PROBLEMS?

NO, BUT I'LL BE BACK LATER.

FINE.

WELL, BYE FOR NOW.

GOODBYE

The computer almost seems literally to understand what you want. It does not really, because the computer has been very elaborately programmed to give you the responses it does. Nevertheless, as time goes by, the conversations that you have with a computer will become so realistic that an observer will be unable to believe that the entity at the other end of the line is not human.

TRANSPORTATION

In the area of transportation computers will help take you where you want to go. You will still own a car, but you will not drive it in the sense that you do now. An electric battery will move it from your garage to the street, but that is where the computer will take over. You will type a coded message telling where you want to go, and a computer-controlled mechanism in the vehicle will take you on your way. Magically, magnetic forces imbedded in the road will move your vehicle along the quiet streets of your community. These streets will merge with larger highways, and your accelerating vehicle will merge also. Soon your car will be surrounded by hundreds of other vehicles travelling in the same direction at speeds of up to 300 kilometers per hour. (A kilometer is about 5/8 of a mile.) These cars will be only a few feet from each other, but there will not be any danger of collision.

As you travel, there will be no need for you to drive, so you can spend your time watching the scenery, reading the paper, doing some paperwork, or just enjoying a second cup of coffee. As your little car approaches its destination, it will gradually be shunted to slower roads until you reach your destination. At that point the computer will turn control back to you, and you may use the car's internal battery again to drive into a parking lot.

Long or short trips may be made in this fashion. A trip across the continent can be made in less than 12 hours. You will pay for this computer service by the kilometer. The final cost to you will be about what you would now expect to pay for gasoline for the same trip.

ENTERTAINMENT

In the area of entertainment, you will have far greater choice over what you may watch or hear on your home entertainment center. You can tune in to news, a sporting event, a dramatic play, an educational program, or simply to a program of good music. You may dial programs you have missed or those you would like to see again. Even the commercials you would like to watch may be selected by you. The cost? You will pay by the program, and the computer will, of course, automatically withdraw funds from your bank account.

At work more and more tasks will be automated. There will be so little for people to do in certain industries that attendance at work will not often be required. Persons will actually compete with each other for the privilege of going to the job to make sure that all the pushbuttons are in proper working order.

MEDICINE

In medicine, computers will help stamp out all forms of diseases so that persons may enjoy healthier, more satisfying lives.

GOVERNMENT

In government, many of the routine activities will be performed by computers. Even some of the major decisions will be computerized. Not being subject to the frailties of human nature, computers will be able to analyze the facts presented by a given situation, analyze the consequences of taking certain actions, and then recommend or actually initiate the actions that seem most appropriate.

It is difficult to predict whether the developments outlined above will occur within the next 20, 30, or 40 years, or even if they will occur at all. Admittedly, our crystal ball is a bit cloudy concerning even what will happen tomorrow. But of this we can be sure: Computers will have a greater impact upon our lives than they do today. Exactly what that impact will be depends, at least to some degree, on how you yourself help bring it about.

SUMMARY

In the future, computers will play an increasingly important role in our lives. In the fields of science, medicine, business, government, and others, computers will increasingly take over the tedious functions performed by humans. Computers may take over so many functions performed by humans that there may come a time when working will be a privilege rather than an obligation.

Persons need not be concerned that computers will some day "take over." Humans can always exercise their option to pull the plug. Of course, if the task of deciding when the plug should be pulled has been delegated to the computer itself, well . . . .

QUESTIONS

1. Discuss the impact that computers may have upon society in the immediate future and in the more distant future.
2. Discuss the advisability or inadvisability of trying to regulate this impact.

29 | GLOSSARY

abacus. A computing device invented around 3000 B.C. Consisting of a frame containing beads strung on reeds or wires, the device is still in use in many countries of the world. In speed and efficiency, it rivals the electric desk calculator.

accounting machine. A device capable of performing arithmetic calculations and of producing reports in some desired format. This EAM device has properties similar to those of a computer, but it is not a computer.

accumulator. A register in the hardware of a computer. This is the main register into which numbers are added, subtracted, multiplied, divided, etc. The content of the accumulator may be stored in memory locations.

address. A number that defines the location of a memory byte or word.

address modification. The nominal address in an instruction can be changed by adding to it the value last assigned to an index register. For example, if the address in an instruction is 1200 and the applicable index register contains the value 300, the effective address will be 1200 + 300, or 1500.

Aiken, Howard. Developer of Mark I.

ALGOL. A compiler language. ALGOL is a scientific language popular in Europe and in universities. The word ALGOL is a contraction of the words *Algorythmic Language*.

assemble. To convert a program written in assembly language to machine-understandable code (zeroes and ones).

assembly language. A formalized code for instructing a computer. The code uses short groups of letters and numbers such as CLA, LDX3, and SHL. These groups are eventually converted to zeroes and ones.

Babbage, Charles. Inventor of "difference machine" and "analytical engine."

BASIC. A compiler language. BASIC is well suited for use in writing programs of modest complexity in both scientific and business areas. BASIC is especially adapted for use on teletype-like terminals in timesharing mode. The word BASIC is a contraction of the words Beginners' All-purpose Symbolic Instruction Code.

basic data processing cycle. Many data processing jobs fall into an easily recognizable pattern. The pattern represents a cycle from "read data," "process data," "write some output," back to "read data" again. The cycle continues until there is no more input data to process.

batch mode. A method by which a computer may be used. The program is physically delivered to the computer center. Output is obtained from the point to which the program was delivered.

binary. A numbering system based upon radix 2. All numbers expressed in binary use only zeroes and ones.

bit. A contraction of the two words *b*inary and d*igit*. A bit is a digit either zero or one.

block. A collection of records on magnetic tape, magnetic disk, or similar device. In the main memory of the computer, a block of records may be stored in a buffer area. The number of records per block is variable, depending upon the requirements of the user.

buffer. A portion of the computer's main memory set aside to receive blocks of records from magnetic tape, magnetic disk, or similar devices. In processing records, the computer obtains them from the buffer one record at a time.

byte. The basic unit of storage in the memory of several computers. A byte usually consists of 8 bits.

card punch. A computer-operated device that punches data upon data processing cards. The information may be punched in Hollerith format (normal data processing characters) or in binary, the language of the computer.

card reader. A device used in a computer system for the purpose of detecting data punched on data processing cards and transferring the data to the main memory of the computer.

character. A single symbol used in data process. The symbol could be a digit or a letter of the alphabet, or a special symbol, such as a comma, dollar sign, asterisk, etc.

characteristic. Part of a floating-point number. A floating-point value is constructed by multiplying the characteristic of the number by the mantissa.

COBOL. A compiler language. The language is well suited to the programming of business problems. The name COBOL is a contraction of the words *Co*mmon *B*usiness *O*riented *L*anguage.

collator. A device having the ability to (1) do sequence checking with cards, to (2) merge two decks of cards in some prescribed fashion, to (3) match card decks, and, to (4) select desired cards from a card deck.

COM. Computer Output Microfilm. Report pages recorded on magnetic tape are transformed to page images on sheets of microfilm called microfiche.

compilation. A process whereby a program coded in compiler language (FORTRAN, COBOL, PL/I, etc.) is converted to machine language (zeroes and ones).

compiler language. A formalized code for instructing a computer in solving some given problem. Compiler languages are English words, such as READ, WRITE, IF, which are eventually converted to machine language (zeroes and ones). *See also* **compilation.**

computer. An electronic system having the ability to compute, to process data, and to provide output in predetermined formats.

computer operator. A person skilled in the submitting of programs to a computer and in the preparation of results for forwarding to programmers.

console. The nerve center of the computer, containing lights, switches, typewriters, and other devices. Computer operators control the operation of the computer from this point.

control. One of the major components of a computer. This is the component that fetches the next instruction of a program to be executed, decodes the instruction, and causes its execution to take place. The other two major components of a computer are "memory" and CPU.

control cards. *See* **JCL.**

control panel. A perforated board upon which wires may be plugged, enabling the control of certain EAM or computer devices.

conversational timesharing. A mode in using a computer system. The user sits at a teletype-like terminal and communicates with a distant computer via telephone lines. The term "conversational" is applicable, since the user and computer type a series of messages to each other, back and forth, until the user's data processing requirements have been met.

conversion. The changing over from one business information system or from one computer to another. Conversion is almost always a major problem in any business concern.

core. Tiny, circular rings constructed of iron. Able to be magnetized to represent zero or one. Each core holds at any one moment the binary digit zero or one. Arrays of cores from the main memory of a computer.

CPU. Central Processing Unit. The central processing unit is that module of a computer that actually computes and that manipulates data stored in the main memory.

data. Characters in the form of numbers, letters of the alphabet, and special symbols that are fed to a computer in order for it to obtain meaningful and useful information from the characters.

data cell. A device upon which data may be stored and retrieved. The data cell employs thousands of short strips of magnetic tape upon which the data are recorded.

debug. Determine what is wrong with a program and eliminate the errors.

decimal. A numbering system based on radix 10. The digits used in the system are zero through nine.

disk. A flat, circular plate upon which data may be magnetically recorded. The data can later be retrieved.

drum. A cylindrical device upon whose surface data may be magnetically recorded. The data can later be retrieved.

EAM. Electric Accounting Machines. Several data processing devices including key punches, card sorters, collators, reproducers, and others are termed EAM devices. Another term having the same meaning as EAM is "unit record devices." EAM devices are used to process punched cards, but they are not computers.

EBCDIC. Extended Binary Coded Decimal Interchange Code.

Employing the 8 bits of the code, one can represent 256 different characters. The EBCDIC code for the letter A, for example, is 11000001.

Eckert, J. P. Co-developer of ENIAC.

electrostatic printer. A high-speed line printer. Report page images are magnetized on paper, and then the magnetized paper is passed through an ink fog. The ink adheres to the magnetized spots. Later, the ink is baked into the paper producing the final output sheets.

ENIAC. Electronic Numerical Integrator and Calculator. First electronic computer, developed by J. P. Eckert and J. W. Mauchley of the Moore School of Engineering at the University of Pennsylvania.

EOF. End of File. When all the records in a file have been processed, the computer is said to have encountered an "end of file" (EOF) condition.

EOF-mark. End-of-file. Files have end-of-file marks that may be detected during file processing operations.

excess-64 method. A method of expressing floating-point numbers. The "64" in the name arises from the fact that 64 must be subtracted from the number's nominal characteristic in order to get the effective characteristic. The effective characteristic ranges from -64 to $+63$.

execution. The computer is instructed to carry out the instructions. Execution is another word for "run."

father file. When a file update program is run, the old master file is termed the "father file." The updated file is termed the "son file." The file that was used to create the father file is termed the "grandfather file."

field. A series of character positions set aside to store data for some individual item. For example, columns 1 through 9 could be set aside, as a field, on a data processing card to hold social security numbers.

file. A collection of related records concerning some business topic. The records are organized according to a key data item. For example, an inventory file could contain all of the data concerning spare parts for a turbine.

fixed-point number. *See* **integer.**

fixed word-length. The memory of a computer is divided into cells of fixed length. The data values to be stored must accommodate themselves to the predetermined sizes. For example, some computers employ memory cells consisting of 36 bits. Both large and small numeric values use all 36 bits.

floating-point. A format for representing numbers. Numbers are expressed as a value of mantissa multiplied by a power (characteristic). The hardware of many computers is able to deal with floating-point numbers, automatically adjusting the assumed position of the decimal point with each use.

flowchart. A pictorial diagram showing what instructions are to be given to a computer in order to solve a given problem. The flowchart also shows the sequence in which the instructions are to be given.

flowchart symbol. Standard shapes used in developing flowcharts. Symbols exist to indicate input and output operations, processing operations, decisions, terminations, and corrections.

FORTRAN. A universal programming language. FORTRAN is well suited for scientific and mathematical programs. The name FORTRAN is a contraction of the words *For*mula *Tran*slator.

grandfather file. *See* **father file.**

hexadecimal code. A method of representing data. The method employs 16 characters ranging from 0 through 9 and from A through F. Each of these characters represents four binary digits (bits) ranging from 0000 through 1111.

HLC. Hypothetical Learning Computer. A fictitious computer developed for this text.

Hollerith, Herman. Fostered the use of punched cards in data processing.

index register. A register in the hardware of a computer. The numeric value stored in the register can be used for counting or for address modification.

information. Meaningful and useful facts that are extracted from data fed to a computer. These facts enable management to make good business decisions.

input data. Numbers, names, addresses, catalogs, etc. that the computer needs to solve a given problem. Input data are the variable part of a job setup; the program instructions constitute the constant portion.

instruction. A command issued to a computer to perform some act, such as add a number to another, or move a number from one area to another.

integer. A whole number without a decimal point. Examples: 26, 17, −42. Integers are also called fixed-point numbers.

interactive mode. A person and a computer engage in a "conversation." During the conversation, the programmer tells the computer what he wants it to do.

interpreter. A device used for printing along the top edge of a punched data processing card the identity of the characters punched on the card.

inter-record gap. A ¾-in. separation between records on magnetic tape. When the tape is read from or written upon, a complete block of records is transmitted at a time. In reading, the gaps define both ends of the block; in writing, gaps are installed at both ends.

Jacquard, Joseph Marie. Used punched cards as control for loom.

JCL. *J*ob *C*ontrol *L*anguage. Cards representing job control language (control cards) are interspersed with source or object card decks and data decks. These cards give information concerning who the programmer is, what charge number he wishes to use, what his location is, etc.

keypunch. A device for punching rectangular (sometimes round) holes in data processing cards. The more universally used keypunch machines are the IBM models 026, 029, and 129.

language. A formalized code involving letters of the alphabet, digits, and special signs, by the use of which a computer can be instructed to take actions of which it is capable.

load and go. A procedure during which a program is submitted to the computer with directions to assemble and execute in sequential, uninterrupted steps.

machine language. A formalized code for instructing a computer. The code uses only zeroes and ones.

mantissa. Part of a floating-point number. A floating-point value is constructed by multiplying the mantissa of the number by the characteristic.

Mark I. First electromechanical computer developed under the direction of Howard Aiken at Harvard University.

Mauchley, J. W. Co-developer of ENIAC.

memory. One of the major components of a computer. The memory is capable of storing characters of data—sometimes several million characters. Data characters stored in memory remain unchanged until the system replaces them with new characters.

MICR. A system whereby characters written in magnetic ink on checks and other documents are recognized by a scanning device and transmitted to the main memory of the computer.

microfiche. A sheet of film about 4 × 6 in. upon which the images of pages of computer output may be recorded. Up to 270 pages of output may be recorded on one sheet of microfiche.

mixed number. A number having a fractional part. Examples: 25.83, −7.163, 146.983.

multiprogramming. Several programs are submitted to the computer's main memory and are executed concurrently. When the computer is operating in multiprogramming mode, several programs can be performing input or output functions while one program actually uses the CPU.

Napier, John. Inventor of Napier's "bones."

Napier's bones. A set of rods with inscribed numeric values. Invented by John Napier in the early 1600's, they were used as an aid in performing multiplications and divisions.

object deck. The deck that contains a program in machine language (zeroes and ones). An object deck is usually obtained as the result of a previous assembly or compilation.

octal code. A method of representing data. The method employs 8 characters, ranging from 0 through 7. Each of these characters represents three binary digits (bits) ranging from 000 through 111.

off-line. The required processing is performed without the processing machine being directly connected to a computer. For example, the output from a computer run may be stored on magnetic tape; the tape is later transcribed to output paper by use of a tape-to-printer device.

on-line. A computer is directly connected and is in control of an on-going process. For example, an on-line computer helps control the power generation at a power generation plant.

one-address computer. A computer that employs only one address in its instruction format. For example, an instruction may be

    ADD X

X represents the address in the instruction. (The value of X is added to the content of the accumulator.)

op. A contraction for the term "operation." An instruction contains an op and one or more addresses.

operating system. A complex software package developed by the manufacturer of the delivered hardware. Its purpose is to enable the computer system to be utilized to its fullest potential. The operating system controls when and how user programs are to be executed.

optical scanner. An optical device that has the ability to look at material written upon forms and transfer the data to the main memory of a computer.

Oughtred, William. Inventor of slide rule.

paper tape. Paper strips upon which programs may be punched off-line preparatory to submitting the programs to a computer. When on-line, a user can also request that the computer punch a program on paper tape so that the user can save the program in his possession.

Pascal, Blaise. Inventor of early calculator.

plug board. *See* **control panel.**

printer. A device used for the printing on paper of the information stored in the main memory of the computer. Printers format and print hundreds of lines of information per minute.

program. A set of instructions executed by a computer in the solution to some given problem.

programmer. A person skilled in the preparation of programs for a computer. *See also* **computer programmer.**

punched card. A card measuring 7-3/8 × 3¼ in. used in data processing. The card is capable of holding 80 characters of data. (Some cards have a capacity of 90 characters.) A smaller data processing card used on the System/3 computer has a capacity of 96 characters.

random method. A method of updating files. Records to be updated in the master file are accessed in whatever order the transactions occur. In random updating, master file records are retrieved from their storage locations (often magnetic disk), updated, and then replaced in their storage positions.

read/write head. A device installed on the arms of magnetic disk units or installed in tape handlers. The device permits the transmission of data from main memory of a computer (WRITE) to magnetic disk or magnetic tape or the transmission of data from those devices to the main memory (READ).

real number. In FORTRAN, numbers that include decimal points. Examples: 67.8, 97., −248.5. The term "real" is synonymous with floating-point.

Glossary

record. A collection of related fields concerning a single individual or thing. For example, in a personnel file, one of the records could give all of the data available for a single employee.

recording density. The number of characters of data stored on magnetic tape is termed its density. The density of a tape may be 800 or 1600 characters per inch, for example.

register. A hardware device in a computer. Numeric values may be assigned to the register. Results of calculations may also be assigned to a register.

remote batch. A method of using a computer. Using telephone lines, a person submits a program to a distant, large computer from a local, small computer. Results are returned to the small computer, again via telephone lines.

reproducer. A device for duplicating decks of cards. The reproducer is capable of giving an exact copy of a master deck, or a copy of the deck may be punched in a different format.

sequential method. A method of updating files. Records are read in sequence from both master and transaction files, and creation of the new master file progresses as those records are accessed. When all records from the master and transaction files have been processed, the new master file has been created and the file update procedure has been completed.

software. Programs that are delivered with a computer system. These software programs enable users to assemble or compile user programs, to execute user programs efficiently, and to use the computer in batch, remote batch, and timesharing modes.

son file. *See* **father file.**

sort. Arrange items in some desired sequence. For example, records in a personnel file may be sorted according to social security numbers in increasing sequence; names in a phone book may be sorted in alphabetical order.

sorter. A device used for placing in some desired sequence a deck of data processing cards.

source deck. The deck that contains a program in assembly language.

source program. The original coded program in assembly language.

stored program concept. Instructions to a compuer as well as data values are stored within the main memory of a computer. The instructions can, thus, be accessed more quickly and may be more easily modified.

system. The procedures that a company uses to achieve certain required objectives.

system commands. Special instructions given to the computer when one operates in the conversational timesharing mode. System commands direct the computer to execute (RUN) programs, list them (LIST), save them (SAVE), and to take over actions of a similar nature.

system design. The planning and creation of a business system.

system study. An investigation made to determine the feasibility of installing or replacing a business system.

tag. A portion of a computer instruction. The tag carries the number of the index register that affects the address in the instruction.

tape handler. A device upon which a tape may be mounted for reading or for writing. Tape handlers may also be referred to as tape drives or tape units.

tape library. A room at a computer center where reels of magnetic tapes are stored under ideal conditions of temperature and humidity. As many as 50,000 tapes can be stored in the tape library of a large computer center.

terminal. A device that can be used by a person to send programs or data to a distant computer. The person uses telephone lines to transmit the programs or data. Often, the terminal is a teletype-like device or a small computer.

three-address computer. A computer that employs three addresses in its instruction format. For example, an instruction may be

ADD X Y Z

(The values of X and Y are added and the result is assigned to Z.)

timesharing. A mode of using a computer. Many persons access a distant computer via telephone lines. The users share the computer's attention.

track. A concentric circle on the surface of a disk. Data are recorded along the circular path of the track. A disk surface may have hundreds of tracks.

turnaround time. The length of time that a person has to wait for results after he has submitted a program to be processed.

two-address computer. A computer that employs two addresses in its instruction format. For example, an instruction may be

ADD X Y

(The values of X and Y are added and the result replaces the old value of Y.)

two's complement. A method of representing negative numbers. A positive or negative number is changed to the opposite sign by changing all 1's to 0's and all 0's to 1's, then binarily adding 1.

unit record devices. Several electric data processing devices, such as keypunch machines, sorters, collators, reproducers and others, are termed unit record or EAM devices. Unit record devices are used to process punched cards, but they are not computers.

unit record principle. When one is using EAM devices, it is desirable to contain entire records on single data processing cards. EAM devices (also called unit record devices) work most efficiently while dealing with files a record at a time.

universal language. A programming language that is available on many computers. Examples: COBOL, FORTRAN, PL/I.

variable names. Labels for numbers used in FORTRAN. A variable name stands for the value assigned to it. EXAMPLES: TEMP, EPSLON, IR.

variable word-length. The memory of a computer, consisting of bytes, can be divided into units exactly suiting the data that are to be stored. Some data items require two bytes of memory storage, others four, others eight, etc. These variable portions of memory are readily allocatable to data items.

von Leibnitz, Gottfried. Developer of early calculator. Disputed inventor of calculus.

von Neumann, John. Devised the stored program concept.

whole number. A number without a fractional part. Examples: 94, −36., 76.0.

wire board. *See* **control panel**.

word. The contents of a computer location. The location may consist of 20, 32, 36, etc. bits, depending upon the design of the computer being discussed.

Index

Accounting machines, 18, 19, 24-28, 32, 39, 240
Accumulator, 103, 106, 109, 110, 120, 240
Address
  in instruction format, 100, 107, 112, 240
  modification, using index registers, 112, 116, 118, 122-24, 240
  or value field on coding form, 115, 116
Aiken, Howard, 5, 6, 8, 241
ALGOL programming language, 154, 167
Alphabetic sequencing, 25
APL programming language, 203
Assembler, 116-24, 203-7, 241
Assembly-language programming, 99, 102, 124-28, 133, 134, 241

Babbage, Charles, 3, 4, 7, 241
Basic data processing cycle, 36, 37, 225, 226, 241
BASIC
  built-in functions, 161
  calculations, 157, 160, 161, 163
  language programming, 154-64, 168, 189, 190, 205, 206, 223, 241
  statement types, 7, 156
Batching period and batched transactions, 217, 219
Batch mode, 184, 241
Billing, automatic, 183, 186
Binary
  addition, 68-71
  digit, definition (bit), 62
  numbers, 59-65, 89, 90, 241
Binary-to-decimal conversion, 85, 86

Bit, definition, 62, 93
Bits, binary, 59-65, 241
Blocks of records, 33-37, 218, 241
Buffers, 34, 35, 37, 241
Business
  applications, 215
  files, 30, 31, 145
  programming, 212-26
  programming language, COBOL, 144-53
Byte, definition, 96-98, 241

Capacity
  data cell, 49
  magnetic disk, 47
  magnetic tape, 45
Card punch machines, 39, 242
Card reader, as I/O device, 24, 43-45, 53, 242
Cards, JCL, batch programming, 176, 243
Card sorter, mechanical, 25, 217
Card-to-tape operations, 45, 50, 178
Central processing unit, CPU, 36
Character positions in records, 34, 37
Changing random records, 225
COBOL
  and flowcharting, 170
  compiler, software, 211
  concepts, 144-53
Coding form
  COBOL, 145
  FORTRAN, 128, 129
Coding forms, programming, 114, 115, 116
Collator, EAM device, 25, 26, 28, 29, 32, 39, 242

252

Index

COM, computer output microfilm, 54-58, 242
Compilation, 132-34, 242
Compilation, FORTRAN, 140, 141
Compiler
  FORTRAN, 133
  language
    definition, 242
    programming, 99
  software, 206-9, 211
Computer
  applications, 11-15
  center, 176, 177, 179, 187
  components, 92, 97
  console, 11, 15, 242
  definition, 9-16
  generations, 6-8
  input/output devices, 43-54
  instruction format, 100
  invention of, 3, 7
  memories, 37, 92-98
  operators, 11, 15, 242
  output microfilm, COM, 52-58, 242
  systems, 10, 11, 15
  usage modes, 175-80
  usage, remote batch, 181, 186, 187
Conditional transfers, 158, 159, 163
Control cards, JCL cards, 243
Control computer component, 92, 97, 242
Control languages, remote batch, 185, 186
Control module in computer, 100, 106
Control panel, 27-28, 243
Control, sequencer in, 101
Conversational timesharing, 175, 179, 188-204, 243
Conversion
  problems, 144, 153
  to new system, 243
Converting
  base 8 numbers to decimal, 89, 90
  binary to decimal, 85, 86
  decimal to hexadecimal, 86
  decimal values to base, 8, 89, 90
  hexadecimal to binary, 87
  to a computer, 39-42
Core, description, 62-65, 243
Costs
  remote operation, 182
  system, 230-34
  timesharing, 189, 203
Couriers, at computer center, 176, 177, 179, 187
CPU
  computer component, 36, 92, 97, 103, 210, 211, 243
  module in computer, 100
  shared use of, 210, 211
Creating a floating-point number, 77, 78, 80
Current system description, 231
Cycle, data processing, 36, 37, 225, 226, 241

Data cell, as I/O device, 47, 48, 243
Data processing
  history, 1-8
  cycle, basic, 36, 37, 225, 226, 241
  in business, 17-21
Data transmission speeds, I/O devices, 43, 35, 47, 51, 52
Debugging
  batch mode steps, 176-79, 243
  FORTRAN programs, 133
Decimal-to-hexadecimal conversion, 86
Decisions, systems design, 228, 234
Decks, source and object, 116, 117, 124, 146, 147
Decoding instructions, 100, 106, 206
Density, recording on magnetic tape, 33, 37
Describing files, 148-50, 152
Difference machine, Babbage's, 3, 4
Disk pack library, 177
Disks used in timesharing, 192, 200
Double precision values, 136
Double word, memory, 112, 136

EAM devices, 18, 19, 22-29, 31, 32, 37, 39, 243
EBCDIC, data representation code, 96, 97, 244
Eckert, J. P., 5-7, 244
Electric Accounting Machinery, 22-29, 243
Electronic computer, invention of, 3, 7
Electronic computers, levels of data processing, 19
Electrostatic printers, 51, 52, 55, 244
End-of-file
  in basic data processing cycle, 37
  in files, 37, 244
ENIAC, 5, 6, 8, 244
Entertainment, use of computers in, 238
Excess-64 method, floating-point, 76, 81, 244
Execution of programs, 117, 178, 244

File
  definition, 30
  key, 30, 37, 218
  processing and maintenance, 30-38, 215-26
Files
  business, 145
  describing, 145, 148-50, 152
  father, son, grandfather, 219, 220
  master, definition, 215
  sorting, 145, 217
  updating, 145, 218, 219
  on magnetic tape, 32, 33, 37
Finance, use of computers in, 236
Fixed word-length memories, 93-97
Flowcharting concepts, 165-74
Flow diagram, system design, 229

254 Index

FORTRAN
  and flowcharting, 170
  compiler, 133
  generations, 141
  program, 183
    keypunching, 130, 131
  survey of, 126-43
FORTRAN V, 142, 143

Games, timesharing, 236
Gaps, interblock, and interrecord, magnetic tape, 33
Goldstein and Burke, 6

Half words, memory, 108, 112, 136
Hard copy, definition, 178
Hardware, contrasted with software, 205
Hexadecimal and octal codes, 82-91
Hexadecimal-to-binary conversion, 87
High-speed printer, as I/O device, 49, 50, 53
HLC
  description, 99-121
  operations, selected, 119-21
Hollerith, Dr. Herman, 4, 5, 7, 22
Hypothetical Learning Computer, 99-121

IBM 026, 029, 129 keypunches, 24
IBM 083 sorter, 25
IBM 088 collator, 25
IBM 129 Card Data Recorder, 24
IBM 407 accounting machine, 26-28
IBM 519 reproducer, 27
IBM 557 interpreter, 26
IBM 2321 data cell, 48, 49
IBM 5496 keypunch, 24
IBM cards, 23
IBM tape handler, 34
ID user, timesharing, 190, 192, 198
Index registers, 104, 110, 108-12, 116, 118, 120-24
Information
  and data, 18
  output from system, 233
Input data
  batch programming, 176
  FORTRAN, 131, 134
Input/output
  devices, computer, 43-54
  shared use of, 210, 211
  symbol, flowcharting, 167, 172
Inputs and outputs, system, 231, 232
Instruction formats, 99-106
Instruction modification, using index registers, 108, 110, 112, 116, 118, 124
Instruction operation (op), 107, 112
Integer numbers, FORTRAN, 136, 142
Integers, 66-72

Integers and floating-point numbers, 82-84
Interactive mode, and BASIC, 155, 163
Interblock gaps, 33-34
Interpreters, 24-29, 39
Interrecord gaps, 33-34
Interrelationships of number systems, 89-90
I/O
  devices, computer, 43-54
  shared use of, 210-11

Jacquard, Joseph Marie, 3, 22
JCL
  cards, 176, 243
  FORTRAN, 131-34
Job preparation
  batch mode steps, 177-78
  computer center procedures, 177-79

K, memory size, 95, 98
Key, file, 30, 37, 215, 216, 218
Keypunch machines, 18, 24, 26, 29, 39
Keypunching a FORTRAN program, 130-31
KODAK KOM-80 microfilmer, 56

Language
  assembly, 205
  COBOL, 242
  machine, 102, 105
  scientific, FORTRAN, 127
Languages
  control, for remote batch usage, 185, 186
  timesharing, 189, 190, 202
  universal, 126, 127
Law enforcement, computer usage in, 14-15
Levels of data processing, 19

Machine language programming, 99, 102-13, 126-28, 133-34, 205
Magnetic disk, as I/O device, 46, 47, 53, 220
Magnetic drum, as I/O device, 47, 53
Magnetic ink character recognition, 50-51
Magnetic tape
  as I/O device, 45, 46, 53
  density, 33, 37
  files upon, 32, 33, 37, 215
  used with COM, 56
Maintaining files, 215-26
Mark I, 5, 6, 8, 241
Manual data processing, 19
Master files, 216-17
Mauchley, J. W., Jr., 5-7
Maximum binary value, 64, 72
Mechanical card readers, 24, 29, 43, 45
Mechanical card sorter, 25, 217
Medicine, computer usage in, 14, 15, 239
Memories, computer, 37, 92-98
Memory sizes, K, 95, 98

Index 255

Memory word, 95, 108, 112
Merging, with collator, 26
MICR, 50, 51
Microfiche, output, 57, 58
Microfilmer, KODAK KOM-80, 56
Microfilm output (COM), 54-58
Microsecond, definition, 94
Millisecond, definition, 94
Mixed numbers, floating-point, 73, 75, 80, 81
Modification, address and instruction, 108-12, 116, 118, 122-24, 240
Modules, computer, 100
Modes, computer usage, 175-80
Mode, remote batch, 181-87
Mode, timesharing, 188-204
Moore School of Engineering, 6
Multiprogramming, 178, 209-11

Napier, John, 2, 7
Negative floating-point numbers, 77
Negative integers, 67, 71
Newton, Sir Isaac, 3
Normalizing floating-point numbers, 80, 81
Numbers
  binary, 60-65, 89, 90
  decimal, 59-60
  floating-point, 73-81
  hexadecimal, 84-87, 90
  integer, FORTRAN, 136, 142
  integers, 66-72
  mixed, floating-point, 73-81
  octal, 88-90
  real, FORTRAN, 136, 142
Number systems, interrelationships, 89, 90

Object deck, 116, 124, 141, 175, 206
  FORTRAN, 133, 134
Object decks and source decks, COBOL, 146, 147, 206
Obtaining output, remote, 183
Octal and hexadecimal codes, 82-91
Octal-to-decimal conversion, 89-90
Off-line
  printing and other operations, 50, 55
  processing, 178
On-line
  applications, 214
  output, 184
  processing, 178
One-address computers, 107, 109, 112
Ones and zeroes, binary bits, 59-65
Op codes for HLC, 115, 116
Ops, HLC, 119
Operating systems, software, 205, 209, 210
Operation in instruction, 100, 102, 107, 112
Operations, HLC, selected, 120, 121

Operators, computer, 11, 15, 242
Optical card readers, 24, 43, 45
Optical scanner, as I/O device, 50
OS (operating system), 209-11
Oughtred, William, 2, 7
Output
  from system, information, 233
  obtained in remote batch, 183-85
  on-line, 184
Output processing, at computer center, 178, 179
Outputs from files, 219

Paper tape, timesharing, 202
Pascal, Blaise, 2, 7
Permanent storage, timesharing, 191-93, 196, 198, 200, 202
Positive integers, 66, 70
Print operations, HLC, 121
Printer
  electrostatic, 244
  high-speed, as I/O device, 49, 50, 53, 55
Printers, special, 52
Processing
  on-line and off-line, 178
  random record, 223
Procedures
  computer center, 177-79
  system design, 228-29
Program
  definition, 6, 102, 105
  file update, 218, 219
Programming
  assembly language, 99, 102, 113-24
  business and scientific, 212-27
  compiler language, 99
  language, COBOL, 242
  machine-language, 99, 107-12, 126
  steps, batch, 175-79
Punched card, 22-23, 29, 242
  files, 31, 32

Random file maintenance, 215, 220-26
Read/Write Heads, 47
Real and integer values, BASIC, 163
Record
  definition, 31
  retrieval, 223
  sequencing, 217-18
  sorting, 217
  structures in files, 32-34
Recording density, on magnetic tape, 33, 37
Records
  blocks of, 218
  description, 215-16
  fields, 31
  on magnetic tape, 33, 37
  randomly stored, 220-21

Index

Registers, index, 103, 104, 110
Remote batch mode, computer usage, 175, 159, 181-87
Reports
  from files, using COBOL, 145
  printed, 50
Reproducer, 24, 27-29
Retrieving records, 223

Saving programs, timesharing, 185, 191-94
Scanner, optical, as I/O device, 50
Scientific programming, 212-14, 225
Selecting, with collator, 26
Self-documentation, COBOL, 144
Semi-automatic data processing, 19
Sentinel values, used in BASIC, 162, 163
Sequence checking, with collator, 26
Sequence numbers, COBOL, 145
Sequencer, in control, 101
Sequencing of records, 217, 218
Sequential file maintenance, 215-20
Serial file
  maintenance, 215, 220
  updating, 215-26
Software, 205-11
Sorter, mechanical, 25, 28, 29, 39, 217
Sorting, 217
Sorting files, using COBOL, 145
Source and object decks, COBOL, 146, 147
Source deck, FORTRAN, 131, 134
Source decks, 116, 175
Source documents, 217
Source program, 116, 124
Statements, FORTRAN, 129
Stored program computer, 101, 106
Submittal form, batch programming, 176
System/3 punched card, 23, 24
System 370, 6
  timesharing, 196-202
System costs, 230-34
System
  design, 228-34
  feedback, 231
  flow diagram, 229
  model, 229
  objectives, 230, 231, 234
  parallel runs, 229
  savings, 230, 234
Synonyms, random file maintenance, 223

Tabulator, Hollerith's, 5
Tape
  density, 33, 37

Tape (cont.)
  handler, as I/O device, 34-37, 45, 46, 53
  library, 177
  magnetic, as I/O device, 45, 46, 53, 56
Tapes and files, 215
Tape-to-printer conversion, 50, 178
Telephone lines, remote batch processing, 182, 183, 186
Telephone usage, timesharing, 188, 202
Terminals, used in remote batch, 181, 183, 186, 187
Timesharing
  conversational, 188-204, 243
  costs, 189, 203
  errors, 195-202
  languages, 189, 190, 202
  processing, 155, 175, 179
Three-address computers, 108, 112
Tracks, magnetic disks, 46, 47
Transmission speeds, I/O devices, 43, 35, 47, 51, 52
Transactions, files, 216, 217, 219
Transfers, HLC ops, 121
Transportation, computer usage in, 14, 15, 237, 238
Turnaround time, remote batch processing, 179-87
Two's complement, 67, 71
Typewriter, as I/O device, 51

Unit record devices, 19, 27, 32, 37, 39
Unit record principle, 31
UNIVAC, 6
UNIVAC keypunch, 24
Universal language, COBOL, 144
Universal languages, 126, 127
Updating files, 215-26
Usage modes, computer, 175-80
User ID, timesharing, 190, 192, 193

Variable word-length memories, 92, 96, 97, 98
Viewers used with COM, 57
Vocabulary
  BASIC, 156
  COBOL, 151
von Leibnitz, Gottfried, 2, 3
von Neumann, John, 6-8, 106

Wire board, 27-28
Word-length, fixed and variable, 92, 97
Working area, timesharing, 190-94, 196, 197, 200

QA
76
D37

DEC 24 1975